Strategic Studies Institute
and
U.S. Army War College Press

STRATEGIC RETRENCHMENT AND RENEWAL
IN THE AMERICAN EXPERIENCE

Peter Feaver
Editor

August 2014

The views expressed in this report are those of the authors and do not necessarily reflect the official policy or position of the Department of the Army, the Department of Defense, or the U.S. Government. Authors of Strategic Studies Institute (SSI) and U.S. Army War College (USAWC) Press publications enjoy full academic freedom, provided they do not disclose classified information, jeopardize operations security, or misrepresent official U.S. policy. Such academic freedom empowers them to offer new and sometimes controversial perspectives in the interest of furthering debate on key issues.

CONTENTS

Foreword vii

1. Introduction 1
   Peter Feaver, Jeremi Suri, Francis J. Gavin, and William Inboden

2. The Political Economy of Retrenchment 7
   Charles Miller

3. Herbert Hoover and the Adjustment to the Depression 69
   Eleanore Douglas

4. Strategic Calculations in Times of Austerity: Richard Nixon 119
   Megan Reiss

5. Jimmy Carter, Ronald Reagan, and the End (Or Consummation?) of Détente 163
   Brian K. Muzas

6. Is it Time for Retrenchment? The Big Debate on American Grand Strategy 221
   Ionut C. Popescu

About the Contributors 257

FOREWORD

In recent years, debates over American grand strategy have often focused on the question of whether the United States should retrench geopolitically or seek to renew its international leadership. This collection of essays puts this pressing question in its proper historical and theoretical context. The authors examine past episodes in which American presidents were confronted with similar choices, and they probe theoretical and policy debates over retrenchment, renewal, and their consequences. The result is a volume that enriches our understanding of how American leaders have, can, and should respond to the challenges and opportunities that characterize international relations.

The Strategic Studies Institute is pleased to offer this collection as a contribution to the ongoing debate on American grand strategy.

DOUGLAS C. LOVELACE, JR.
Director
Strategic Studies Institute and
   U.S. Army War College Press

CHAPTER 1

INTRODUCTION

Peter Feaver
Jeremi Suri
Francis J. Gavin
William Inboden

American strategic debates are rarely new. They generally replay inherited conflicts of vision and interpretation in new settings. The consistent, almost obsessive, focus on "enduring dilemmas" has led historians like Arthur Schlesinger, Jr., to emphasize the "cycles of American history," especially as they relate to politics and defense policy.

American policymakers are preoccupied with one of these cyclical strategic debates today: In times of economic difficulty, should the United States retrench its international presence, or should it renew itself abroad? Those who advocate for retrenchment emphasize the need to reduce military expenditures, reallocate resources at home, and redefine a more modest definition of the national interest. Those who call for renewal claim that the threats to American prosperity are growing, that reduced expenditures will invite more threats, and that the United States has the capacity to expand its military activities and grow its domestic resources at the same time. Now, as in the 1870s, the 1920s, the late-1940s, and the 1990s, Americans confront a familiar choice between reducing inherited international commitments or investing in new potential sources of international value.

This is, of course, a false choice. The cycles of American history are potentially harmful because they encourage comfortable but distorted debates between polarized positions. The partisan nature of American society heightens polarization as one political party embraces a position, and the other feels required to take the exact opposite side. Electoral politics encourage conflict rather than consensus in American strategic doctrine, especially during periods of uncertainty and budgetary pressure. The *déjà vu* feel to the debate introduces other distortions, as participants in the debate invoke poorly supported "lessons of history" and short-hand references to previous periods that strip away the nuance and other insights from academic research.

The chapters commissioned for this volume aim to improve the current debate over American grand strategy. They begin with recognition of the cyclical tendencies in American strategic debates, and an understanding that policy rarely actually matches the polarities of public rhetoric. Instead, the chapters show that politicians are usually strategic synthesizers, seeking areas for overlap and hedging in their strategies as they simultaneously prepare for new foreign adversaries and cut the costs of their international commitments. Strategy is less about clarity and choice than about a creative management of contradictions. Strategy is always a compromise among alternatives that appear more irreconcilable in presentation than in practice.

These observations are especially true for the historical and contemporary debates surrounding retrenchment and renewal in American foreign and defense policy. Since the early-20th century, when the United States established itself as a major international actor, the country has never chosen exclusively to retrench or to renew. Each President has sought some of both. The same is true today. The key question is how to balance the two and, more specifically, where to retrench and where to renew. Which commitments can the United States cut without undue harm? Which commitments must the United States expand to protect vital interests? The issues of balance and selection are the issues that motivate the analysis in the forthcoming chapters.

Our goal in commissioning these chapters (initially presented at a workshop at Duke University in November 2012) was to help policymakers making retrenchment and renewal trade-offs today by clarifying how policymakers have sought the correct balance in the past. We commissioned five essays to synthesize the vast literature, with an eye to creating a single handy reference for the current debate. The essays cover several disparate literatures—political science, economics, current policy debates, and the historical scholarship on three presidential periods most often invoked in the current debate over retrenchment and renewal: Herbert Hoover, Richard Nixon, and Ronald Reagan. We chose to examine how leaders have conceptualized the trade-offs, and how they have reacted to moments of apparent crisis—when the pressures to reexamine long-standing commitments were particularly strong. Beyond the rhetoric frequently deployed in public discussions, we sought to bring more rigorous analysis and empirical detail to an assessment of how policymakers have thought about retrenchment and renewal at what appear to be key strategic turning points in the last century. In some cases, the essays show that prevailing conventional wisdom about past periods differs from what the empirical record shows; in other cases, the essays identify insights that could more fruitfully inform the current debate.

Chapter 2, written by Charles Miller, reviews the vast literature in economics and political science to provide a framework for understanding how leaders think about trade-offs between security threats and economic capabilities. Miller articulates what he calls the "retrenchment dilemma," which is the fear that reducing foreign commitments will embolden U.S. adversaries, just as expanding foreign commitments will undermine domestic order and prosperity. Miller provides a model for weighing these countervailing pressures at different moments, and he concludes that some periods (like today) probably merit serious retrenchment in expensive international commitments.

Eleanore Douglas builds on these insights in her detailed examination of President Hoover's policies during the Great Depression. No President faced greater pressures to retrench than Hoover after the stock market collapse in October 1929. Of course, Hoover sought to slash already limited American military and economic commitments abroad. He did, however, focus on new mechanisms for renewing American power at home, according to Douglas. She argues that the renewal plans in Hoover's program contributed significantly to the growth of American power a decade later under a different President.

Megan Reiss examines the controversial presidency of Nixon in a similar light. Reiss reminds readers how the domestic unrest, rising inflation, and disappointments of the Vietnam War forced Nixon to scale back traditional American activities abroad. Nixon, however, turned this pressure for retrenchment into new opportunities for renewal, according to Reiss. Nixon opened relations with China, relied on greater allied assistance abroad (the "Nixon Doctrine"), and pursued détente with the Soviet Union—actions that increased American power. Nixon renewed American standing in the world by re-defining American foreign policy. His great failing, according to Reiss, was an inability to manage his policies with consistency and attention to unforeseen consequences.

Brian Muzas compares Nixon's successor, Jimmy Carter, with Reagan. Muzas shows that both Presidents faced pressures simultaneously to reduce American commitments and renew containment of an expanding communist threat, especially after the Soviet invasion of Afghanistan in December 1979. Muzas also points to what he calls "existential austerity" — the feeling among many Americans in the late-1970s that the country had lost its confidence and its purpose. In this troubled environment, Reagan inspired a new-found mission. He painted a roadmap for renewal that allowed for withdrawal from costly commitments and a doubling-down on worthwhile strategic endeavors, especially challenging Soviet power. Reagan's strategy worked better than Carter's because it matched elements of retrenchment with promises of renewal that increased national confidence and capability.

Ionut Popescu extends this analysis into the post-Cold War world. He cogently outlines the axes of debate between proponents of retrenchment and renewal since 1991. Popescu shows a strong continuity in the arguments made by different groups. He analyzes the different trade-offs required by different policy proposals. Popescu's chapter makes it clear that current policymakers cannot accept either retrenchment or renewal, but must work somewhere in between.

That is the key takeaway from these excellent chapters. The United States has a cyclical tendency to follow too much expansion with too much retrenchment, and vice versa. Policymakers often overcompensate, at least in their rhetoric, for the actions of their predecessors. Successful policy must avoid this temptation, as it judiciously mixes opportunities for cost-saving cuts with continued commitments to extended security for the nation and its diverse interests. A superpower facing budget difficulties must show discipline, discernment, and continued determination to defend its values.

CHAPTER 2

THE POLITICAL ECONOMY OF RETRENCHMENT

Charles Miller

In 1774, King Louis XVI of France ascended to the throne of Versailles. While on the surface Europe's most powerful kingdom, France faced a severe financial crisis. Millions of livres were owed to the King's creditors, at increasingly onerous interest rates. The origin of the debt lay in the Seven Years' War, but Louis added to it substantially through French participation in the American Revolutionary War. Eventually, in order to stave off a default, the King called a meeting of the Estates-General to discuss a new tax code designed to repair France's position. Instead of fixing the problem, however, the recall of the Estates-General set off the chain of events which culminated in the French Revolution and the deposal and death of the King (Ferguson 2004).

Britain faced a financial crisis of a similar magnitude 166 years later, which was kept secret from the public and overshadowed by the concurrent military crisis. Adolf Hitler's armies had overrun Western Europe and seemed poised to invade Britain itself. In the corridors of Whitehall, however, a stark fact faced British policymakers—Britain was running out of money. In fact, British credit was so extended that the British were compelled to ask for an emergency soft loan from the Free Belgian Government to continue to pay for the supplies of food and military equipment from the United States which were keeping Britain in the war. Had Congress not swiftly passed the Lend-Lease

Act, allowing the British to purchase American supplies on soft American loans, the Nazis would have been able to knock Britain out of the war without a single German soldier having to set foot on British soil (Barnett 1986).

Freshest in memory for contemporary observers, of course, is the case of the Soviet Union. While the collapse of the Soviet Empire resulted from a number of factors, one key factor was the simple inability of the Soviet fiscal state to keep pace with American rearmament (Schultz and Weingast 2003).

Fiscal solvency and economic strength are key prerequisites for a state to be able to pursue all its other grand strategic goals. States which are not fiscally solvent risk internal collapse (like France and the Soviet Union) or defeat in war (as Britain nearly did), after which their ability to pursue grand strategic goals is greatly reduced. Even if things do not come to such a dramatic pass, a higher defense burden should, *ceteris paribus*, be expected to reduce economic growth in the long run by diverting investment from the civilian economy. National wealth being a key component of power, slower growth should, in turn, reduce a state's strategic freedom of maneuver over time.

Retrenchment is a policy designed to achieve a number of goals. Some political scientists choose an expansive definition—McDonald and Parent, for instance, claim that retrenchment involves pruning foreign policy liabilities, renouncing existing commitments, defining particular issues as less than critical, and shifting burdens onto allies (McDonald and Parent 2011). Retrenchment could also involve changes to force posture and structure—a shift from counterinsurgency (COIN) or expeditionary force capabilities toward a conventional defensive posture (or vice versa), for instance. Retrenchment may even involve changes in a nation's self-conception—for instance, Britain's withdrawal "East of Suez" in the 1970s marked a definitive break with the conception of Britain as an independent global power. I contend that many of these actions can, in fact, be reduced to even simpler aims. States retrench in order to free up two things—money and leaders' time and attention—to address internal political problems. Both are scarce and critical resources.

At the same time, however, retrenchment is not without costs. Following World War I, the United States cut back its military forces dramatically from wartime levels and withdrew them from Europe (Layne 2006). At the time, Germany and the nascent Soviet Union were prostrate, Italy and Japan were Western Allies, and the British and French had apparently emerged victorious and stronger than ever. The American decision, therefore, would have struck many observers at the time to be the correct one to restore U.S. fiscal solvency. Yet, this was illusory. German and Soviet weaknesses were transient. Japan and Italy moved away from liberal democracy toward militaristic fascism. Britain's and France's power to halt these developments was insufficient—their post-war territorial gains had only temporarily masked a long-term economic and demographic decline. Readers should not need to be reminded of what happened next.

After World War II, the United States chose differently. While the U.S. Army was reduced from its wartime levels, the U.S. military did not revert to its interwar strength. Moreover, U.S. forces remained in Western Europe and Northeast Asia to "keep the Germans down and the Russians out" (Layne 2006). As we know, of course, there followed the most sustained period of global peace the world has yet seen (Pinker 2011). Germany and Japan democratized and gradually gained the trust of many of their neighbors. The Soviet Union was first contained and then finally collapsed of its own contradictions.

The decision over whether or not to retrench is not an easy one. Retrench too much, and a state may put its security at risk and, paradoxically, make war more likely. Retrench too little, by contrast, and a state may hasten its economic and hence political decline and waste scarce resources which it may need in the future. In light of this, it is reasonable to expect political science to provide guidance to policymakers and to the public on when retrenchment is appropriate. This chapter is intended to do just that.

This chapter contends that there is no strategy which is right for all circumstances. Both retrenchment and renewal bring with them costs and benefits. Policymakers asking whether retrenchment is the correct strategy at a given point in time must consider two main factors—the security position and the fiscal/economic position. As outlined in the following pages, the combination of these two factors determines whether retrenchment is appropriate. When the short- to medium-term security threat is high, renewal is the best option, even if the fiscal/economic position is weak. Incurring high debt, inflation, and damaging domestic savings are undesirable, but are preferable to national extinction. By contrast, the combination of a low security threat and strong finances is indeterminate, although policymakers certainly have latitude to retrench if they choose to do so. However, retrenchment is clearly the best option where the fiscal position is poor, **and** the security situation is good. In this case, there is less need to devote resources to defense and a higher need to repair the state's fiscal position. (See Figure 2-1.)

		Strong	Weak
Medium-Term Security Threat	High	Renewal	Renewal
	Low	Renewal/Retrenchment	Retrenchment

Figure 2-1. Fiscal/Economic Position.

I argue that the current circumstances are those of a historically benign security situation combined with grave economic and fiscal difficulties. Consequently, retrenchment is the best path. If we accept this, however, a second question arises—How can retrenchment be done well? What might help or hinder it? Does the political science or political economy offer creative solutions which would allow the United States to retrench without curtailing its global commitments? The pessimistic conclusion of this chapter is "no." Most of the ways political economists and scientists suggest for states to cut costs without curtailing commitments have already been tried. If any more "easy wins" existed, it would be strange if policymakers had not already tried them. Consequently, successful retrenchment will have to involve cutting commitments.

WHAT IS THE SECURITY SITUATION?

For political scientists and analysts, retrenchment can be a dangerous strategy in security terms. International relations theorist Robert Gilpin claimed that great powers rarely pursue retrenchment because it "signals weakness" and thus invites challenges from other powers (Gilpin 1983). Charles Krauthammer makes a similar but distinct argument. Krauthammer claims that "international relations abhors a vacuum," and that, if the United States were to retrench, this would tempt other powers to challenge America militarily. The closer other states approach the United States in military power, the higher they will rate their chances of success in a conflict and hence the more willing they will be to fight (Krauthammer 2009).

Although the two arguments point to the same conclusion, they derive from distinct viewpoints in international relations. The Krauthammer argument is a straightforward application of balance of power and hegemonic stability theory. According to this view, a preponderance of power by one state such as the United States reduces the probability of conflict. The reasoning is easy enough to follow. No matter how much rival states may wish to fight the United States over some issue, they are very unlikely to do so if the United States is so much more powerful than they are. By contrast, as the margin of American supremacy over other states narrows, so does the probability that these states would be able to defeat the United States militarily. Knowing this, they are more likely to challenge the United States and potentially start fresh wars.

Gilpin's argument rests on the importance of signaling and resolve. Dating back to Thomas Schelling, this school stresses the importance of building and maintaining reputation in international politics (Schelling 1960). The signaling school of international relations often stresses that outward measures of a state's power are less important in determining war and peace than intangible factors such as a reputation for resolve. In this view, it is pretty well known how much the United States and other states spend on defense and how many soldiers, tanks, and aircraft they have. These facts are already "priced in" and accounted for in state behavior. What is less apparent is how much states actually care about the main issues of international politics. Slobodan Milosevic, for instance, would clearly have been foolish to think that the Yugoslav Army could defeat the United States if both sides went all out for victory. What Milosevic was counting on, in this view, is the possibility that the United States did not care enough about Kosovo to incur the costs necessary to beat the Serbs.

For the signaling school, it follows from this that uncertainty over resolve is a key cause of international conflict. To complicate matters, a U.S. President cannot assuage such concerns simply by stating that the United States is "prepared to bear any burden, undertake any task." Anybody can **say** they are highly resolved, especially given that a reputation for resolve has obvious benefits in terms of getting one's own way and deterring challengers. The trick is to undertake certain actions which are costly to oneself and which, therefore, separate genuinely resolved, tough states from weak states just pretending to be resolved. This is known in the literature as "costly signaling" (Spence 1973).

It is easy to see from here why some believers in signaling might claim retrenchment is a bad idea. Keeping up the same level of defense spending and foreign commitments in the face of an economic decline is, for them, a costly signal that the United States is genuinely highly resolved to maintain its global preeminence. Conversely, cutting defense spending in the face of relative decline is a signal of weakness—it reveals some information outsiders did not know about the President's (or the American elite's or the American people's) true resolve to remain global top dog.

Thus retrenchment could have two malign effects on the prospects for America's power position and global peace and stability. First, rival states (perhaps China or Russia) will note that the United States has less material capacity. Second, even more ominously, they will infer that the United States lacks resolve and so would not even be prepared to use the full extent of its remaining capacities, if push came to shove. Both factors would tempt these rivals to challenge America's security interests, with potentially disastrous consequences. These two claims have provoked a heated response from many political scientists.

Empirically, the balance of power argument has come under a great deal of criticism. Statistical tests of the proposition that a preponderance of military power in favor of one nation deters conflict have revealed mixed results (Bennett and Stam 2004). Theoretically, signaling theorists have claimed that the balance of power, in terms of observable military capabilities, simply affects the division of spoils among states rather than the likelihood of war—as states become weaker, they simply concede more in interstate bargaining rather than fighting (Fearon 1995).

Even if one were to accept the power preponderance argument, however, analysts such as Krauthammer often fail to state just how much relative power is enough for the United States. The United States currently spends as much on defense as the next 11 states combined. If the United States spent as much as all states in the world combined, say twice over, it would be even less vulnerable to challenge than it currently is—but would this additional invulnerability actually be worth the economic costs involved? Conversely, the United States spent less on defense as a proportion of world spending in the 1990s than it does now—

even though the United States was even then spoken of as a "hyperpower" whose conventional capabilities dwarfed the rest of the world's.[1] The 1990s were also an unprecedentedly peaceful era.

Moreover, Krauthammer and others need to specify who the enemies are who will challenge global peace, if the United States retrenches. Even before Hitler's rise to power, the potential long-term threat from Germany was clear—Europe's most populous country, with one of the most advanced economies and arguably the most efficient Army on the planet, hosted a strongly revanchist right wing and a fledgling, unstable democracy. Who today could play the disruptive role in the international system which Germany, Japan, Italy, and the Soviet Union played in the 1930s? The international relations theorist Stephen Walt points out that a security threat is primarily a combination of two things—capabilities and intentions (Walt 1990). Surveying the modern global system, which actors have the combination of capabilities and intentions to pose a potential threat to the United States and the liberal world order if the United States were to retrench? In terms of current military power, the United States simply dwarfs the rest of the world.

The U.S. share of global military expenditure, as calculated by the Stockholm International Peace Research Institute (SIPRI), is shown in Figure 2-2. SIPRI calculates military spending in international rather than purchasing power parity dollars, which is the correct metric, given that this measures a state's ability to buy either advanced weapons or the materials to make them on the global market. By this measure, the United States spends more on defense than the next nine powers combined, five times that of the next biggest spender, China, and 10 times that the third biggest, Russia. Current figures for Iran are not available, but in the last year in which SIPRI provided data, the United States outspent Iran on defense more than 84 times over. Of the remaining top 10 spenders in 2011, four were solid U.S. allies—Britain, France, Japan, and Germany—and three were at the very least friendly powers—Brazil, India, and Saudi Arabia.[2]

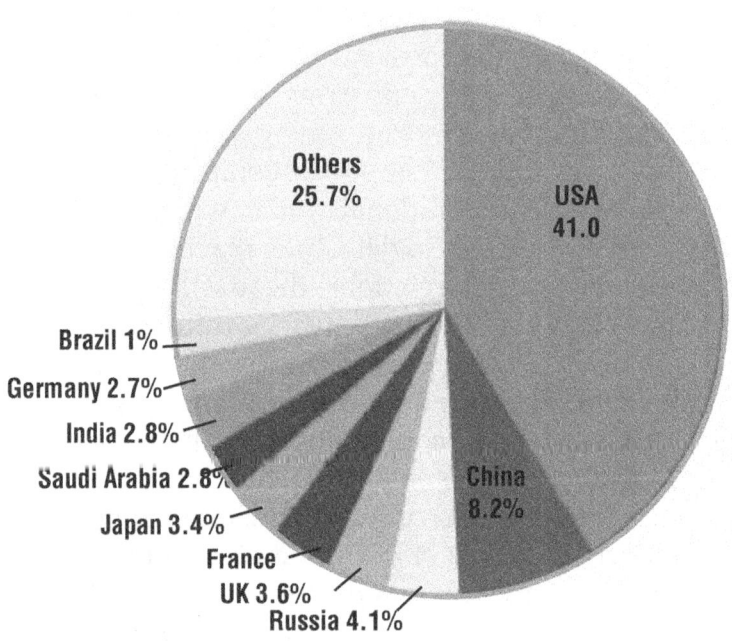

Figure 2-2. Shares of World Military Spending for the Top 10 Spenders, 2011.

What about **potential** military power? If the United States retrenched, who might be tempted to mount a challenge? The European Union (EU) collectively boasts a larger population and economy than the United States, key sinews of global power. Japan is also highly developed with a large population, though considerably smaller than the United States. However, Europe and Japan are American allies and show little appetite to overturn the global order. The concern amongst U.S. policymakers is more that the Europeans and Japanese will not contribute enough toward maintaining global security, not that they will actively undermine it.

On the other hand, there are some states whose goals are thought to be incompatible with the United States and who are most likely in the near future to be active military opponents. These are, of course, the surviving members of the "axis of evil"—Iran and North Korea. However, while these states' **intentions** may be as malign as those of previous American enemies, their actual and potential **capabilities** are vastly inferior. According to the latest World Bank figures, the United States boasts a population of 311.6 million people and a gross domestic product (GDP) in international dollars of $15.09 trillion. Iran, by contrast, has a population of 74.8 million and a GDP of $331 billion,[3] while North Korea has 24.45 million people and an estimated GDP of $28 billion.[4] To put this in perspective, America's population is three times that of Iran and North Korea combined, while America's GDP is over 48 times that of Iran's and almost 539 times that of North Korea's. It is very difficult to imagine a scenario in which North Korea or Iran could even potentially rival the United States in terms of capabilities, irrespective of whether the U.S. retrenches. This would require rapid and sustained economic growth in these countries, something which is unlikely in itself and even more unlikely without also triggering political changes which may render these states less hostile to the United States anyway (such as democratization).

Now, the threat from Iran or North Korea could be regional rather than global. Neither country has the potential to be the new Nazi Germany or Soviet Union, but they could cause localized problems for the United States by, for instance (in the case of Iran), disrupting Middle Eastern oil supplies, acquiring nuclear weapons, or sponsoring terrorist groups.

While this is a more realistic concern, there are a number of reasons to doubt that U.S. retrenchment would spark off a serious Iranian challenge. Cutting off or restricting oil flows would ultimately also damage the Iranian economy. As the 1973 Organization of the Petroleum Exporting Countries (OPEC) oil crisis showed, while interruptions to global oil supplies may profit oil-producing nations in the short term as prices increase, in the long run, it does them little good as the global economy slows and oil-producing countries look to conservation and alternative energy sources (Yergin 1991). A nightmare scenario in which Iran cuts off Middle Eastern oil supplies or rapidly raises prices is therefore unlikely precisely because this would undermine the revenues which help the Iranian regime stay in power.[5]

As for the pursuit of nuclear weapons and sponsorship of terrorist organizations, there is a strong argument to be made that U.S. retrenchment would make either of these behaviors less likely rather than more. While the reasons behind Iran's pursuit of nuclear weapons cannot be known with certainty at this stage, many international relations scholars have pointed out that fear of a U.S. invasion is one of them (Waltz 2012; Sagan, Betts, and Waltz 2007). If Iran wants nuclear weapons to deter an American attack, then a reduction in America's ability to attack Iran through retrenchment would **reduce** Iran's incentives to acquire them. Iran's sponsorship of groups such as the Mahdi Army or Hezbollah could also be seen in similar terms. In this view, Iran's goal is to use such organizations to tie down American and Israeli resources in Iraq and Lebanon, respectively, so that they cannot be used against Iran itself. Such a strategy would be similar to that of the United States itself in sponsoring the Afghan *mujahedeen* against the Soviets in the 1980s or of the Allies in sponsoring partisan campaigns against the Germans in occupied Europe. If this is correct, then a reduced American military presence in the Middle East would not embolden Iran, but rather serve to dampen down its more worrying behavior (Waltz 2012).

Of those actors with the motive to challenge the United States, the stateless terror group, al-Qaeda, is the most clearly malevolent. Yet al-Qaeda's capabilities are not commensurate with its ambitions. The events of September 11, 2001 (9/11) understandably gave rise to the belief that in modern conflict, nonstate actors may, in fact, pose greater risks to international security than traditional states. However, with the benefit of over 10 years of hindsight now, the weaknesses of nonstate actors have also been revealed. Unable to mobilize the level of resources that a state can, even the deadliest nonstate actors are too weak to inflict damage on the scale of a Nazi Germany or Soviet Union. As many risk analysts have pointed out, the risks posed by al-Qaeda to Americans are smaller than many other more mundane factors which attract hardly any public attention (Bailey 2011; Mueller and Stewart 2011). Again, of course, it is hard to estimate how much these risks might rise for a given level of reduction in U.S. defense spending. How the probability of future terrorist attacks might respond to changes in U.S. policy is hard to estimate precisely because terrorist attacks are so rare, giving us little past data to go by. Nonetheless, even taking the most pessimistic estimates as valid, terrorism still constitutes a less severe risk to life and limb for the average American than other risk factors which receive a lower budgetary priority. For instance, Ronald Bailey examined all the foiled cases of terrorism on U.S. soil since 9/11 as documented by the Heritage Foundation. Bailey then supposes that these attacks had succeeded in killing an average of 100 Americans each **and** that there had been another successful 9/11-level attack. Even under these assumptions, the United States would still have spent approximately 20 times the amount per life saved on preventing terrorism than on the average Federal protective regulation. This is all the more striking, given that Bailey does not include the wars in Iraq and Afghanistan as counterterrorism spending (Bailey 2011).

So having examined the security situation, there is a spectrum of capacities and intentions. On the one hand, there are actors who have the capacity, but not the motive, to challenge the United States (the Europeans and Japan), and on the other, those who have the motive, but lack the capacity (rogue states and terrorist organizations). In the middle, however, are the ambiguous cases—states which have, or may in the future have, the capacity to challenge the United States and whose intentions are unclear. These are America's erstwhile Cold War rivals, Russia and China.

Russia is a large middle-income country and hence has more potential power than Iran or North Korea, but it also faces severe internal demographic challenges, including falling life expectancy. With a shrinking population, Russia has also experienced falling potential military power. Its improved economic performance under Vladimir Putin is more reflective of a natural resource boom than of higher productivity or better quality institutions — the factors which make for long-term, sustainable economic growth and provide a solid foundation for military power. As an indication of this, investment analyst Ruchir Sharma notes that Russia still ranks 120th out of 183 countries on the World Bank's ease of doing business rankings (Sharma 2012).

China, rather than Russia, is the most credible candidate to emerge as a peer competitor to the United States. With a population of 1.344 billion people, the Chinese outnumber Americans by over four to one.[6] As it stands, China's economy is almost half the size of America's,[7] and the gap is famously closing. In terms of potential power, then, China is the most plausible future threat. Yet even here, there are a number of unanswered questions. China's rulers are alleged to believe that the days when they will be able to challenge American power lie decades in the future (Friedberg 2011). In the meantime, many things could happen. For one, China's current rapid economic growth could come to a halt. Many analysts recall that Japan was once considered to be the rising power poised to eclipse the United States, not long before Japan entered a period of prolonged economic stagnation (Kristof 1997). In the Chinese case, analysts point to coming demographic problems as the population ages (Sharma 2012) and also to political interference in the economy and weak property rights protections (Acemoglu and Robinson 2012) as factors which could slow or halt China's economic rise.

Assume, however, that China's economy does continue to grow rapidly. This leads to the possibility that

China will transition to democracy. One of the most solid findings in comparative politics is that wealthier countries are more likely to be democratic than poorer ones (although the reasons why are unclear) (Pzeworski et al. 2000). Similarly, one of the most solid findings in international relations is that democracies do not go to war with one another (although, again, no one is sure precisely why) (Bennett and Stam 2004). If China's economic rise does continue, one of the likely consequences of this may be Chinese democratization, one of the likely consequences of which, in turn, is improved relations with the United States. Consequently, Chinese economic growth may put China into the same category as Europe and Japan—states with the capacity, but not the motive, to challenge the United States. Indeed, this is precisely the hope of American leaders who press for engagement with China (Friedberg 2011).

However, let us assume that China continues to rise to a position in which it is capable of challenging the United States, and it does so while the Communist Party remains in power. What then? The question now arises—what would the Chinese leadership gain by engaging in security competition, let alone war, with the United States? After all, few countries have gained more from the current global system than China. What issues are there which are important enough to the Chinese to cause them to fight the United States or American allies such as Japan, risking highly profitable economic ties or even nuclear war?

The answer for "China pessimists" such as John Mearsheimer is clear. One need not assume especially aggressive motives or an expansionist ideology on the part of China to see why its rise will not be peaceful. Rather, as China rises, it will seek to improve its own security position by establishing hegemony over East Asia, which will mean ejecting the United States from the region. The United States, however, cannot countenance this exclusion because it would give the Chinese a free hand to begin interfering in America's own backyard, the Western hemisphere. Chinese and American interests over East Asia will ultimately be irreconcilable, even if both sides are rational and concerned only with their own security (Mearsheimer 2005.)

Whether one accepts Mearsheimer's pessimism or not, the sheer size of China makes it the biggest long-term potential security challenge the United States faces. It is true, as Michael Beckley points out, that China's size alone does not guarantee that it will be a world power. Beckley points out that 19th century China was the world's largest country and economy, but was politically prostrate and picked over by the Western powers (Beckley 2011). True as this is, China's disarray in the 19th century was a historical aberration. Would anyone care to bet that, in the future, China will continue to arrange its internal affairs as badly as it did in the heyday of European imperialism? In fact, power is the product both of a state's population and how efficiently it mobilizes its national resources, broadly construed. If efficiency were the only relevant criterion, Switzerland and Norway would be military behemoths. China's population means that it does not have to be as efficient as most other countries in order to be as powerful. To be as powerful as the United States, for instance, China would only need to be one fourth as efficient.

Without democratization, moreover, China's true intentions will remain opaque compared to the EU or Japan. Yet even if the pessimistic view of China is correct, this is a challenge which lies sometime in the future. It is not clear that higher defense spending today, especially if it comes at the expense of fiscal solvency, is the correct way to deal with it.

The previous analysis on America's relative power position sheds light on whether retrenchment might "signal weakness." The concepts of signaling and resolve have engendered lively controversy in international relations. The premise of the signaling school was questioned by Darryl Press. Press pointed out that the signaling theory rests on the idea that reputation is portable from one issue to another—that is, that the Chinese will make inferences about likely U.S. behavior over Taiwan from its decisions with respect to Iraq. Yet, Press showed that states tend not to make such "dispositional" inferences from other states' behavior (Press 2005). Rather, they believe that behavior over one issue reveals information only about a state's valuation of that particular issue and nothing else. For instance, Press showed that, contrary to historical mythology, the only inference which Hitler drew from the Munich agreement was that Britain and France did not care about Czechoslovakia, not that they were generally "weak." Hitler did not, so Press claimed, draw any inferences from Munich about how the British and French would react to an invasion of Poland, for instance. In Press' view, states such as China would not conclude from U.S. retrenchment that the United States was "weak." They would simply believe that the United States was trying to save money, something which is rather obvious anyway. Nor would a withdrawal from, say, Afghanistan, be interpreted as meaning the United States would be less willing to defend Taiwan.

Yet, Press' skeptical view has, in turn, been challenged. Anne Sartori points out that the importance of a reputation for resolve very much depends on what assumptions one makes about linkages between issues (Sartori 2012). If, as Press contends, states believe different issues to be entirely unconnected, then clearly a reputation for resolve is pointless. At the same time, as Sartori insightfully points out, if issues are **too** interconnected, then a reputation for resolve is also pointless. Take, for instance, the domino theory justification for the war in Vietnam—that, by fighting hard over a relatively unimportant issue like Vietnam, the United States will gain a reputation for resolve which will make it less likely that the Soviets might, for instance, invade Western Europe. The problem, as Sartori points out, is that when one examines this logic carefully, it can be interpreted as saying the United States is actually "weak"—it wants to fight a less costly war in Vietnam in order to avoid fighting a more costly war in Europe. If the Soviets had actually bought the domino theory, then they would have drawn precisely the opposite conclusion from America's war in Vietnam to that which American policymakers wanted to give. The Soviets would not have concluded that America was so highly resolved that it would have incurred huge losses even over a comparatively unimportant country as Vietnam. Rather, they would have perceived America as a "weak" actor, using Vietnam as an elaborate bluff to escape the costs of a full-scale war in Germany.

Sartori, however, goes on to explain that a reputation for resolve is most important when issues are seen as being moderately connected. If issues are too strongly connected, then supposedly costly signals are also interpreted as bluffs. If issues are not connected at all, then a state's behavior over one issue will have no impact on its interactions with other states over separate issues. Yet, if issues are somewhat but not entirely connected, then building a reputation for resolve through costly signals is, Sartori claims, useful.

While Sartori's work does go a long way toward clarifying a conceptually tough issue, it, of course, leaves open the question—what kind of world are we actually in? To what extent are issues actually linked? Thus, while the political science literature on signaling has clarified many key issues, it remains frustratingly divided over whether building a reputation for resolve is something over which the United States should incur costs.

Yet, in light of the contemporary situation, the concern over resolve is less pertinent. When Schelling laid the framework of signaling theory in the Cold War, the material balance between the United States and the Soviet Union was very even. Consequently, the difference between victory and defeat for one side or the other could plausibly come down to which side was more highly resolved. Yet, America's conventional superiority since the end of the Cold War has been so overwhelming that even a lowly resolved America can prevail over most opponents—the United States defeated Yugoslavia over Kosovo and deposed Muammar Gadhafi's regime in Libya, for instance, without suffering a single combat fatality. Resolve is not as crucial an asset in a unipolar as in a bipolar world.

In short, the security situation in 2012 was very benign in a historical perspective. There was no Soviet Union, or a Nazi Germany, even in prospect. There were actors which wished the United States harm, such as North Korea and al-Qaeda, but they were not very powerful. There were actors which were powerful (at least potentially), but they did not wish the United States harm, such as Europe and Japan. There were actors which were somewhat powerful and whose intentions were unclear. One of these—Russia—had far less potential power than it appeared at first glance and will likely have even less in the future. The other—China—may have been a threat if several factors came together at the same time: China continuing to grow without democratizing and its leaders perceiving a benefit in challenging the United States. Even if this happens, it is a long-term future challenge, not one requiring a military buildup today.

Having examined the first question in detail, let us look at the second—what do the fiscal and economic positions suggest?

WHAT IS THE FISCAL AND ECONOMIC POSITION?

According to one realist view of international relations expressed by McDonald and Parent, retrenchment results from the "structural pressures of the international system" (McDonald and Parent 2011). Put in less abstract terms, this means that states which do not reduce their defense expenditure when their relative power position worsens run an increased risk of being selected out of the international system. Why is this?

Governments who wish to maintain a higher level of defense spending on a stagnating economic base may need to borrow more funding. Increased borrowing, however, normally leads to increased interest rates,[8] which have numerous baleful consequences (Furceri and Sousa 2011). First, states which have to pay more to borrow are less likely to prevail in security competition and war. In the former case, Kenneth Schultz and Barry Weingast demonstrate that in long-term competition, the lower borrowing costs of 18th-century Britain and the 20th-century United States helped them to outlast their respective strategic competitors, France and the Soviet Union (Schultz and Weingast 2003). Recent work by Patrick Shea also convincingly suggests that higher borrowing costs are significantly associated with defeat in "hot" wars as well as "cold" security competition (Shea 2014).

A second problem is that interest payments themselves come to take up a substantial share of government spending. This reduces both the amount that states can spend on defense directly and also reduces what they can spend on other areas which may in the long run promote economic growth—for instance, public infrastructure, research and development, and education. As the Center for Strategic and Budgetary Assessments shows, interest payments are already coming to take up a significant share of Federal government spending (Krepinevich, Chinn, and Harrison 2012).

A third problem is that government borrowing "crowds out" private investment (Pass, Lowes, and Davies 2005). The insight here is that capital is just like any other good—when demand increases, the price increases too. Government borrowing represents an increase in demand for capital, meaning that the price of capital must also rise. In other words, private corporations must offer higher interest rates to bondholders or higher returns to stockholders in order to compete with the government for capital. Some companies will, of course, not be capable of doing so and may go to the wall.

Alternatively, government may seek to maintain current levels of defense expenditure by increasing taxes. This, however, is also problematic. One reason is that higher taxes may reduce incentives for work and increase those for tax evasion—an effect described through the famous and controversial "Laffer Curve." The Laffer Curve states that there comes a point at which further increases in taxation reduce government revenue through these perverse incentives (Knowles 2010). This is displayed in Figure 2-3 as the point t*. While most economists accept the principle behind the Laffer Curve, very few believe that the United States today is at the point at which increased taxation would reduce government revenue (Trabant and Uhlig 2006). In fact, the top marginal rates have been far higher historically at times when the U.S. economy has grown more quickly than it is growing today—for instance in the 1950s (Hungerford 2012). Consequently, it is important not to overstate this point in discussing retrenchment.

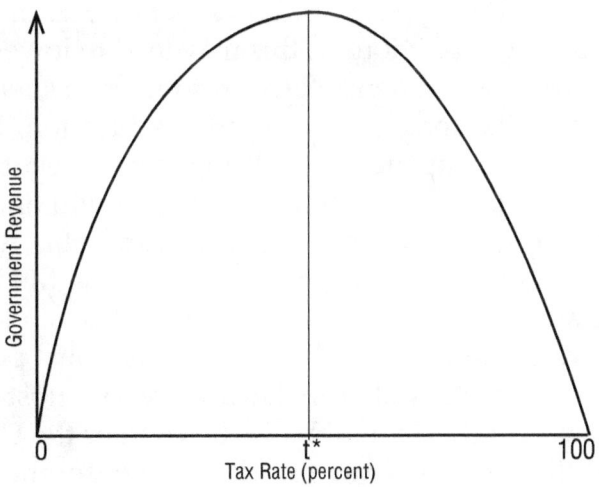

Figure 2-3. The Laffer Curve (from Knowles 2010).

More compellingly, higher taxation to fund defense can reduce economic growth in the long term because of the diversion of funds from private and public civilian investment, as noted by Robert Pape (Pape 2009). One tax dollar spent on defense is a tax dollar not spent on education, civilian research and development (R&D), or transport. One dollar taken by the Federal government in taxation is no longer available for private investors to sink into a new Google or Microsoft. Now, of course, it has often been pointed out that defense R&D investment has numerous positive spin-offs for the civilian economy, of which the Internet is the most obvious. However, this argument runs into the objection — if the U.S. Government wants to sponsor R&D in the private civilian sector, would it not be more efficient to do so directly rather than as an unintended consequence of defense spending?

A final option open to governments in the face of reduced resources is to maintain defense spending by cutting other types of public expenditure. In some cases, as noted previously, this may lead to lower economic growth and hence fewer resources to spend on defense in the long run. Arguably, education, R&D, and transport expenditure fall into this category, although, the precise amount of future growth one gets per dollar spent in these areas is disputable. Other forms of government expenditure, such as Medicare or Social Security, do not contribute quite so obviously to future economic growth and hence national power. Such expenditures also make up a very substantial proportion of the Federal budget. Whether the United States should choose to prioritize defense ahead of other public policy objectives is, however, beyond the scope of this review.

In light of this, then, the surprising fact in the political economy of defense literature is that there is little clear evidence that increased defense spending really does reduce growth. Emile Benoit, the first economist to examine the question empirically, came to the conclusion that defense spending **increases** economic growth (Benoit 1973, 1978). However, others have criticized Benoit's methodology and grounding in economic theory (Ram 1995). It should be noted that increased economic growth can lead to increased defense spending, which can lead analysts to conclude erroneously that the causal relationship goes in the opposite direction. Ward and Davis, analyzing data from the United States between 1948 and 1996 and using a model taking into account the positive spillover effects from defense expenditure on civilian economy, concluded that defense spending does lower economic growth significantly (Ward and Davis 1992). However, as Rati Ram notes in his review of the copious literature on the subject, economists have produced different results on the subject, depending on which countries they examine, which years, and how their models are specified. In approximately equal numbers, they have concluded that defense spending increases economic growth, that it lowers economic growth, and that it makes no difference (Ram 1995).

Other than providing fodder for the old joke that if you put two economists in a room, you will get three opinions, what are we to make of this? For the reasons outlined previously, it seems quite likely that defense expenditure should lower growth, so why is the evidence so inconclusive? If there is no strong evidence that defense spending lowers growth, is the whole premise behind retrenchment wrong? Can we simply spend as much as we like on defense without worrying about the economic consequences?

Here an analogy with another economic finding may be in order. Economists in the 1950s discovered an inverse relationship between inflation and unemployment. That is, when unemployment goes up, inflation goes down, and vice versa. Policymakers drew the conclusion from this correlation that it was possible to "trade off" unemployment and inflation against each other. The problem was that the relationship only held when individuals were not aware of it and did not consciously try to take advantage of it. When policymakers announced that they were happy to allow inflation to increase in order to combat unemployment, employees demanded higher wages to compensate, which increased prices, which increased inflation further in a vicious cycle. By ignoring the fact that relationships between variables in economics are the result of individuals' conscious choices, policymakers ended up getting higher inflation without lower unemployment (Carlin and Soskice 2006).

Similarly, when examining the weak relationship between defense spending and economic growth, it must be remembered that most policymakers have believed that excessive defense spending lowers growth and so can be expected to take care not to increase it beyond levels which they think the economy can bear. Where they have been compelled to increase defense expenditure in spite of a sluggish economy, they may have taken care to reduce other forms of government spending to keep the tax burden and budget deficit under control. In short, we may see little evidence that defense spending hurts economic growth precisely because few policymakers have been foolish enough to risk the health of their economies by overspending on security. This leads to a paradoxical conclusion. If policymakers were naively to read from Benoit and Ram and begin spending freely on guns and bombs, we may actually start seeing strong evidence for the first time of a negative effect of defense expenditure on growth! In short, the surprising lack of evidence of a negative effect of defense spending on economic growth should not lead us to conclude that retrenchment is unnecessary. Rather, retrenchment is necessary when a state faces deficit and debt problems. In the long run, states need to align revenue and spending. If they do not, they will face higher interest rates and/or higher taxes, which will divert investment from the productive sectors of the economy that are the wellspring of national power.

While the international security situation provides the United States with a great deal of room for maneuver, this can hardly be said of the fiscal and economic situation. According to the Congressional Budget Office, if current trends in taxes and spending continue, public debt will reach 101 percent of GDP by 2021 and 187 percent by 2035. As Krepinevich, Chinn, and Harrison report, this could seriously jeopardize the U.S. ability to borrow, even in a national emergency. Krepinevich, Chinn, and Harrison quote Erskine Bowles, Co-Chair of President Obama's deficit commission, as saying that the national debt is a "cancer" which will "destroy the nation from within." The debt problem will be all the more serious as the "baby boomer" generation retires and begins drawing benefits, changing America's worker to retiree ratio from the current 3.2 to 2.1 by 2035 (Krepinevich, Chinn, and Harrison 2012).

Defense spending is not the only contributing factor toward fiscal problems, of course, but it is a major one. As Krepinevich, Chinn, and Harrison note, increases in defense spending account for 16 percent of America's shift from surplus to deficit over the 2000s, compared with 4 percent for increases in Social Security, Medicare, and Medicaid. Defense is a smaller contributor to the current fiscal crisis than revenue shortfalls, but in accounting for nearly one-fifth of the change, it is scarcely insignificant (Krepinevich, Chinn, and Harrison 2012). In the absence of a pressing military threat, therefore, defense spending has to bear part of the burden of adjustment.

This then raises the question—if retrenchment is the way ahead, how best can it be done? What are the factors which make it more or less likely to work well? Can efficiencies be found allowing defense spending to be reduced without reducing commitments?

HOW TO DO RETRENCHMENT

The political science and political economy literature reveals a number of principles which can help to guide successful retrenchment. The problem is that, of these principles, many are already being enacted. Consequently, it will be very difficult to maintain all U.S. current commitments under retrenchment. Some will have to be deemed lower priority. The first principle is what defense economist Keith Hartley called **substitution** (Hartley 2011). As this principle has a number of different applications, it will receive the most prolonged attention. The intuition is to examine all the goals of security policy and determine whether, for each goal, there is a cheaper way of achieving the same effect. In the civilian economy, an example of substitution would be if the price of driving were to increase but the price of public transport remained the same, more individuals would choose to get to work by bus or train than by car.

The second principle, outlined by the Center for Strategic and Budgetary Assessments, is that of **cost imposition**. Here, the idea is to arrange your defense spending so as to force your adversaries to compete in areas which cost them relatively more than they cost you (Krepinevich, Chinn, and Harrison 2012). A few examples to follow will help to make this clear.

The third principle is to remember that **sunk costs are sunk**. The economic principle of sunk costs suggests that individuals should consider only future costs and benefits when deciding on a course of action—recouping past investments should not figure in the costs (Arkes and Blumer 1985). This is a prescriptive-logical principle of how people **should** behave, not an empirical claim about how people **do** behave. There is both experimental and archival evidence that citizens and policymakers do not treat sunk costs as sunk—yet, this does not mean that they are right to do so. Identifying common cognitive errors in decisionmaking still serves a useful purpose in advancing better public policy.

The final principle is probably the most important, and so will be left to the Conclusion. This is the principle that Hartley refers to as the **principle of final outputs** (Hartley 2011). I will discuss this principle more in the subsequent pages. The principle of final outputs simply boils down to this, however—it is very hard to determine how best to retrench without answering fundamental questions about what defense expenditure is ultimately **for**.

Substitution.

Substitution in defense policy could play out in a number of ways. The first and most obvious is through external alliances (Trubowitz 2011). Instead of the United States spending money to balance against China, persuade Japan, Australia, South Korea, and Vietnam to do it instead. If there is instability in former European colonies in the Middle East, have the British and French take care of it. In fact, some political scientists such as Stephen Walt argue that should the United States cut defense spending, it will compel allies to do more. This logic dates back to Mancur Olson and Richard Zeckhauser's *Economic Theory of Alliances*, which claimed that American allies under-contribute toward defense because they believe the United States will take care of the responsibility for them (Olson and Zeckhauser 1966). It follows that, if the United States were to signal an intention to reduce its defense spending, America's Asian and European allies would have to step into the breach. This, according to Walt, would represent a win-win for the United States — security is still provided, but the United States does not have to pay quite so much for it (Walt 2012).

While logically appealing, there are certain drawbacks to this position. First, America's allies may also be in decline or straightened economic circumstances. Today, this is especially the case in Europe. Second, America's allies may not be capable of providing the necessary level of security by themselves. In World War II, the United States first intended simply to supply the British who, it was hoped, could deal with the actual fighting against Nazi Germany. Britain, however, was simply not strong enough to do so (Barnett 1986). Similarly, in the early Cold War, the United States first intended to leave European security primarily to Europeans, but again found that they were not strong enough alone to stand against the Soviet Union (Ferguson 2004). Thus, while there is a great deal of sense in increasing dependence on allies, the process can only be taken so far.

A second form of substitution is also potentially controversial. This involves the use of private military companies instead of regular military. Here, the United States has already taken the practice as far as it can. In theory, the use of private military companies could cut costs significantly for a number of reasons. First, as with any service, competition among a number of providers would be expected to stimulate greater effort and provide strong incentives to reduce costs. Second, for a number of military functions which have civilian analogues such as engineering, logistics and maintenance, private companies might be thought to have a comparative advantage over a government agency because they are obliged to compete and survive in the marketplace. Third, the greater specificity of the contract between the Department of Defense (DoD) and a private contractor relative to a soldier might be thought to reduce costly "shirking." This is because there are more clear "redlines" on what constitutes a violation of the contract and hence less ambiguity for a potential shirker to exploit.

In light of this, it might be instructive to pose a provocative thought experiment—why not use private contractors for all military functions? Would this not achieve security goals at a greatly reduced cost? The political science and political economy literature suggests that the answer to this question is unambiguously "no." There are many good reasons why private contracting in defense policy can only go so far.

The first follows from the nature of the private military market. This market is, in fact, similar to the armaments industry, whose dynamics were well-described by William Rogerson. American armaments manufacturers are in the position of producing products for essentially one buyer—the U.S. Government and whichever foreign powers to whom the U.S. Government allows arms makers to sell (Rogerson 1995). This situation is known in economics as a "monopsony." Similarly, the U.S. Government is unlikely to be happy if XE or Control Risks is selling military services to Russia, China, or Iran. This dependence on one buyer makes both the armaments and the private military industry vulnerable. If the U.S. Government does not buy their services, they have few other profitable outlets. If the U.S. Government does not provide some kind of security, a "retainer," for companies which do not win the current contract, they would normally exit the market and leave the winner of the contract with a de facto monopoly. Yet, it would be prohibitively expensive for the United States to pay for the upkeep of three or four private armies, each with their own training, recruitment, and promotion systems and legacy costs. Consequently, if the United States did contract out all "fighting services" to private military companies, it would most likely very quickly replace the current public "monopoly" with a private one. More seriously, there would be more insidious dangers in contracting out "fighting services" to private military companies.

At present, service in the U.S. military is unquestionably regarded as more than an economic transaction. Soldiers rightly enjoy very high levels of public esteem. Young boys dream of becoming soldiers, not actuaries. Marines in uniform boarding civilian aircraft are given rounds of applause. Investment bankers and personal injury lawyers are not.

Soldiers often earn less than comparably qualified individuals in civilian life in part because they are "paid" in honor and esteem. A brilliant essay by economic philosopher Geoffrey Brennan suggests that this is how it should be (Brennan 1996). Professions such as the military which receive relatively more esteem and honor will attract individuals who value honor and esteem more than money. Professions such as personal injury law which receive relatively more money and less esteem will attract individuals who value money more than esteem. For the military, this is the best outcome – individuals who care more about esteem and honor than money can be trusted to stand and fight where naked self-interest might suggest running. They will also be less corruptible and less prone to abusing civilians.

The danger with excessive use of private military companies is that it may replace the honor and esteem on which the military profession is founded with a purely economic transaction and so end up attracting the wrong "types" into service. Consider, for instance, the connotations of the term "mercenary" relative to that of "soldier." Consider also the widespread complaints among professional soldiers about the attitude and behavior of military contractors, especially toward Iraqi civilians. In short, military contractors are not a great substitute for professional soldiers. For support functions, they may help to reduce costs, but there are sound political, scientific, and economic reasons why combat should remain a state monopoly.

A less controversial means of applying substitution to the military is through increased use of reservists. This is a large part of the British Government's defense plans (Hartley 2011). Reservists are obviously less costly as they are not full-time soldiers, but at the same time, they do not have the same experience or incentive to perform, given that the military is not their only or primary career. Reservists make the most sense in branches of the service which policymakers expect to use only infrequently. Again, however, increased use of the National Guard is already a part of U.S. defense adjustment.

A final way in which substitution can be applied to defense is, ironically, by reducing reliance on military means to achieve political ends. Diplomacy, espionage, and subversion are three potential alternatives (Trubowitz 2011). For instance, since 9/11, the military has been a significant component of the war on terrorism. The theory is that by building capable, stable states in the Islamic world, the military can "drain the swamp" and deny terrorists a safe haven from which to launch attacks on the United States (Kilcullen 2004).

Part of the problem, however, is that terrorists can substitute, too. If Afghanistan is denied to them as a safe haven, then they may move to the Tribal Areas of Pakistan. If the "costs" of using these areas becomes too high, they may then move to Yemen, Mali, or the southern Philippines (Rose 2009).

This raises the question—is a dollar spent on "global COIN" the cheapest way to achieve a given reduction in the risk of a terrorist attack on the United States? Are there cheaper ways to achieve the same effect? Part of the appeal of the drone war for its advocates is the potential they see in it for getting a greater bang in terms of threat reduction for a vastly reduced buck, relative to COIN. The counter to this view is that successful drone attacks depend upon good intelligence, which in turn requires boots on the ground, both to gather this intelligence and to protect informers (Biddle 2009).

Drone strikes are also problematic for the issue of civilian casualties. Although administration figures dispute the proposition that drone strikes cause more civilian deaths than COIN operations, it is at the very least plausible that missiles fired from a distance make accidental deaths more likely (Cavallaro, Sonnenberg, and Knuckley 2012). If civilian deaths cause increased radicalization and hence recruitment into terrorist organizations, they may, in fact, prove counterproductive (Brooks 2012).

Political economists generally tend not to make ethical judgments themselves (Sen 1970). This does not mean to say that political economists do not believe in ethical judgments, but that it is not the domain of their subject. Questions such as how one trades off the lives of soldiers versus civilians, or civilian casualties from drone strikes versus civilian casualties from terrorism, are thought to be more the domain of moral philosophy and political theory. Nonetheless, it would not be impossible to include the risk to civilians as an explicit cost factor in the cost-benefit analysis of terrorism. As we shall see, welfare economics does so frequently with respect to other areas of public policy (Stern 2006).

Alternatively, it may be that cutting terrorists off at the source is not the most effective place in the terrorist "production line" to intervene. The basic errors in security procedures in the State Department and intelligence agencies identified by the 9/11 Commission suggests that a dollar spent in law enforcement, border security, and espionage may have a bigger marginal effect in terms of risk reduction than military intervention overseas (9/11 Commission Report 2006).

The question, of course, is whether, given the amount already spent on Homeland Security since 9/11, more spending here will have much of an impact either (Mueller 2006; Mueller and Stewart 2011). As the risk analyst Howard Kunreuther pointed out, counterterrorism expenditure of any kind is paying for "small reductions in probabilities that are already extremely low" (Kunreuther 2002).

In short, the process of substituting law enforcement, diplomacy, and espionage for COIN is already underway. Consequently, many of the savings it promises have already been realized. Moreover, given that the baseline risk of terrorism is already low, any counterterrorism spending can only buy a tiny additional reduction.

Cost Imposition.

Krepinevich, Chinn, and Harrison note a clever means used by great powers in the past to get more value for their defense dollars (Krepinevich, Chinn, and Harrison 2012). This refers to a strategy of asymmetric cost imposition. In this strategy, states concentrate their spending on areas in which their principal adversary is at a comparative disadvantage. By comparative disadvantage, I mean that one's adversary must spend more proportionately simply in order to maintain parity.

There are two particularly striking instances of this. The first is the British dreadnought program of the pre-World War I era. German ships had to leave port via the Kiel Canal, and, in order to maintain parity with the British, the Germans not only had to spend to build more dreadnoughts, they also had to spend on widening the Kiel Canal to allow dreadnought-sized vessels to pass through. Consequently, a given dreadnought cost the Germans more proportionately than the British. Similarly, the U.S. decision to pursue stealth bomber technologies imposed an asymmetric burden on the Soviet Union. With one of the world's longest borders, the Soviets were compelled to spend large amounts on anti-aircraft defense, further weakening the Union of Soviet Socialist Republics' (USSR) fiscal position.

Krepinevich, Chinn, and Harrison note that the United States is not publicly committed to asymmetric cost imposition on anyone (Krepinevich, Chinn, and Harrison 2012). In many ways, this is understandable. It may not be diplomatically astute to state explicitly that the United States is spending on a particular project in order to impose asymmetric costs on Russia or China. Nonetheless, in the competitive realm of international relations, states often look to exploit others' vulnerability, even if they do not make a song and dance out of doing so. The Chinese are not investing in anti-access, area denial capabilities in order to combat Uighur separatists (Friedberg 2011). Consequently, it would not contravene Marquis of Queensberry rules for American strategists to examine discreetly where they might compel China to compete in areas of comparative disadvantage. For one thing, it should be noted that the United States is still far ahead of most potential rivals in terms of high technology equipment. In spite of hype to the contrary, China, and even more so Russia, are simply not as innovative as the United States on the production frontier of the world economy. Very high technology would therefore seem to be one area in which the United States would be competing at a comparative advantage.

As for the threat from nonstate actors such as al-Qaeda, asymmetric cost imposition appears to have been little explored. Previous literature mostly concerns how al-Qaeda has been able to pursue such a strategy against the United States through measures such as suicide bombing and improvised explosive devices. Yet this does not mean that this strategy cannot also be wielded against al-Qaeda by the United States. If we conceive of terrorism as a "production line" running from recruitment all the way to the completion of an attack, there must be some points which are costlier to the terrorist group than others. Is training the costliest part of the line, or is it infiltration into the target zone? If careful research into terrorist finance can provide consistent information on this, then strategies can be devised to compel terrorist groups to concentrate more time and effort on the most expensive part of their operations.

Sunk Costs are Sunk.

Behavioral economists are well known for a number of discoveries casting doubt on the rational actor model of the social sciences. One of their earliest findings concerned an intriguing facet of decisionmaking — when deciding on a course of action, we tend to take into account not just future costs and benefits, but those costs which we have already incurred. The sunk costs fallacy should not be confused with simply sticking with a course of action in which one has incurred costs — if the expected benefits of this course of action still exceed the costs, sticking with it is entirely rational. The fallacy is when unfavorable new information arises about the costs of the course of action (or favorable information about the benefits of some alternative) of which the decisionmaker was not aware when making the initial decision **and the decisionmaker sticks with the initial decision anyway**.

Daniel Kahnemann gives a good example of the sunk costs fallacy in operation. Suppose a company has spent $50 million on a given project when it finds out that it will need an additional $60 million which was not originally budgeted to complete it. At the same time, however, a different project would also require $60 million but would provide a higher return. The sunk costs fallacy would be to invest the $60 million in the pre-existing project, even though the expected return is lower, because one believes that in doing so one has "recovered" one's initial investment (Kahnemann 2011).

Political scientists and business analysts have detected traces of the sunk costs fallacy in numerous political and commercial decisions. Large-scale capital projects are especially prone to the "sunk costs fallacy." The British and French Governments are known to have persevered with the construction of the supersonic Concorde jet in spite of mounting doubts about its commercial viability because of the money they had already invested in it (Arkes and Ayton 1999). Yet sunk costs do not refer only to money. Jeffrey Taliaferro explains both the French and the American decisions to stay in Vietnam after the prospects for success had diminished with reference to the sunk costs fallacy (Taliaferro 2004). Both sets of policymakers, in Taliaferro's view, believed that they had to stay the course in Vietnam in order to ensure that the blood and treasure which they had already expended there would not have been in vain.

"Sunk costs" reasoning cannot necessarily tell policymakers whether they should continue with a given project. Yet, it can offer useful guidance on the decisionmaking process itself. The guidance is this—costs, whether human or financial, which have already been incurred, should not factor as future benefits into decisionmaking about various courses of action. In examining what to do about a given project, policymakers should engage in the following thought experiment—if somehow we had arrived at the position we are in without the United States having expended anything on the project so far, would the current and future benefits outweigh the current and future costs?

Of course, ignoring sunk costs might be rational from the point of view of the state, but irrational from the point of view of an individual leader. To return to Kahneman's example, the executive who gave the green light to the $50 million project may have strong incentives to bring it to fruition so as not to appear incompetent. There is indeed experimental evidence to back this up—Michael Tomz, for instance, shows that voters reacted negatively to political leaders who initiated U.S. involvement in a crisis and then subsequently backed down (Tomz 2007).

Where this situation arises, the interests of the political leadership and the country as a whole have diverged. Even if the "cost overrun" was not due to incompetence on the part of the leader, it may be time for him or her to be replaced. Indeed, in the business case, Kahnemann explicitly recommends that the Board of Directors take action to remove chief executive officers who are personally invested in failing projects (Kahnemann 2011). A new leader is less likely to have the same attachment to the previous project and also less likely to face electoral punishment for abandoning it. Indeed, if the new leader was publicly opposed to the project from the start, he would be more likely to face electoral punishment for inconsistency if he did **not** abandon it.

Moreover, where the sunk costs are financial rather than human (that is, they refer to the development of new weapons projects rather than military operations), there is evidence that political leaders can treat sunk costs as sunk without fear of negative consequences. This is especially the case if the leaders in question can frame the issue as one of getting value for money for the taxpayers against special interests. Robert Gates, for instance, is one of the most popular and respected U.S. Defense Secretaries, in spite of, in the words of Lexington Institute's Loren Thompson, "prevailing on every major program kill he chose to pursue."[9] Perhaps, however, the causal relationship runs in the opposite direction—Gates was willing and able to kill more programs precisely because he already commanded so much respect across the political spectrum. This question calls for additional research to determine whether financial sunk costs are more readily ignorable than human ones.

Yet the idea that sunk costs really are a fallacy has not been without its critics. McAffee, Mialon, and Mialon (2010) point out that there are many reasons why rational decisionmakers may choose to incorporate sunk costs into their calculations. Here I will outline those which are most relevant to national security policy. The first is that past investments may have a cumulative effect on the probability of a given project succeeding (McAffee, Mialon, and Mialon 2010). Many projects in national security may be of this type—economic sanctions or COIN could fall into this category, for instance. Perhaps the "hearts and minds" projects already paid for are about to turn into a flood of tip-offs about the whereabouts of insurgent leaders, turning the tide of the campaign. Perhaps the target of the sanctions is teetering on the verge of economic ruin and getting ready to throw in the towel. It is quite conceivable that all the past costs a policymaker has incurred are about to "break the back" of the problem, and that turning away at this stage would be to snatch defeat from the jaws of victory. Properly considered, however, this line of argument is not too different from the standard rational actor prescription. If success requires "just one more push," then the net future benefits of a course of action will exceed the net costs. The only difference is that sunk costs factor into the cost-benefit calculation through their effect on the probability of success rather than as a stand-alone benefit.

Second, there may be reputational consequences to ignoring sunk costs which transcend the costs and benefits of the specific issue at hand. Acquiring and maintaining a reputation for sticking with projects which have run into difficulty may induce others to cooperate with you. Many projects require investments of time and effort by multiple partners to succeed. If one partner has a reputation for abandoning projects as soon as the numbers no longer stack up, then others may be reluctant to commit their own resources to working alongside them (McAffee, Mialon and Mialon 2010).

These are important qualifications in applying sunk costs reasoning to decisionmaking. By refining and clarifying the issue of sunk costs, they help decisionmakers to ask themselves the right kinds of questions in examining ongoing projects. Such questions might include, Do I really think that one more push will solve this problem, or am I simply trying to recoup my past investment? How are potential allies judging my persistence in this project? A further objection may also be raised—if sunk costs reasoning really is deeply rooted in human psychology, is it realistic to make policy recommendations based on individuals ignoring sunk costs? The United States may be able to cut spending on air transportation if soldiers were able to grow wings and fly, but this obviously is not going to happen.

Fortunately, there is evidence that making individuals aware of common heuristic errors can serve to change their behavior. Kahnemann points out that graduate students in economics and business who are taught about the sunk costs fallacy are significantly more likely to walk away from failing projects (Kahnemann 2011). Increasing knowledge of the faulty heuristics of baseball scouts led to the "sabermetric revolution" dramatized in the book and movie, "Moneyball." Starting with the Oakland A's, baseball teams came to recognize the value of data analysis as opposed to "gut feel" in selecting players (Lewis 2003).

Similarly, the hope is that increasing awareness of the "sunk costs fallacy," with the caveats mentioned previously, can help to sharpen the thinking not only of policymakers themselves but of their audience — the public and media who hold them accountable. In short, then, the existing political science and political economy literature offers some interesting suggestions about how retrenchment can be done well. Before moving on to the final and perhaps the most important recommendation, let us first examine a few notes of caution from the literature on retrenchment.

A different school of thought on retrenchment disagrees with the likes of Krauthammer and Gilpin on the desirability of retrenchment, but believes that it is likely to be hijacked by domestic interests. These scholars take their cue from the public choice school of political economy. Public choice was a reaction against an implicit view which political scientists and economists had taken of their role in political life — "whispering in the ear of the sovereign." In other words, social scientists had believed that there was one unitary individual called the "state" who wanted the best for its inhabitants, and the role of the social scientist was simply to find out what was the best policy so that this "benevolent social planner" could enact it (Buchanan 1972). This assumption was almost precisely analogous to the unitary actor view of the state in realist international relations theory. The problem, as public choice theorists realized, is that the state is not a unitary actor but rather a collection of individuals and groups who each may have interests contrary to that of the "state" as a whole (Snyder 1991; Trubowitz 1998; Narizny 2007). It may, for instance, be the case that the "United States" would do better to cut programs X and Y and spare program Z, but perhaps programs X and Y have more lobbying power or have struck a deal to join forces to shift the costs of retrenchment onto program Z.

It is not hard to see numerous examples of such problems in the contemporary United States. Congressmen fight to maintain military bases in their districts, even if these make little sense from the point of view of overall national defense. Political leaders come to power through the support of domestic constituencies which may or may not favor increased spending on national defense (Trubowitz 2011). Defense firms make campaign contributions to candidates from both parties to protect their contracts. Even the military itself can act as a lobby — service branches possess numerous strategies, such as off the record briefings, which they can use to punish politicians who propose scrapping favored projects (Rogerson 1995).

The latter problem can be seen as a special case of a more general issue in public choice — the "expert problem." An "expert problem" is where a customer requires expert information about how much of a given product or service to buy, but the expert in question stands to gain financially from the purchase. Think for instance of a dentist or a car mechanic—the average customer knows less than the mechanic or the dentist about what work needs to be done and, knowing this, the dentist or mechanic can gain by recommending more work than the customer actually needs (French 1986). Such expert problems are seen by some political scientists as plaguing security and defense spending. Military officers obviously know better than most civilians what their service branch needs in terms of technology, but at the same time they may wish to have more equipment than the United States taken as a whole really needs. This need not necessarily reflect any private, personal gain they may get from the purchase by DoD of military equipment, but simply an intrinsic desire to have the most up to date, technically advanced equipment regardless of whether it is needed. Given the high levels of respect which the U.S. public has for military officers, expert problems in this particular area could be especially acute. John Mueller believes that expert problems are especially common in the intelligence and counterterror community (Mueller 2006).

So although expert problems and political logrolling are likely to arise and complicate efforts to secure successful retrenchment, what does the political science and political economy literature say about when they are likely to be most acute and what can be done about them? First, political scientists and economists are skeptical about appeals to "political will" among policymakers and "the watchfulness of a well-informed citizenry" (Eisenhower 1961). Daniel Drezner has written that asking politicians to display political will is to ask them to stop being politicians (Drezner 2011). Suppose a political leader does arise who champions the national interest and displays political will in standing up to special interests—political scientists would claim it is likely he will simply be defeated and removed from office by someone less scrupulous. The well-informed citizenry concept is also problematic—as pointed out by political scientists going back to Mancur Olson, individual citizens are at a disadvantage relative to special interests because any one particular issue is worth less to them than it is to the interest group (Olson 1982). Consequently, it is the interest group as a whole which is more likely to get organized and get what it wants. In fact, political scientists are concluding that even becoming well-informed about the issues is too costly for the average voter. The average voter has a close to zero chance of determining the outcome of an election, so it is in his or her self-interest to devote his or her time to getting on with his or her own job, rather than absorbing a great deal of information about differing candidates' political positions—a stance termed "rational ignorance" by political scientist Anthony Downs (Downs 1957). Only individuals who derive some "extra-rational" intrinsic pleasure in learning about politics for its own sake actually will choose to do so.

Conversely, some political scientists believe that the structural pressures of the international system will eventually give such strong incentives to domestic interest groups to cooperate that they will be able to agree on a program of successful retrenchment. In this view, domestic disagreement only comes into play when there is little external pressure for the state to act in a unitary manner (McDonald and Parent 2011).

Unfortunately, this may be resting on an overly optimistic reading of realism. While realism is a very large tent incorporating many points of view, one of its most theoretically compelling strands suggests that it works through a process of selective adaptation similar to that of Darwinian evolution. In other words, realism does not suggest that any individual state will sort out its domestic difficulties when it comes under pressure from the international system. Rather, it claims that those which, for whatever reason, put aside their domestic difficulties will survive, and those which do not, will not (Feaver 2000). The latter claim is much less reassuring than the former.

Peter Trubowitz points out that there is a further micro-foundation for realism—political leaders do not want their states to be bested in international competition as this in itself will hinder their prospects for political survival (Trubowitz 2011). Nonetheless, it is less clear that a failure in the long term to retrench would have the same consequence—in fact, quite the opposite. A political leader could, for instance, increase defense spending through borrowing in the short term to triumph in international conflict and then pass the costs on to his or her successor. In short, the pressures of the international system cannot be relied upon themselves to produce successful retrenchment. As Trubowitz himself notes, domestic factors are also key (Trubowitz 2011).

Which domestic structural factors, then, might push the United States toward successful retrenchment and which would push it away? Let us start with the negative side of the ledger. Hendryk Spruyt suggests that a political system with a large number of "veto points" might have difficulty pursuing successful retrenchment. This means that a political system which puts power in the hands of many different groups who can hold up decisionmaking will find it harder to divest itself from unwieldy foreign commitments. Spruyt contrasts the protracted and difficult process of decolonization by France and the Netherlands with the more painless British transition. As the French and Dutch political systems had many "veto players" from different parties—individuals who can put a stop on political decisions—they came to be held hostage by colonial lobbies who wished to hold on to imperial possessions long after France and Holland had lost the power necessary to do so. By contrast, the British system centralizes power around the Prime Minister and his cabinet. Party discipline is very strong. Consequently, as soon as the British Government had decided that the Empire was a strategic liability, they were able to divest themselves of it relatively quickly (Spruyt 2005). Of course, the United States does not have a colonial empire from which to extricate itself. However, the U.S. political system, with the division of power among legislative and executive and lower levels of party discipline, make the United States more prone to capture by special interests looking to put a hold on retrenchment.

Even if it were desirable, however, constitutional reform to reduce the number of "veto players" in the U.S. system is clearly not in the cards. So let us consider the positive side of the ledger. Jack Snyder's *Myths of Empire* suggests that economic concentration is a key factor in fostering overstretch and preventing successful retrenchment. States such as Germany and Japan—which had highly concentrated, monopolistic economies, tended toward overstretch. This is because these large monopolistic conglomerates could cooperate in fostering expansion overseas even where it was against the interests of the state as a whole. For instance, German industry supported naval rearmament, which antagonized Britain, while German agriculture supported protective tariffs, which alienated

Russia. Industrial and agricultural concerns struck an informal deal to support each others' preferred foreign policy, even though it would have benefited Germany as a whole to placate at least one in the Anglo-Russian duo (Snyder 1991).

However, the United States has always had a less concentrated, more diverse economy than Germany or Japan. There are a number of economic interests in the United States which would most likely be opposed to retrenchment, but there are also many others which would be either in favor or neutral on the subject. Moreover, the anti-retrenchment interests are simply not as big or influential in relative terms in the United States as in Imperial Germany or Japan. It should not, therefore, be beyond the wit of pro-retrenchment political leaders to build successful coalitions in favor of a well-designed retrenchment policy.

Opinion polls conducted by Gallup for Dartmouth's Benjamin Valentino tentatively support this conclusion. Valentino's polls find that there is no majority support for cutting any of the specifically named big ticket items in the Federal budget—Social Security, Medicare, or defense. However, defense is by far the most popular of the three as a target for cuts amongst all Americans and even marginally among Republicans; 35.4 percent of the overall sample support defense cuts versus only 9.7 percent who are in favor of cuts in Social Security and 11.8 percent for Medicare. A majority of Americans, including a majority of Republicans, also believe that the United States can no longer afford to maintain all of its commitments to defend all of its allies—though, as is often the case with such polls, when it comes to discussing abandoning specific commitments, support drops. Surprisingly, the poll also shows that a majority of Americans believe that the global security situation is more dangerous than during the Cold War. Given that the majority of international relations scholars would not concur with this assessment, changing this perception may be one particularly effective way of building public support for retrenchment.[10]

CONCLUSION

As could be surmised from the discussion previously, insights from the relevant literature suggest that intelligent American retrenchment is in the interests of the United States and of international security more generally. The security situation is benign, while the fiscal situation is not.

Economically, excessive defense spending diverts money from more productive uses in the civilian sector, undermining future potential power. Even though the U.S. Government borrows at relatively good rates today, absent retrenchment, this may not continue in the future. Good creditworthiness being a key component of national strength, this also has clear implications for security and foreign policy.

The security situation, by contrast, provides U.S. policymakers with some slack. Because violent crises such as Syria or Libya frequently arise and preoccupy the policy community, it can be easy to miss the wood for the trees and forget that the world of today is one of striking peacefulness by historical standards (Pinker 2011). We do not have data on Roman, Habsburg, or Ming Dynasty military manpower or defense expenditures, so it is impossible to say for sure, but there is a strong case to be made that America's post-Cold War military superiority is historically unprecedented. Most other actors in the international system are either potentially powerful but friendly (like the EU or Japan) or hostile but weak (like North Korea). Only China combines power potential with uncertain intentions, but this is a challenge requiring fiscal solvency for the future rather than a large military buildup today.

Of course, U.S. military superiority and the current peacefulness of global politics are not uncorrelated. That is why retrenchment should not mean isolationism 1930s-style. Rather, a policy somewhere between "selective engagement" and "offshore balancing" suits the needs of the hour best. Maintain peace between the great powers and keep the global trading system open, but avoid entanglement in peripheral ventures which sap U.S. strength unnecessarily.

Retrenchment will not be easy, given the number of vested interests involved in continued high defense spending, the multiple veto points in the American political system, and the existence of "expert problems." Nonetheless, there is room for skilled political leadership to build coalitions in favor of intelligent retrenchment.

There are some ways in which the United States can get more bang for its defense buck, though many others have been or are being implemented already. One way is to adopt the idea of asymmetric cost imposition. As the United States itself did with Soviet air defense in the 1970s, the United States today should look at its potential allies and rivals to determine their areas of comparative disadvantage and subtly shift U.S. defense spending to take advantage of these situations.

American policymakers (and voters) also need to have a clear understanding of the sunk costs fallacy. Projects cannot be justified partly with reference to sums already spent on them. Sunk costs are sunk and cannot be recovered. The only relevant question is whether the present and future benefits of a project outweigh the present and future costs.

This leads to the final principle, which is perhaps the most important. Substitution, asymmetric cost imposition, and forgetting sunk costs can only go so far. If there were lots of easy ways to retrench, policymakers would probably have discovered most of them already. Rather, it is impossible to discuss retrenchment solely as a cost cutting exercise without asking very fundamental questions about what defense spending is actually for (Hartley 2011). What is the good which defense dollars are designed to buy?

This is the principle of final outputs.

Examples in other areas of public policy help to make this concept clear. Mayors, for instance, often boast about the number of police officers they hire. Yet the principle of final outputs suggests that this is not the correct metric by which to judge crime policy. Police officers hired are an **input**, not an output measure. The important metric, therefore, is not the number of police hired, but the level of crime.

Right now, similar output metrics elude U.S. defense policymakers. Yet this does not mean to say that it should always continue to do so. Of course, defense policy is designed to achieve a number of different objectives—protecting U.S. citizens overseas, forestalling terrorist attacks, keeping sea lanes open, preventing nuclear proliferation, and so on. This is entirely correct. However, determining whether taxpayers are getting value for money in terms of defense spending will need to involve putting some numbers on these goals to put the benefits on the same scale as the costs. This would involve asking questions like: How much of a reduction in risk of an East Asian war is affected by the current U.S. military presence? How much likelier would this be if the United States were to downsize its presence by a given amount? What would be the costs of such a conflagration?

As long as the benefits of a given policy remain nebulous, it is easier for self-interested parties either to exaggerate or to downplay them. Compelling individuals to put actual numbers on their arguments would help, at a minimum, to rule out genuinely implausible scenarios. Explicitness also helps in accumulating and refining our understanding. It is quite likely that the first exercise in explicit cost-benefit analysis of U.S. defense policy would result in hotly contested figures and projections. Yet, this is to the good. If a critic believes a given prediction to be wrong, perhaps he or she has a better one and a compelling argument for why it is better. If the argument in favor of the revised figure is genuinely better, it should be adopted, and so our knowledge progresses and predictions improve.

Such exercises in cost-benefit analysis for long-term, complex global challenges already have been undertaken. For instance, the British Government's Stern Report, a cost benefit analysis of policies designed to halt or slow climate change, explicitly assigned probabilities and numbers to various long-term scenarios across the globe (Stern 2006). Long-term meteorological projections are notoriously difficult, but, nonetheless, the Stern Report was able to base very plausible and consistent calculations on them. Similarly, the Copenhagen Consensus—established by the Danish economist Bjorn Lomborg and including many eminent political scientists and economists such as Douglass C. North, Thomas Schelling, Jagdish Bhagwati, Robert Fogel, and Paul Collier also has sought to use cost-benefit analysis to gauge the long-term, worldwide impact of policies designed to tackle a variety of problems ranging from conflict and disease prevention to financial instability.[11] Could not a similar application of cost benefit analysis to U.S. national security strategy pay dividends? Would such a report become politicized? Of course, but at least it would compel all sides to make explicit the assumptions which underlie their views, rather than hiding behind a veil of vagueness.

It may strike many readers as foolhardy and ambitious to imagine such an undertaking. After all, we live in an exceptionally complex world in which prediction is very difficult. Yet prediction and scenario planning should not be avoided simply because they are hard. If the world were radically unpredictable, a domain of true "uncertainty" rather than risk, there would be no basis to prefer any policy over any other (Sunstein 2005). We would have no basis to believe that the current U.S. defense policy is any better than disarming completely, or declaring war on the entire planet. Given that hardly any voices in the current debate seriously make the previous arguments, the difference between those who are skeptical of long-term prediction and assessment and those who believe it necessary, if difficult, is actually one of degree rather than of kind. To say that the world is complex and that it is very difficult to predict the future is simply a more sophisticated way of saying, "I don't know." Neither political leaders nor the public at large need expensively trained political scientists, economists, or historians to hear that. As Samuel Huntington pointed out:

If you tell people the world is complicated, you're not doing your job as a social scientist. They already know it's complicated. Your job is to distill it, simplify it, and give them a sense of what is the single, or what are the couple, of powerful causes which explain this powerful phenomenon.[12]

REFERENCES

Acemoglu, Daron; and Robinson, James A. 2012. *Why Nations Fail: The Origins of Power, Prosperity, and Poverty.* New York, NY: Crown Business.

Arkes, Hal R.; and Ayton, P. 1999. "The Sunk Cost and Concord Effects: Are Humans Less Rational than Lower Animals?" *Psychological Bulletins,* Vol. 125, pp. 591-600.

Arkes, Hal R.; and Blumer, Catherine. 1985. "The Psychology of Sunk Costs." *Organizational Behavior and Human Decision Processes,* Vol. 35, No. 1, pp. 124-140.

Bailey, Ronald. 2011. "How Scared of Terrorism Should You Be?" *reason.com,* September 6, 2011.

Barnett, Correlli. 1986. *The Audit of War: The Illusion and Reality of Britain as a Great Nation.* London, UK: McMillan.

Beckley, Michael. 2011. "China's Century? Why America's Edge Will Endure." *International Security,* Vol. 36, No. 3, pp. 41-78.

Bennett, Scott D.; and Stam, Allan C. III. 2004. *The Behavioral Origins of War.* Ann Arbor, MI: The University of Michigan Press.

Benoit, Emile. 1973. *Defense and Economic Growth in Developing Countries.* Lexington, MA: Lexington Books.

Benoit, Emile. 1978. "Growth and Defense in Developing Countries." *Economic Development and Cultural Change,* Vol. 26, No. 2, pp. 271-280.

Biddle, Stephen. 2009. "Is There a Way?" *New Republic*, October 20, 2009.

Brennan, Geoffrey. 1996. "Selection and the Currency of Reward," Robert E. Gordon, ed., *The Theory of Institutional Design*, New York: Cambridge University Press.

Brooks, Rosa. 2012. "Take Two Drones and Call Me in the Morning." Available from *foreignpolicy.com*.

Buchanan, James M. 1972. *Theory of Public Choice: Political Applications of Economics*. Ann Arbor, MI: University of Michigan Press.

Carlin, Wendy; and Soskice, David. 2006. *Macroeconomics: Imperfections, Institutions and Policies*. New York: Oxford University Press.

Cavallaro, James; Sonnenberg, Stephan; and Knuckey, Sarah. 2012. "Living under Drones: Death, Injury and Trauma to Civilians from U.S. Drone Attacks in Pakistan." Available from *livingunderdrones.org*.

Downs, Anthony. 1957. "An Economic Theory of Political Action in a Democracy." *Journal of Political Economy*, Vol. 65, No. 2, April 1957, pp. 135-150.

Drezner, Daniel. 2011. "Political Leadership and the Eurozone." Available from *foreignpolicy.com*.

Eisenhower, Dwight D. 1961. "Eisenhower's Farewell Address to the Nation." January 17, 1961. Available from *mcadams.posc.mu.edu/ike.htm*.

Fearon, James D. 1995. "Rationalist Explanations for War." *International Organization*, Vol. 49, No. 3, (Summer), pp. 379-414.

Feaver, Peter. 2000. "Brother, Can You Spare a Paradigm? Or, Was Anyone Ever a Realist?" *International Security*, Vol. 25, No. 1, pp. 165-193.

Ferguson, Niall. 2004. *Colossus: The Price of America's Empire.* New York: Penguin.

French, S. 1986. "Calibration and the Expert Problem." *Management Science,* Vol. 32, No. 3, pp. 315-321.

Friedberg, Aaron. 2011. *A Contest for Supremacy: China, America and the Struggle for Mastery in Asia.* New York: W. W. Norton & Co.

Furceri, Davide; and Sousa, Ricardo M. 2011. "The Impact of Government Spending on the Private Sector: Crowding Out Versus Crowding In Effects." *Kyklos,* Vol. 64, No. 4, pp. 516-533.

Gilpin, Robert. 1983. *War and Change in World Politics.* New York: Cambridge University Press.

Hartley, Keith. 2011. "Defense Economics: Achievements and Challenges." Working Paper. Barcelona, Spain: Institut de Economica de Barcelona.

Hungerford, Thomas L. 2012. "Taxes and the Economy: An Economic Analysis of the Top Tax Rates since 1945." Washington, DC: Congressional Research Service.

Kahneman, Daniel. 2011. *Thinking, Fast and Slow.* New York: Farrar, Straus and Giroux.

Kilcullen, David. 2004. "Countering Global Insurgency." *Journal of Strategic Studies,* Vol. 28, No. 4, pp. 594-617.

Knowles, Michael. 2010. "Laffer Curve Revisited." *Yale Economic Review,* Vol. 6, No. 1, p. 8.

Krauthammer, Charles. 2009. "Decline is a Choice." *The Weekly Standard,* Vol. 15, No. 5.

Krepinevich, Andrew; Chinn, Simon; and Harrison, Todd. 2012. *Strategy in Austerity.* Washington, DC: The Center for Budgetary and Strategic Assessments.

Kristof, Nicholas. 1997. "Japan's Full Story: Inside and Outside of the Cabinet." *Foreign Affairs*. November/December.

Kunreuther, Howard. 2002. "Risk Analysis and Risk Management in an Uncertain World." *Risk Analysis*, Vol. 22, No. 4, pp. 655-664.

Layne, Christopher. 2006. *The Peace of Illusions: American Grand Strategy from 1940 to the Present*. Ithaca, NY: Cornell University Press.

Lewis, Michael. 2003. *Moneyball: The Science of Winning an Unfair Game*. New York: W. W. Norton.

McAffee, R Preston; Mialon, Hugo M.; and Mialon, Sue H. 2010. "Do Sunk Costs Matter?" *Economic Inquiry*, Vol. 48, No. 2, pp. 323-336.

McDonald, Paul K.; and Parent, Joseph M. 2011. "Graceful Decline? The Surprising Success of Great Power Retrenchment." *International Security*, Vol. 35, No. 4, pp. 7-44.

Mearsheimer, John. 2005. "China's Rise Will Not Be Peaceful At All." *The Australian*. November 18, 2005.

Mueller, John. 2006. *Overblown: How Politicians and the Terrorism Industry Inflate National Security Threats, And Why We Believe Them*. New York: Free Press.

Mueller, John; and Stewart, Mark G. 2011. *Terror, Security and Money: Balancing the Risks, Benefits and Costs of Homeland Security*. New York: Oxford University Press.

Narizny, Kevin. 2007. *The Political Economy of Grand Strategy*. New York: Cambridge University Press.

Olson, Mancur; and Zeckhauser, Richard. 1966. "An Economic Theory of Alliances." RAND Paper, Santa Monica, CA.

Olson, Mancur. 1982. *The Rise and Decline of Nations: Economic Growth, Stagflation and Social Rigidities*. New Haven, CT: Yale University Press.

Pape, Robert A. 2009. "Empire Falls." *The National Interest*, January/February.

Pass, C.; Lowes, B.; and Davies, L. 2005. "'Crowding out Effect' in Collins Dictionary of Economics." New York: Collins.

Pinker, Stephen. 2011. *The Better Angels of Our Nature: Why Violence Has Declined*. New York: Viking.

Powell, Robert. 2008. "Deterring and Defending against Strategic Attackers: Deciding How Much to Spend and on What." Working Paper.

Press, Darryl. 2005. *Calculating Credibility: How Leaders Assess Military Threats*. Ithaca, NY: Cornell University Press.

Pzeworski, Adam; Alvarez, Michael E.; Cheibub, Jose Antonio; and Limongi, Fernando. 2000. *Democracy and Development: Political Institutions and Well-Being in the World, 1950-1990*. New York: Cambridge University Press.

Ram, Rati. 1995. "Defense Expenditure and Economic Growth." Keith Hartley and Todd Sandler, eds. *Handbook of Defense Economics Volume 1*. New York: Elsevier. pp. 251-277.

Rogerson, William. 1995. "Incentive Models of the Defense Procurement Process." Keith Hartley and Todd Sandler, eds. *Handbook of Defense Economics Volume 1*. New York: Elsevier. pp. 309-346.

Rose, Charlie. 2009. "A Look at U.S. Strategy in Afghanistan With Andrew Exum." PBS Broadcast, July 27, 2009.

Sagan, Scott D; Betts, Richard; and Waltz, Kenneth. 2007. "A Nuclear Iran: Promoting Stability or Courting Disaster?" *Journal of International Affairs*, Vol. 60, No. 2, pp. 135-xiv.

Sartori, Ann. 2012. "International Reputation with Dynamic Resolve." Working Paper.

Schelling, Thomas. 1960. *The Strategy of Conflict*. Cambridge, MA: Harvard University Press.

Schultz, Kenneth A.; and Weingast, Barry R. 2003. "The Democratic Advantage: Institutional Foundations of Financial Power in International Competition." *International Organization*, Vol. 57, No. 1, pp. 3-42.

Sen, Amartya. 1970. *Collective Choice and Social Welfare.* San Francisco, CA: Holden-Day.

Sharma, Ruchir. 2012. *Breakout Nations: In Pursuit of the Next Economic Miracles.* New York: W. W. Norton.

Shea, Patrick E. 2014. "Financing Victory: Sovereign Credit, Democracy, and War," *Journal of Conflict Resolution*, Vol. 58, No. 5, pp. 771-795.

Snyder, Glenn. 1997. *Myths of Empire: Domestic Politics and International Ambition.* Ithaca, NY: Cornell University Press.

Spence, Michael. 1973. "Job Market Signaling." *Quarterly Journal of Economics*, Vol. 87, No. 3, pp. 355-374.

Spruyt, Hendrik. 2005. *Ending Empire: Contested Sovereignty and Territorial Partition.* Ithaca, NY: Cornell University Press

Stern, Nicholas. 2006. *The Stern Review on the Economics of Climate Change.* London, UK: HM Treasury.

Sunstein, Cass R. 2005. *Laws of Fear: Beyond the Precautionary Principle.* New York: Cambridge University Press.

Taliaferro, Jeffrey. 2004. "Power Politics and the Balance of Risk: Hypotheses on Great Power Intervention in the Periphery." *Political Psychology*, Vol. 25, No. 2, pp. 177-212.

Tomz, Michael. 2007. "Domestic Audience Costs in International Relations: An Experimental Approach." *International Organization*, Vol. 61, No. 3, pp. 821-840.

Trabant, Mathias; and Uhlig, Harald. 2006. "How Far Are We From the Slippery Slope? The Laffer Curve Revisited." CEPR Discussion Paper 5657. London, UK: Centre for Economic Policy Research.

Trubowitz, Peter. 1998. *Defining the National Interest: Conflict and Change in American Foreign Policy.* Chicago, IL: University of Chicago Press.

Trubowitz, Peter. 2011. *Politics and Strategy: Partisan Ambition and American Statecraft.* Princeton, NJ: Princeton University Press.

Yergin, Daniel. 1991. *The Price: The Epic Quest for Oil, Money and Power.* New York: Simon and Schuster.

Walt, Stephen. 1990. *The Origins of Alliances.* Ithaca, NY: Cornell University Press.

Walt, Stephen M. 2012. "Should we give Iran the bomb?" *Foreign Policy* blog, June 26, 2012.

Waltz, Kenneth. 2012. "Why Iran Should Get The Bomb." *Foreign Affairs*, July/August 2012.

Ward, Michael D.; and Davis, David R. 1992. "Sizing up the Peace Dividend: Economic Growth and Military Spending in the United States, 1948-1996." *American Political Science Review*, Vol. 86, No. 3, pp. 748-755.

ENDNOTES - CHAPTER 2

1. See *www.nytimes.com/1999/02/05/news/05iht-france.t_0.html*.

2. See *www.sipri.org/databases/milex*.

3. See *hdr.undp.org/en/statistics/hdi/*.

4. See *https://www.cia.gov/library/publications/the-world-factbook/*.

5. In fiscal year 2008-09, 65 percent of Iranian Government revenue came from the oil industry. See *iranprimer.usip.org/sites/iranprimer.usip.org/files/The%20Oil%20and%20Gas%20Industry.pdf*.

6. See *hdr.undp.org/en/statistics/hdi/*.

7. Ibid.

8. Economists such as Paul Krugman point out that increased U.S. borrowing at present has not resulted in higher interest rates—in fact, the real interest rate on U.S. Treasury bonds is currently negative. However, this results from the special circumstances of the current global economy in which investors view American sovereign debt as the best of a very bad bunch. As former President Bill Clinton pointed out, once the world economy recovers and investors begin to perceive safer and more profitable investment opportunities elsewhere, America's currently low borrowing costs should increase substantially absent action on the deficit.

9. See *www.huffingtonpost.com/2011/04/25/robert-gates-defense-joint-strike-fighter-program_n_853489.html*.

10. See *www.dartmouth.edu/~benv/files/poll%20responses%20by%20party%20ID.pdf*.

11. See *www.copenhagenconsensus.com/research-topics*.

12. See *www.foreignpolicy.com/articles/2011/01/05/remembering_samuel_huntington*.

CHAPTER 3

HERBERT HOOVER AND THE ADJUSTMENT TO THE DEPRESSION

Eleanore Douglas

The interwar period in American history provides an unparalleled opportunity to examine the dynamics of retrenchment and renewal. Herbert Hoover, as one of the main architects of the 1920s Republican strategy of retrenchment, is indelibly associated with the strategy and with its subsequent crisis and failure during his presidency. Less well examined are Hoover's own differences with the traditional Republican heritage of laissez-faire and his subsequent attempts to change the strategy of retrenchment in the face of the Depression crisis, establishing the initial policy foundations for what would subsequently become—under Roosevelt—a vigorous strategy of domestic renewal. Despite these efforts at adaptation, Hoover's strong adherence to his own political philosophy and his cautious, methodical approach not only limited his freedom of action in formulating a successful response to the Great Depression, but also fatally undermined the potency of those steps he did take.

INTRODUCTION

As discussions over a series of "fiscal cliffs" extend into another year in Washington, so too does the heated debate over strategies of retrenchment and renewal. On the one side are those who see America's military and economy perilously overstretched by the foreign policy commitments and actions of the past decade. They see the rise of new powers, the rise of the developing world, and argue that a redefinition of our interests is required to accept with grace our declining relative position. They call for a broad-reaching strategy of retrenchment, namely, one that:

> ... decreas[es] the overall costs of foreign policy by redistributing resources away from peripheral commitments and toward core commitments. Concretely, declining great powers select from a wide menu of policy options ... economizing expenditures, reducing risks, and shifting burdens.[1]

Retrenchment can also be understood from a domestic policy perspective as a shifting and redistribution of state resources vis-á-vis society. A strategy of domestic retrenchment thus implies a dramatic decrease in the scope and scale of domestic government activities and expenditures.[2]

On the other side are those who see a fundamental misperception at the root of America's current economic woes. They argue the primary cause of our fiscal problems is not defense spending, which takes up only a small percentage of our gross domestic product (GDP). Instead, they point to ballooning entitlement expenditures reinforced by America's gently aging population. Observing the same rise of new forces in the international environment, they emphasize the dangers of premature retrenchment. They foresee it opening strategic vulnerabilities to our national security, reducing opportunities for influence, and with these trends, the probability of real decline. These advocates for a strategy of renewal call for the maintenance of critical defense expenditures and a reaffirmation of foreign policy commitments to address the shifting constellations of international power.[3]

Critical to both discussions is retrenchment's indelible link with decline: either as a rational response to decline, or as a key precipitate of decline. Retrenchment, however, is not always historically linked to decline. One of the most significant periods of retrenchment in U.S. history followed hard upon the heels of World War I and was subsequently followed by an even more dramatic period of renewal and the rise of the United States to global preeminence during World War II. The interwar period also contains the major example of retrenchment taken too far, providing the elbow room required for the rise of Germany and Japan during the 1930s. Even so, some argue that the partial American retrenchment of the 1920s, with its peculiar balance of economic engagement and political-military withdrawal, helped to lay important foundations for America's later reemergence in a position of global preeminence.

Central to understanding the dynamics of this American interwar period of retrenchment, its strengths, and its limitations is the figure of Herbert Hoover. Hoover and his political philosophy in many ways exemplified the best aspects of the Republican retrenchment strategy of the 1920s. His approach seemed successful during an extended period of American economic growth and relative international quiescence. Unlike more traditional proponents of laissez-faire government, Hoover adopted a strategy of retrenchment explicitly offered a positive vision for action in response to modern problems and even crises. Hoover faithfully adhered to his approach as the austerity crisis of the Great Depression unfolded. In response to the failure of retrenchment policies either to prevent or to mitigate the conditions of the Depression crisis, Hoover slowly adapted, building the first innovative elements of what might be termed a program of domestic economic renewal. He also tried and failed to prevent the collapse of the international liberal economic system and, with it, America's remaining ties to international engagement. He also continued to scale back U.S. security commitments in the face of events to focus on the economic crises at home and abroad, despite evidence of dramatic changes to key elements of the post-war international security architecture. In so doing, some have argued that Hoover signaled too strongly America's lack of interest in maintaining the stability of the international system and opened the door to the rise of new threats from Japan and Germany.

THE REPUBLICAN RETRENCHMENT LEGACY OF THE 1920S

The American retrenchment of the 1920s had its roots in a number of different factors. The bloody engagement of World War I provoked an emphatic response from the American public which subsequently recoiled from the idea of further costly entanglements in European problems. The failure of President Woodrow Wilson's proposed League of Nations to garner decisive support in the U.S. Congress seemed only to confirm this shift away from the domestic indulgence of international commitments and collective security. Second, the considerable expansion of government structure and expenditures incurred by World War I produced deficits that were, for the time, impressive and prompted a perceived need to get the country's budget and finances back on track.[4]

The retrenchment of the period was not merely a redefinition of America's international commitments and activities; it contained a re-scoping of America's domestic governance structure as well. Domestically, it represented the political reaction to 2 decades of energetic progressive political reforms and policy experimentation. Characterized by one historian as an illustration of Newton's third law of physics, the republican policies of the 1920s reflected a dramatic political swing away from the heady reformism, trust-busting, state-interventionism, and grass-roots activism of the prior 20 years.[5] Another argues that "with the war over, traditional fears of big government had reasserted themselves and been spurred along by taxpayers and regulated interests who believed that they stood to gain from shrinking the public sector."[6] With the collapse of the Russian state to Bolshevism and the embrace of socialistic policies in other European countries, there was also a desire to defend the validity of the capitalist model of economic development, to avoid anything that resembled state-socialism, and to seek out alternative models for handling modern problems in a non-statist fashion.

The New Era retrenchment strategy entailed a number of distinct policy positions that were more-or-less consistently carried out by a succession of Republican administrations, culminating with Hoover's presidency in 1928. This "New Era" in American history has been seen as a period of international withdrawal so radical that it has often been characterized by the term isolationism. As one European scholar has argued, it is difficult to understand what isolationism could mean if it is not descriptive of this rather dramatic shift in U.S. foreign policy.[7] On the other hand, some historians have been at great pains to point out that the 1920s—in contrast with other decades, and the 1930s in particular—was a period of impressive and energetic growth in American international economic and cultural engagement. While there remained a hard-core of "stand pat," isolationist conservatives in the Republican party, the administrations of Warren Harding and Calvin Coolidge turned away from only the most formal and symbolic international political and security instruments, namely the League of Nations, and instead pursued normal international relations and tackled major issues through the less formal mechanisms of conferences, disarmament, and "economic diplomacy."[8] Some have suggested that this represented a clever and pragmatic maneuver by internationalists within the Harding and Coolidge administrations to continue international engagement by other means in spite of the lack of domestic political support. The retrenchment strategy of the 1920s was not a unilateral withdrawal on all fronts, but envisioned a substitution of more profitable economic engagement for the riskier political and security engagements of former times.[9]

The most significant aspect of the retrenchment of the 1920s was the rejection of the League of Nations by the U. S. Congress. They promoted ". . . peace through disarmament as an alternative to Wilson's program of peace through world government."[10] The Washington Conference of 1921 was a masterful hat-trick of retrenchment diplomacy, successfully refining U.S. obligations and interests through the Four- and Nine-power treaties governing spheres of interest in the Far East. The conference also saw the most dramatic international downsizing of military force structures for almost half a century in its culminating effort, the Washington Naval Treaty. This retrenchment of defense expenditures proved fatal to the long-term maintenance of British Imperial interests, and thus is often looked at as a prime example of how retrenchment can readily be provocative of decline. While not fatal, the treaty also proved to be problematic to the United States, as it was not matched with a political resolution of the status of the Philippines. Left ambiguous, America's force posture was sufficient to suggest that the Far East remained a "core" interest, while nonetheless providing insufficient means to protect that interest.

One of the major international institutions supported by the Republican retrenchment of the 1920s was the international monetary gold standard of exchange. "It was widely assumed that there was simply no other workable basis on which currencies could be rendered reliable and on which the international economy could function. . . ."[11] Without a gold standard, Hoover noted, "No merchant could know what he might receive in payment by the time his goods were delivered."[12] With 59 countries on the gold standard before World War I and the total global supply of gold filling only a modest two-story townhouse, "few people realized how fragile a system this was, built as it was on so narrow a base."[13] Aggravating this situation was the imbalance of gold reserves between the world's major powers after the war, with the United States controlling over 60 percent of the total.[14]

Reinforcing America's support for a return to the international gold standard and hopefully a return to profitable economic growth by Europe and the United States was a policy of dollar diplomacy. Reflecting a preference for the private backing of international finance, dollar diplomacy:

> . . . hoped to mobilize private American capital for European reconstruction without engendering domestic

inflation, sacrificing conservative fiscal policies, compromising anti-statist principles, or risking the politicization of economic relationships.[15]

Investment expanded rapidly beyond Europe, and the Republican administrations of the 1920s implemented a level of "voluntary" State Department review of these otherwise private loans. Intended to encourage better behavior in both investors and recipients, the system proved confusing and opaque. It produced the worst compromise between self-regulation and oversight. The system ". . . did not preclude unproductive loans; yet, it engendered the belief that the government had a responsibility to protect loans it did not formally disapprove."[16] Unfortunately, the sheer volume of investment abroad proved itself to be a source of instability.

Economically, the Americans were anything but isolationist during the 1920s, investing as much as $80 billion across the globe and almost doubling the volume of foreign trade by 1929.[17] The State Department and Department of Commerce established a number of fact-gathering agencies and commissions of experts. They promoted international conferences and consultation to support the efforts of American businesses to expand. The Bureau of Foreign and Domestic Commerce alone expanded from six to 23 offices across the country during that period.[18] While U.S. trade was expanding at a remarkable pace, Europe's significance as a trading partner declined relative to Latin America and the Far East.

Tariffs were, in part, a response to uncertainty within the American business community about how the nation should best protect its economic and commercial needs in an increasingly interdependent world.[19] They were also a necessity borne of the rigors of domestic politics. Policymakers justified this policy, so contradictory to their international economic goals, by arguing a prosperous domestic market would increase the total market for imports regardless of tariffs. The prosperity and economic growth of the 1920s was such that conditions did not immediately contradict this assertion. But as one scholar noted, "It was impossible to sell to the world, lend to the world, and refuse to buy from the world without eventually courting disaster."[20]

Cultural exchange was a significant side effect of the economic exuberance of the 1920s. The most popular products of commercial trade—motor cars, films, radio—were not only useful items in and of themselves, but also proved to be influential vectors for artistic expression and a major medium of American cultural transmission to the rest of the world.[21] Less tangibly, in their travels American businessmen brought with them their professional values, ideas, and organizational models. One historian notes that concepts of business efficiency, professional organization, and voluntary cooperation were exported almost as vigorously as American films and music.[22] In addition to culture and the arts, the pursuit of diplomacy and engagement by indirect means also produced a powerful wellspring of grass-roots organizations and values activism on such topics as women's rights, prohibition, disarmament, and peace.

A major domestic objective of the post-war Republican retrenchment was domestic tax relief. Secretary of Treasury Andrew Mellon focused on the outsize rates applied to the wealthy, reducing them from 73 percent to 25 percent, and reduced estate taxes to better support bequests given by wealthy donors to public institutions, charities, and schools.[23] There was, at the same time, a strong desire to reduce the total level of public debt in the United States. These two domestic priorities directly influenced America's unwillingness to contemplate European war-debt relief for almost the entire decade.[24]

The retrenchment strategy of the 1920s was also plagued by a number of contradictions. While the United States was not keen to take a leadership role in the international economy, its size and weight ensured it would have an influence regardless of its desire. Without proper recognition of that fact and responsibility taken, the directional influence of the United States on the international system was haphazard, as often destabilizing as it was constructive. There were also a number of tradeoffs implicit in the retrenchment policies of the 1920s, defending the repayment of war debts so as to relieve the domestic tax burden, for example. These tradeoffs were rarely reexamined as global conditions shifted and changed. America's approach further suffered from a basic lack of coordination due to the diffusion of responsibility within the executive branch, the small size of the federal government, and the deep professional and political divide between Washington, the political capital, and New York, the financial capital.[25]

HOOVER AND AMERICAN INDIVIDUALISM

The figure of Hoover is critical to understanding dynamics of this retrenchment strategy, its strengths, and its limitations. Born into the relative poverty and communal strength of a Quaker society in 1874, Hoover was orphaned before the age of 10. Accepted into the "Pioneer" class of the newly established Stanford University at the age of 21, he studied geology and mining. He worked on the U.S. Geological Survey during the summers, helping to map out parts of Sierras around Lake Tahoe. After graduating in 1895, Hoover spent a few months pulling ore carts for an American mining firm before convincing a San Francisco law firm specializing in mining disputes to take him on as the equivalent of a research assistant. At the age of 23, Hoover was technically 13 years too young for his first major post as an "Inspecting Engineer" for the distinguished London firm of Bewick, Moreing & Co. Hoover concealed his youth and embarked upon his assignment to Western Australia and to China, where he evaluated, managed, and reorganized a variety of mining enterprises with great success and even greater profit. Within 5 years, he was made a partner of the firm and rapidly moved into the specialty of mining finance. Hoover subsequently opened one of the largest silver mines of the 20th century in Bawdwin, Burma. He started an Australian zinc mining operation, which later became a major portion of the modern firm, Rio Tinto, one of the largest mining enterprises in the world. He also advised on a rich mining and industrial cooperative enterprise at Kyshtim, Russia, all before his 40th birthday.[26]

Having reached a point of uncontested financial and professional success, Hoover turned his attention toward public service. With the outbreak of World War I, he won his first public role as Head of the Committee for the Relief of Belgium (CRB). After overseeing food relief to German-occupied Belgium and France for 3 long and brutal years, Hoover returned to Washington to take up the role as Food Administrator when the United States finally entered the conflict. When the Armistice was signed, Hoover accompanied the U.S. delegation to head the American Relief Administration (ARA), which coordinated relief and reconstruction operations throughout Europe in the wake of the unexpected peace. Hoover subsequently helped to organize a massive food relief program to Russia in response to the civil-war spawned famine there. By 1921, there was no private citizen better known across the globe for his competence, energy, and achievements in the face of humanitarian crisis.[27]

Hoover announced himself to be a Republican during the 1920 presidential campaign. As a former member of Woodrow Wilson's war cabinet and a vocal supporter of the League of Nations (with reservations), it had not been clear on which side of the political spectrum Hoover would ultimately come down. Despite his vaunted humanitarian credentials and international business reputation, many in the Republican Party remained perennially concerned about his political views. Hoover represented a new generation of Republicanism, one that embraced a number of progressive values and ideas about government's role in society, and one that discomfited the older laissez-faire elite, such as President Coolidge and Secretary Andrew Mellon.[28] Hoover served on presidential cabinets from 1917 until his accession to the presidency, and spent 8 years as one of the most influential and energetic Secretaries of Commerce in U.S. history. He was bound up with and reflected many of the main planks of the Republican retrenchment policies of the era. His personal political philosophy, however, in many ways also exemplified the most appealing aspects of the Republican retrenchment strategy of the 1920s.[29]

Hoover's own approach to retrenchment evolved from his personal and professional experiences.

Hoover's philosophy finds its clearest public expression in a pamphlet he published in 1922 entitled "American Individualism." Articulating the objectives of Hoover's approach, Hoover described what he saw as the unique character of America's society:

> Our individualism differs from all others because it embraces these great ideals: that while we build our attainment on the individual, we shall safeguard to every individual an equality of opportunity to take that position in the community to which his intelligence, character, ability, and ambition entitle him; that we keep the social solution free from frozen strata of classes; that we shall stimulate effort of each individual to achievement; that through an enlarging sense of responsibility and understanding we shall assist him to this attainment, while he in turn must stand up to the emery wheel of competition.[30]

Moving beyond simple negative injunctions on the preservation of liberty, Hoover tried to characterize the deeper purpose and positive vision enabled by that same liberty.

Hoover then described how this objective was to be realized in daily life in terms that the ordinary American could understand:

> We have long since realized that the basis of an advancing civilization must be a high and growing standard of living for all the people, not for a single class; that education, food, clothing, housing, and the spreading use of what we so often term non-essentials, are the real fertilizers of the soil from which spring the finer flowers of life.[31]

At the heart of this vision was the engine of private voluntarism and cooperative organization. Hoover argued that:

> there are in the cooperative great hopes that we can even gain in individuality, equality of opportunity, and an enlarged field for initiative, and at the same time reduce many of the great wastes of over-reckless competition in production and distribution.[32]

It was through this cooperative mechanism that Hoover increasingly sought to find a third way between unfettered capitalism and state socialism, to build the bridge between self-interest and the public interest, between the individual and the state. Hoover hoped that the promotion of close cooperation between capital and labor, between government and business, would enable the realization of their mutual interests and the elimination of conflict.[33]

This spirit of private voluntarism and cooperative organization dominated both his domestic and foreign policy approaches, respectively termed "cooperative individualism" and "independent internationalism."[34] In both spheres, Hoover also believed that the influence of professional experience and academic expertise would help to depoliticize intractable problems and make them more amenable to solution. Hoover saw the role of the federal government in American society as primarily one of coordinating and supporting the independent actions of individuals and groups. The federal government ought to provide reliable information and advice, to support public education and the advancement of science, and to enable the more efficient conduct of business and society. As one scholar has put it:

> The invisible hand of the marketplace would be complemented, but not supplanted, by the 'visible hand' of cooperative planning to control the business cycle, increase efficiency, and raise living standards.[35]

In a presidential campaign speech, Hoover described it as follows:

> It is as if we set a race. We, through free and universal education provide the training of the runners; we give to them an equal start; we provide in the government the umpire of fairness in the race. The winner is he who shows the most conscientious training, the greatest ability, and the greatest character.[36]

Politically and professionally moderate, Hoover viewed his strategy as a positive map to the middle course between the tyranny and bloated bureaucracy of statism and the injustices of laissez-faire capitalism. Yet, as with so many "middle ways," it was not always clear where the boundaries of appropriate action lay. For example, a state-owned warehouse for marketing agricultural commodities was an example of unacceptable state intervention, but a private, or even public-private, board could lend public funds to a farming cooperative to build that same warehouse.[37] To others, it was not always obvious where the acceptable midwife state ended and the unacceptable nanny state began. His view of foreign relations similarly suggested that the government should play a limited role of guidance over the wider diversity of cooperative efforts in the international community. Critically, the U.S. Government should avoid political commitments and entanglements that might destroy the natural fruits of voluntary international cooperation and commerce. "Independent," however, did not mean total disengagement. Hoover once described America's international position as that of being enmeshed in a "... great but delicate cobweb on which each radius and spiral must maintain its precise relation to every other one in order that the whole complex structure may hold."[38]

Hoover's conception of international economic engagement tended to prioritize self-sufficiency over free-market efficiency. With the objective of a better-controlled economic expansion, Hoover tried to march the line between interdependence and independence. He encouraged U.S. businesses to seek markets outside of Europe, hoping to reduce America's commercial dependency on Europe. He supported the monopolistic practices of American companies in their foreign endeavors to give them an edge against European competition. He also sought to guarantee supplies of certain strategic materials like tin and rubber in the interest of lessening the potential for future economic conflict. Finally, Hoover believed that prioritizing the health of America's domestic economy would, of itself, benefit global economic growth and trade. He firmly believed that protecting the standard of living of Americans through tariffs would enable them to demand more global imports in the future and help to stimulate the growth of global trade.[39]

Hoover had a complicated attitude toward coercion. His general attitude toward the use of force is perhaps best expressed in a pre-war radio broadcast: "We cannot slay an idea or an ideology with machine guns. Ideas live in men's minds in spite of military defeat. They live until they have proved themselves right or wrong."[40] Yet he was not a pacifist, despite his Quaker upbringing. While working in China during the Boxer rebellion, Hoover volunteered with the European forces sent to relieve the international settlement of Tientsin. Nonetheless, Hoover remained staunchly opposed to the use of economic sanctions. Hoover's experience of World War I had taught him that sanctions were far more aggressive than most people realized and often produced unintended effects. He argued that the Allied embargo of Germany during World War I had been a mistake. It had unified the German people and given them financial relief from an otherwise deeply unfavorable trade balance. It had forced a radical overhaul of the German economy, which, in his view, had the unintended consequence of producing a greater level of efficiency and potential post-war strength.[41]

Hoover, whatever his philosophical views on the role of government, was a very active individual. As one scholar has commented:

> Hoover strewed around phrases about individuality, but he could not control his own sense of agency. He was by personality an intervener; he liked to jump in, and find a moral justification for doing so later.[42]

Despite the Republican administration's emphasis on economy and restraint, Hoover and those sympathetic to his outlook were busily building a very active, cooperative community with public finances.

> These additions outweighed retrenchment elsewhere, and many Americans accepted them as a superior kind of national progressivism meeting social needs that could not be satisfied by the bureaucratic and 'class legislation' proposals emanating from Congress.[43]

HOOVER AND THE CRISIS ON A THOUSAND FRONTS

As Hoover began his presidency, there were few hints of the tectonic events that would soon overtake it. As he entered the office in March 1929, Hoover felt that his approach already had gathered quite an impressive record of success. In 1929, real GDP had increased more than 6 percent, the unemployment rate was about 3 percent, and the United States produced $47 billion in manufactured goods and imported only $854 million.[44] Hoover was sufficiently confident in his own and the Republicans' achievements to declare the end of poverty as one of his main campaign objectives. Even the shadow of a rapidly overheating stock market could not sour his mood. Hoover felt that his strategy had already been tested by the grinder of recession in 1921-22 and that he had developed tools adequate to counter a normal economic downturn.

Many of the early policies of the Hoover administration were an extension of the retrenchment policies that had previously existed. Much of what was enacted in the first 2 years of his presidency originated in the initiatives of his first few months, prior to the stock market crash, prior to the onset of the Depression.[45] In some cases, these policies strengthened already well-trodden measures, such as disarmament and international disengagement. In other cases, they were intended to soften the perceived domestic impact of earlier policies, reaching out to farmers with cooperatives and with a new tariff.

After winning the election, Hoover was the first President-elect to conduct a goodwill tour of Latin America, visiting the capitals of nearly a dozen countries. Meeting with local representatives, he delivered expressions of respect and mutual interest. Speaking in Ampala, Honduras, Hoover noted:

> In our daily life, good neighbors call upon each other as evidence of the solicitude for the common welfare and to learn of the circumstances and point of view of

each that there may come both understanding and respect.... This should be equally true among nations.[46]

His words were followed up with a policy of fiscal restraint and of military withdrawal. The subsequent release of the Clark Memorandum in March 1930 disavowed the famous Roosevelt Corollary which had formed the basis for many prior American interventions to the south. Hoover's initiative formed the foundation for what would later become the "Good Neighbor" policy under Franklin Roosevelt and substantially narrowed the scope of existing U.S. security commitments and obligations in Latin America. In Hoover's Latin American policy, we can find the most positive illustration of his vision for "independent internationalism."

Hoover also took the Republican retrenchment position on international disarmament and military expenditures and strengthened it even further. Some might say he eventually took it to its natural extreme. Hoover viewed military preparedness largely in terms of national economic preparedness. He also viewed national defense and disarmament as "... inextricably intertwined, for the most economical means of assuring preparedness was to encourage other nations to join the United States in reducing arms levels."[47] Disarmament served not merely the purpose of freeing up national budgets for enhanced economic growth and better fiscal discipline, but it also reinforced the integrity of the delicate web of treaties put in place by Secretary of State Charles Hughes and most recently, Secretary Frank Kellogg and Foreign Minister Aristide Briand.

A disarmament conference was scheduled for January 1930 in London, United Kingdom (UK), after the prior naval conference in Geneva in 1927 had broken up in disarray. Hoover decided to help the London agreement along by using his personal influence with Ramsay MacDonald, who became the first sitting UK Prime Minister to visit the United States in early-October 1929. The London Disarmament Conference focused on cruisers, the object of a minor arms race since the early-1920s. The conference agreement, signed on April 22, 1930, was hailed as a welcome end to an anticipated Anglo-American naval arms race and achieved a comfortable "parity" between the two powers. However, it failed to entice either Italy or France to join and overlooked the relative gains made by the Japanese. Hoover also was disappointed by his inability to get agreement on the immunity of international food shipping, which he saw as vital for humanitarian reasons and as a means to enable much larger naval cuts in the future.[48]

Early in his presidency, using a skillful bureaucratic maneuver, Hoover also managed the rare feat of dramatically cutting the defense budget without publicly appearing to do so. It began with a simplified "pocket budget" initiative intended to make the federal budget more understandable to the public. As part of this, Hoover added all the costs associated with veterans, as well as the principal and interest on the national debt that had grown since World War I, to the defense portion of the federal budget. This dramatically increased the publicly reported size of the military portion, which took up 72 percent of the projected 1931 fiscal year budget and made comparatively more reasonable his calls for moderation.[49]

In tempering the effects of retrenchment, one of Hoover's first acts was to call a special session of Congress to address the needs of the American farmer.

From this session, came the Agricultural Marketing Act, which set up a Farm Board with funding of $500 million, and the early drafts for what would eventually be signed as the Smoot-Hawley tariff. The Farm Board was designed from Hoover's classic model of cooperative individualism and efficiency and applied to agriculture. He envisioned it as the solution to American farmers' lack of clout in the market and their "inequality" with Eastern manufacturers. The Farm Board was intended to address two inherent problems with agriculture: the overproduction problem, which plagued wheat and cotton, and the lack of efficiency and resilience in the agricultural sector more generally. To address these problems, the Farm Board encouraged and financially supported the establishment of small farming cooperatives across the country. Hoover also encouraged the mechanism of national commodity associations whereby cooperatives could channel their resources more efficiently to try to stabilize the market. The Farm Board also had the slightly more controversial and interventionist authority to make purchases in agricultural commodity markets to stabilize prices in a crisis.[50]

Infamous for its role in freezing international trade, the Smoot-Hawley tariff oddly was also inspired as a Republican campaign measure to provide relief to the farmers. Heavily dependent on the unpredictable international market to absorb their surplus, American farmers had not experienced the benefits of the policies of the 1920s that most Americans had. The bill's agricultural backers originally hoped the new tariff would "equalize" the treatment of tariff protections between agriculture and industry (the bill ultimately increased more manufacturing than agricultural tariffs), as well as provide a means of discretely embedding price support measures. These "debentures" were specifically eliminated by Hoover, but the final bill retained a Tariff Commission and flexible tariff review authority that Hoover felt were essential to conducting "rational" trade policy. Unfortunately, the record of review of the prior Tariff Commission throughout the 1920s was not one to prompt optimism in even the most fervent of technocrats.[51]

Given Republican Party sponsorship of the bill and the length of the deliberations, it is not clear whether there was a real option to veto the heavily log-rolled measure. While the total increase in tariff rates brought about by Smoot-Hawley was not as extreme as the Fordney-McCumber tariff reform of 1922, it increased an already high average tariff rate to 40.1 percent, peaking in 1932 at 59.1 percent, the second highest recorded value in U. S. history.[52] It also proved unfortunate that the bill had taken so long to develop. When it was eventually signed into law on June 17, 1930, the Smoot-Hawley tariff was seen as a gratuitous and insulting gesture to a world teetering on the brink of recession. Many make the case that Hoover's background in international business and finance should have convinced him, if anyone, of the bill's potentially damaging impact, but Hoover's stance on protectionism was long-standing. The Smoot-Hawley tariff was to have unanticipated consequences that would materially affect global trade for the remainder of the decade.[53]

In October 1929, the New York Stock Exchange experienced a handful of the most severe shocks in its history. Economists, bankers, and politicians had long expected a correction, and the early response at the highest levels was one of relief. If nothing else, it halted the seemingly endless drain of European currencies westward across the Atlantic Ocean. One of the common misperceptions of this period is the idea that the stock market crash caused the Great Depression: it did not. The collapse of America's primary capital market eventually did come to affect millions of ordinary Americans, but a great deal more had to occur before the unraveling of the American economy was to become inevitable. Nonetheless, the crash did have an immediate impact on public and business confidence that needed to be addressed.[54]

Hoover responded to the crash, believing it to be little more than a traditional, albeit severe, economic downturn. Given his prior work supporting the development of countercyclical ideas and policy instruments, Hoover was confident and felt well-positioned to handle the crisis in a fashion that was consistent with his philosophy and the prior Republican approach. He called for a series of national "Conferences for Continued Industrial Progress," drawing in leaders from major business, banking, railroads, utilities, construction, agriculture, and labor. These conferences undertook developing cooperative terms of agreement that would preserve employment and wages and prevent a disruption of production. Instead of reducing production, cutting jobs, cutting wages, and maintaining prices to the extent possible, Hoover proposed that businesses maintain jobs and wages and continue to produce even while the market for their goods was melting away. As one scholar has noted:

> Hoover was asking the businessmen to forswear all their natural inclinations. . . . It is surprising, perhaps, that they agreed to follow his plan, and even more surprising that, so far as wage rates were concerned, they generally made an effort to comply.[55]

These efforts have been singled out as one of Hoover's more jejune and least successful attempts to maintain the economy.

Hoover carefully deployed all the measures that he had previously worked out in the 1921-22 recession. He accelerated the initiation of and appropriation for already authorized Federal construction contracts. He increased and sped up plans for new construction to include the new Department of Commerce building. Unfortunately, federal construction at this time was but a small amount of the total construction industry, only $210 million in 1930.[56] Only a handful of state and local governments followed suit, and even fewer in the private sector. By the end of the year though, it appeared that things might be turning around. The stock market largely had recovered. Employment and production appeared to be responding in a fashion consistent with previous economic cycles. Early in 1930, Hoover had little notion that he would not be able to oversee a rapid and energetic recovery.[57] Over the next 2 years, Hoover clung tenaciously to many of the central elements of his vision in formulating a government response to the crisis: the cooperative, the information exchange, and the private relief agency supported with public funds.

In the summer of 1930, a record-breaking drought struck the agricultural sector. American agriculture—already laid low by years of debt overhang, overproduction, and low commodity prices—was hit badly. In response to the drought, Hoover established an Emergency Commission and secured a relationship with the American Red Cross, which had a network in many of the affected states. With starter funding and private donations, Hoover hoped the Red Cross network would be able to respond to the disaster in as competent a fashion as their response to the great Mississippi floods had been under Hoover's supervision in 1927. The partnership with the Red Cross quickly proved to be problematic. While the Red Cross had a network of officials in place and had already pledged resources to provide aide, they dispersed relief with a frustrating slowness rooted in their own attempts to avoid stifling the private flows of charity.[58] Hoover, meanwhile continued to make distinctions with which few could sympathize. Concerned to avoid even the appearance of direct government handouts, Hoover argued endlessly with Congress over the particulars of agricultural relief over the next few years. Most famously, Hoover approved loans for feed and seed, but refused to provide food or relief directly to farmers. No longer recalled as the great humanitarian, "... Hoover would be subject to the taunt that he was willing to feed the area's livestock but not its starving farmers."[59]

Hoover's endeavors to encourage private charity and community responses to the continuing economic depression were also met with far less success than he had ever experienced. The President's Emergency Committee on Employment (PECE) acted as a national advisory board, an investigative office, and a public relations agency, all in hopes of stimulating local charity, cooperative projects, and matching donors with needy recipients. Despite having 3,000 local committees across the country, its efforts proved insufficient to the scale and complexity of the unemployment problem then unfolding. Another famous mechanism of local charity, the community chest, dramatically increased its draw as the Depression deepened. While 1932 was their biggest year for donations, the total was still only $35 million, a fraction of what was needed to provide relief.[60]

The National Credit Corporation (NCC) was perhaps Hoover's last and most dramatic attempt to imbue a community with the proper spirit of cooperative self-help. Announced in October 1931, in the wake of a second wave of bank closures, the NCC was the product of extraordinary and painstaking behind-the-scenes negotiations between Hoover and New York's private bank leaders. It was intended to develop an approved pool of liquid capital to be reinfused into the banking system as needed. Private bankers seemed to be neither willing nor able to accumulate and deploy capital in even the modest amounts requested. At that stage, however, Hoover had already turned to other policy instruments.[61]

During the winter of 1930, the United States and the international economy had reached a darker turning point. By the early-1930s, the outflow of American liquidity to international markets had shuddered to a halt. The international exchange system, constructed on an unbalanced foundation and made dependent upon American investment, had already sustained severe stress as a result of the speculative stock bubble on the New York Stock Exchange (NYSE). It had not only withdrawn American investment from Europe but also drew in scarce European capital before the bubble broke. Germany, whose finances had been sustained on the famous and fragile "revolving door" of the Dawes plan, was in a particularly precarious state. In December 1930, the immigrant-owned and enticingly titled "Bank of United States" in New York collapsed due to a mix of overexposure to the stock market, social prejudices, and the Darwinian theories many bank managers used to appraise distressed institutions at the time. The largest commercial bank failure in American history at that time, it wiped out

$286 million from 440,000 depositors and threatened a wave of bank collapses.[62]

In the spring of 1931, rumors of a German economic customs union with Austria created public fear and furor. French opposition to the rumored plan appears to have fatally undermined investor confidence in Austria's largest and most distinguished bank, the Credit-Anstalt. The collapse of the Credit-Anstalt produced a dangerous run on Germany's currency and threatened to pull out the peg from beneath the City of London. Long a hawk on the matter of war debts, Hoover put forward a bold proposal to suspend war debt and war reparations payments for a year and to put together a negotiated "standstill" agreement with private bankers on the withdrawal of existing interstate debts. Given the controversial nature of this temporary moratorium in domestic politics, Hoover hesitated. He also failed to consult the French, delaying the agreement even further. While the moratorium eventually was agreed to, it put only a finger in the dike. The German currency soon experienced another run such that Germany suspended its international exchange. The rising waters then passed on to London where, in September 1931, the Bank of London took the UK off the gold standard. Then it rushed toward the U.S. banking system, which had been weakened by both the drought and the prior flurry of bank failures, and created a much more serious chain of bank-failures. Some 2,200 banks closed by the end of 1931, wiping out some $1.7 billion in deposits.[63]

The 1931 collapse of the international gold exchange standard and the rolling waves of banking crises from Europe across the Atlantic and to the Pacific Oceans did more than almost anything else to transform the depression into the Great Depression. John

Maynard Keynes whimsically described the essential problem of the gold standard:

> Almost throughout the world, gold has been withdrawn from circulation. It no longer passes from hand to hand, and the touch of the metal has been taken from men's greedy palms. The little household gods, who dwelt in purses and stockings and tin boxes, have been swallowed by a single golden image in each country, which lives underground and is not seen. Gold is out of sight—gone back into the soil. But when the gods are no longer seen in a yellow panoply walking the earth, we begin to rationalize them; and it is not long before there is nothing left.[64]

In Hoover's words, the movement of gold and credit in 1931 was like, ". . . a loose cannon on the deck of the world in a tempest-tossed sea."[65] The extreme movements and uncertainty surrounding the gold-exchange standard in 1931 and its dictates, and the contradictory policies of the Federal Reserve Banks, produced what Milton Friedman termed a "deflationary wringer," bringing Keynes's prophecy most horribly to life. In retrospect, many economists argue that the most significant cause of the Great Depression was this deflation, noting that ". . . the actual money supply available dropped by nearly 4 percent between the end of 1928 and the end of 1930."[66]

An economy's need for liquidity was something that Hoover instinctively recognized and understood as an international businessman. As the crisis of 1930-31 began to unfold, Hoover moved quickly to shore up both the international monetary system abroad, and to first protect and then to revive the banking system at home. Under these clear crisis conditions, Hoover began to adapt his traditional approach, moving from retrenchment to what might be viewed as the start of a program for domestic renewal. The seeds were already to be found in some of his cooperative and early countercyclical efforts, for example, the expansion of federal construction projects and the Farm Board's purchasing authority. However, the crisis of 1930-31 generated new policies of renewal that took Hoover far from his comfort zone.

Most important, the failure of the privately organized NCC prompted Hoover to establish the Reconstruction Finance Corporation (RFC). Modeled on the War Finance Corporation of the Wilson era, Hoover originally conceived a broad mandate for the RFC, which was modeled on the War Finance Corporation of the Wilson era. He drafted provisions authorizing lending to industry, farmers, and local communities, in addition to banks. Some of these components were held up by Congress until the fall of 1932, due both to partisan tensions and to genuine concerns as to the radical nature and far-reaching effects of this new legislation. A temporary "crisis" agency, the RFC would continue for 20 years and lend some $50 billion before it finally closed. Unfortunately, the RFC was not able to accomplish much in the immediate crisis, as most new borrowers used the funds to extend old loans or to make extremely conservative investments.[67]

In addition to the RFC, Hoover submitted the Glass-Steagall Act of February 1932, which broadened the definition of collateral acceptable for Federal Reserve System loans, thereby expanding the available liquidity in the American banking system. He also initiated legislation calling for a mortgage discounting service similar to what the Federal Reserve provided for banks. It called for mortgages to be eligible as security for loans at 12 new Home Loan Banks. Congress did not pass this measure until July 1932. In the interim, home foreclosures continued to eliminate even more liquidity from the economy.[68]

Many identified the establishment of the RFC as a critical turning point in the scope of domestic government, even at the time. Now that direct federal relief had been justified and provided to the banks, ". . . the president had implicitly legitimated the claims of other sectors for financial assistance."[69] Hoover's continuing stance against direct relief for unemployment and drought became increasingly hard to sustain. Given the intent of Hoover's philosophy to find a third way between laissez-faire capitalism and state socialism, perhaps the most damning evidence of Hoover's failure is to be found in information uncovered by *Business Week* at the time. The number of visitors requesting visas to visit the Soviet Union doubled in 1930 and doubled again the following year. Some even applied for work visas and declared their intent to remain in the Union of Soviet Socialist Republics (USSR).[70] In response to growing calls for unemployment relief, Hoover reluctantly passed the Relief and Reconstruction Act of July 21, 1932, providing the RFC with an additional $1.5 billion in funds for "self-liquidating public works" and an additional $300 million to states for the relief programs of their choice. With this measure, Hoover's stance against direct government intervention was almost entirely overthrown, yet he continued to resist similar "emergency" measures on a variety of fronts. [71]

Many of Hoover's policies of domestic renewal were expanded upon by the subsequent Franklin Roosevelt administration. Many of Hoover's own appointed administrators were carried over. Some of the legislation prepared by the Hoover administration, after being blocked by an unfriendly and uncooperative Congress, quickly found passage in 1933. As scholars have noted, there were a number of similarities between Roosevelt's and Hoover's policies for countering the Depression crisis at home. One historian has argued that, "To a considerable degree the differences lay in divergent definitions of what constituted an emergency or a necessary supplement rather than in divergent theories of what constituted liberal governance."[72] It was a disagreement of means, not of ends. On the other hand, Hoover and Roosevelt did take distinctly different approaches to the question of international economic engagement and renewal under austerity conditions.

Late in his presidency, Hoover threw himself most energetically into perhaps vain efforts to prevent the collapse of the liberal international economic system. He followed the moratorium and standstill agreement of 1931 and the subsequent collapse of the gold exchange standard with calls and preparations for a World Economic Conference to take place in June 1933 after he had left office. At this conference, everything that had previously been off-limits—i.e., war debt renegotiations and reparations—would be open for discussion as an incentive to save the international exchange standard. "By trading debt payments for the stabilization of currencies, Hoover hoped to eliminate exchange controls, revive international commerce, stimulate American exports, and raise commodity prices."[73] Exchange stability was critical to U.S. interests at this point partly because the United States was still on the gold standard and partly because ". . . it was a principle for preserving economic internationalism at a time when more and more nations were abandoning it in favor of economic nationalism."[74] While

Hoover argued loudly that the primary causes of the crisis were to be found abroad, he also believed that the quickest means to recovery lay in revitalizing the international economic system.

In 1932, Hoover was swimming against the public and the political stream. Commentators and politicians demonstrated a desire to focus on the home front. The idea of bringing back internationalism seemed premature, if not foolish. "In order to prevent the economic crisis from growing worse, it seemed imperative to reduce foreign commitments and ties as much as possible."[75] President Roosevelt did not attend the summit that had been organized with such fervor by his predecessor, and publicly jettisoned the agreement his attendant advisors had worked out. In the eyes of some historians and economists, the World Economic Conference has marked the point ". . . when the United States abandoned any pretense of international cooperation and decided to generate a recovery on its own. The result was a disastrous backlash against globalization."[76] Whereas the retrenchment of the 1920s had been a broad substitution of international economic engagement for political and military engagement, the retrenchment of the early Depression saw a withdrawal from almost all forms of international engagement to focus on the foremost challenge of domestic economic renewal.

HERBERT HOOVER'S LEGACY

Hoover, a methodical and private man by nature, unfortunately failed to respond to the Depression crisis with the kind of leadership the American public required. He gave the public the impression of being out of touch with real conditions, unsympathetic to the troubles of the country as a whole, and reluctant to shift course in response to events. His inability to shift his approach to the farming crisis damaged his humanitarian reputation, but it was his handling of the Veteran's March on Washington, DC, that definitively sunk what remained of his reputation and most likely cost him the presidential election.

Until 1932, Hoover had enjoyed a good relationship with veterans. He had established the Veterans Administration on July 21, 1930, built 25 new veterans hospitals, and increased the provision of benefits to 420,000 veterans whose disabilities were not directly linked to their service.[77] The summer of 1932 saw thousands of veterans marching on Washington and calling for an early payment of their bonuses. Hoover opposed early payment, but Congress authorized loans to be disbursed immediately against the bonus amounts. Their aims attained, the veterans were ordered to disperse from the capital region. Upon being given presidential instructions on July 28, 1932, to enforce an orderly dispersal, Army Chief of Staff General Douglas MacArthur exceeded his orders and participated in what appeared to be, to all witnesses, an armed rout. This was followed up with the gratuitous burning of the veterans' encampment. While MacArthur's actions were in blatant disregard of the President's instructions, he refused to take public responsibility for having done so. What is perhaps more surprising was that Hoover proved willing to buy into MacArthur's and Secretary of Defense Hurley's explanation that the action had been a justified response to a radical communist plot and publicized this explanation. When a Department of Justice investigation failed to find any evidence of such plot, or indeed of radical communists among the bonus-marchers, public opinion swung decisively against the President.

There is also evidence that Hoover was too quick to declare victory and to attempt a return to the familiar tenets of his retrenchment strategy of old, prematurely undermining some of the more successful steps of his renewal approach. A central tenet of classical economics, Hoover believed that the most important thing he could do to restore confidence was to balance the federal budget—a central tenet of classical economics. After trying and failing to get the Federal Reserve to lower its interest rates and inject additional liquidity into the economy, Hoover succumbed to growing domestic political pressure to reimpose fiscal discipline on the federal government. Over the previous 4 years, the U.S. Government had run up bills pursuing various measures to counter the impact of the depression, totaling $900 million for the 1931 fiscal year budget.[78] The democrats had even made balancing the budget a central plank of the presidential election platform in 1932. While the Revenue Act of 1932 proved to be an extremely progressive tax bill, it also inarguably raised taxes at exactly the wrong time to reinforce the momentum for an economic recovery. Partly due to Hoover's errors, we now know how difficult it is to get the timing of a return to ordinary fiscal constraints after a period of crisis: too late, and you have undermined confidence in the long-term viability of the entire system; too early, and you have choked off the recovery. Yet for all their folly, the new tax rates were also left untouched throughout the New Deal period and for many years thereafter.

Another more portentous choice was Hoover's decision to continue to scale back U.S. security commitments to focus on the economic crises at home and abroad, despite evidence of dramatic changes to key elements of the existing post-war international security architecture. Hoover's proposals at the World Disarmament Conference in 1932 were viewed by contemporaries as the product of political opportunism, and as a potentially dangerous signal of reluctance. While Secretary of State Henry Stimson recommended a passive observational stance to an event for which few outside the disarmament activist community cherished any high ambitions, Hoover approached the World Disarmament Conference in April 1932 as an opportunity for him to contribute both toward the global good and the immediate economic relief of European and American budgets. Hoover distributed a rather audacious proposal: a one-third reduction across all armed forces with the abolition of bombers, tanks, large guns, chemical warfare, submarines and battleships, and 25 percent of aircraft carriers.[79] While the proposal boosted conference morale and created a flurry of publicity and political attention, it produced little by way of material progress to the negotiations. The disappointed Stimson observed it was:

> a mistake and a proposition that cut pretty deep. . . . But, really, so far as a practical proposition is concerned, to me it is just a proposal from Alice in Wonderland. It is no reality, but is just as bad as it can be in its practical effect.[80]

While an unusual way of understanding a balance of power, many military officials and policymakers at the time viewed the credible fulfillment of treaty terms, even under conditions of general disarmament and military decline, as important. Even as the overall numbers declined, the balance could only be preserved if signatories were willing to build up to their treaty-protected numbers.[81] Far from restraining an ambitious ship construction program, the disarmament conferences under Hoover sought desperately to push other nations to accelerate their own reductions as a way of minimizing the U.S. construction program. By the end of Hoover's administration, the United States was dangerously underfulfilling its role in lowering the bar of the global balance in a stable fashion.

On September 18, 1931, some brigades of Japanese troops decided covertly to provoke what was later called the "Mukden Incident," which provided the excuse for the Japanese to seize Manchuria. Tied up with fairly serious domestic problems, the United States confined itself to declaring its outrage and hoping for the League of Nations to prove itself equal to the occasion. However:

> The Manchurian crisis had worldwide implications. At stake was the survival of the series of postwar agreements based on principles of law and morality that successive Republican presidencies vowed would take the place of the discredited prewar system of armaments, secret diplomacy, and recurrent wars.[82]

Secretary of State Stimson promulgated a declaration of nonrecognition of the belligerently acquired territory, subsequently termed the "Hoover-Stimson Doctrine." The Japanese, not impressed by the international community's protests, seized Shanghai on January 28, 1932. Stimson recommended sanctions or a show of force. Concerned that such actions would be themselves both acts of belligerency and ineffective, Hoover disagreed. He was later persuaded to assent to a multilateral deployment of ships in the region to protect the international settlement of Shanghai. In failing to do more, some have argued that Hoover signaled America's lack of interest in maintaining stability in the rest of the world and opened the door to new threats from rising, revisionist powers only a few years later.

Hoover's strategy of disarmament and economy in military expenditures was predicated on the continuation of the global trend of arms limitations, disarmament, and the disavowal of the use of force. For as long as these trends continued, it allowed the United States to benefit from its international influence and economic engagement without incurring messy obligations. However, the Mukden Incident and the subsequent Japanese invasion and occupation of Manchuria undermined these assumptions. It became more difficult to justify Hoover's minimalist interpretation of U.S. security interests as largely being confined to the Western Hemisphere. The gap between existing American forces, and even their treaty-approved force levels, became increasingly visible. The gap between U.S. diplomatic support for international treaties, and what they were willing to do to defend them became more clearly apparent.[83]

While he perhaps understood it better than most other individuals at the time, it is also not clear in retrospect whether Hoover grasped the essential nature of the Depression crisis. Hoover's relentless drive to try to save the gold standard at all costs in 1933 is revelatory of this partial blindness. Defensible in terms of economic orthodoxy and even internationalism, Hoover's vehement defense of the gold standard flew in the face of what others were rapidly learning through experience. Britain's economy and finances had rebounded with surprising strength following their abandonment of the gold standard in 1931. Economists also credit Roosevelt's far less justifiable lapse from gold with reinvigorating the American economy between 1933 and 1937. However, the gold standard—much like the cooperative, the private relief agency, and the extra-legal agreements—was a central element of what Hoover thought had been most successful in his approach. A prisoner of his own success, Hoover was unable to turn around and recognize the gold standard as being the part of the problem, much less its source.

CONCLUDING THOUGHTS

There are those who have recently looked back to Hoover's strategy of cooperative individualism and independent internationalism and to the retrenchment strategy of the 1920s as a source of inspiration. The approach, after all, embodied a radically different vision of the relationship of the federal government with both American society and the larger global community. Hoover's starting point was an extraordinarily rich, participatory community life—a community life which many work toward today through their participation in what many term "civil society": those forms of nongovernment activity and social organization, professional associations built around values and self-regulation, the propagation of new codes of social responsibility. There are also those who also more recently might applaud his critique of international interventionism, if not his skepticism of collective security and his unshakable belief in disarmament.

The Depression crisis of 1929-33 is not necessarily a fair test of Hoover's strategy, but it nonetheless remains an important test. It is not fair because the crisis was unprecedented in both scale and intensity at the time, and remains so with the perspective of history. It is also important to remember how primitive and emergent the state of economic knowledge was at the time. Yet, we must also understand that the objective of the retrenchment strategy of the 1920s was not the husbanding of resources in anticipation of a cyclical change in conditions or taking up the matter of renewing America's global position at some future date. The objective of the Republican retrenchment strategy of the 1920s was small government, full stop. By 1928, that objective had largely been attained. A key factor in the failure of the federal government's response to the Great Depression between 1929 and 1933 was a sheer lack of wherewithal in its budget, structure, and capabilities to influence, much less counter, the meltdown of the economy and society occurring around it. In short, small government proved insufficient to this most terrible of tests.[84] While Hoover himself envisioned a more dynamic government response to the natural cycles of the economy, he believed that a more cooperative society of private endeavor, backed with public support, would provide the necessary resilience to these cycles and changes in fortune. This cooperative society did exist to an impressive degree in 1928, but this too failed most spectacularly under the extraordinary pressure of the crisis.

Finally, the aspiration of "independent internationalism" had its dark side as well. While the Good Neighbor Policy highlights the positive elements of international respect and disengagement, Hoover's trade policies ultimately sacrificed internationalism for the sake of independence. His embrace of protectionism, as a means of enhancing domestic self-sufficiency, growth, and lessening U.S. dependence, backfired by providing the excuse other governments, economically threatened by the growth of American trade in the long-term and the Depression in the near term, to abandon economic liberalism.[85] The fragmentation of world trade into regional, national, and imperial blocs had a significant effect on the length and speed of America's economic recovery. Furthermore, in focusing to such a degree on preserving independence of action, Hoover failed to make a positive case to the American public as to why internationalism remained important.

By 1933, the bargain struck by the Republican retrenchment strategy of the 1920s and by Hoover had crumbled under the force of the economic crisis. In the years that followed, the United States (and indeed most of the developed world) would follow a path of more complete withdrawal, a retrenchment far more radical than almost any experienced before, turning inwards to focus on competing strategies for domestic renewal. In the same period, the balance between disarmament, diplomacy, and the use of force, having weakened dramatically through neglect, would come unglued entirely, leaving the field open for powers whose strategies of domestic renewal required aggressive expansion. It was only after conflict had been joined by these revisionist forces that America returned to take up a more active role in the international community, sending first money, then equipment, and finally soldiers down the paths blazed and across the global networks built by an earlier generation of American businessmen and nongovernmental organizations.

REFERENCES

Ahamed, Liaquat. "Currency Wars, Then and Now: How Policymakers Can Avoid the Perils of the 1930s." *Foreign Affairs*, Vol. 90, No. 2, 2011, pp. 92-103.

_____. *Lords of Finance: The Bankers Who Broke the World*. New York: Penguin Press, 2009.

Boyce, Robert W. D. *The Great Interwar Crisis and the Collapse of Globalization*. Basingstoke, UK: Palgrave Macmillan, 2009.

Brooks, Stephen G.; Ikenberry, G. John; and Wohlforth, William C. "Don't Come Home, America: The Case against Retrenchment." *International Security* Vol. 37, No. 3, Winter 2012/13, pp. 7-51.

Burner, David. *Herbert Hoover: A Public Life*. 1st Atheneum Ed. New York: Atheneum, 1984.

Clements, Kendrick. *The Life of Herbert Hoover: Imperfect Visionary, 1918-1928*. The Life of Herbert Hoover. Vol. 4, New York: Palgrave, MacMillan, 2010.

Davies, Thomas R. *The Possibilities of Transnational Activism: The Campaign for Disarmament between the Two Wars*. Boston, MA: Martinus Nijhoff Publishers, 2007.

Foster, Anne L. *Projections of Power: The United States and Europe in Colonial Southeast Asia, 1919-1941*. American Encounters/Global Interactions. Durham, NC: Duke University Press, 2010.

Hamilton, David. *From New Day to New Deal: American Farm Policy from Hoover to Roosevelt, 1928-1933*. Chapel Hill, NC: University of North Carolina Press, 1991.

Hawley, Ellis Wayne. *The Great War and the Search for a Modern Order: A History of the American People and Their Institutions, 1917-1933*. The St Martin's Series in 20th-Century US History. 2nd Ed. New York: St. Martin's Press, 1992.

Hicks, John Donald. *Republican Ascendancy, 1921-1933*. The New American Nation Series. 1st Ed. New York: Harper & Row, Publishers, 1960.

Hofstadter, Richard. *The American Political Tradition and the Men Who Made It*. New York: Vintage Books, 1954.

Hoover, Herbert. *American Individualism*. Garden City, NY: Doubleday, Page & Company, 1922.

Iriye, Akira. *The Globalizing of America, 1913-1945*. The Cambridge History of American Foreign Relations. Vol. 3, William Cohen, ed., Cambridge, UK: Cambridge University Press, 1993.

Irwin, Douglas. *Peddling Protectionism: Smoot-Hawley and the Great Depression*. Princeton, NJ: Princeton University Press, 2011.

Kagan, Robert. "Not Fade Away: The Myth of American Decline." *The New Republic*, January 11, 2012.

Kennedy, David M. *Freedom from Fear: The American People in Depression and War, 1929-1945*. The Oxford History of the United States. New York: Oxford University Press, 1999.

Leffler, Melvyn P. *The Elusive Quest: America's Pursuit of European Stability and French Security, 1919-1933*. Chapel Hill, NC: University of North Carolina Press, 1979.

Louria, Margot. *Triumph and Downfall: America's Pursuit of Peace and Prosperity, 1921-1933*. Westport, CT: Greenwood Press, 2001.

MacDonald, Paul K.; and Parent, Joseph M. "Graceful Decline? The Surprising Success of Great Power Retrenchment." *International Security*, Vol. 35, No. 4, 2011, pp. 7-44.

Nash, George H. *The Life of Herbert Hoover: Master of Emergencies, 1917-1918*. The Life of Herbert Hoover. Vol. 3, 1996.

_____. *The Life of Herbert Hoover: The Engineer, 1874-1914*. The Life of Herbert Hoover. Vol. 1, New York: W. W. Norton & Co., 1983.

_____. *The Life of Herbert Hoover: The Humanitarian, 1914-1917*. The Life of Herbert Hoover. Vol. 2, New York: W. W. Norton & Co, 1988.

Rhodes, Benjamin D. *United States Foreign Policy in the Interwar Period, 1918-1941: The Golden Age of American Diplomatic and Military Complacency*. Praeger Studies of Foreign Policies of the Great Powers. Westport, CT: Praeger, 2001.

Rosenberg, Emily S. *Financial Missionaries to the World: The Politics and Culture of Dollar Diplomacy, 1900-1930*. American Encounters/Global Interactions. Durham, NC: Duke University Press, 2003.

Shlaes, Amity. *The Forgotten Man: A New History of the Great Depression*. 1st Harper Perennial Ed. New York: Harper Perennial, 2008.

Wilson, Joan H. *Herbert Hoover: Forgotten Progressive*. Library of American Biography. Boston, MA: Little, Brown, 1975.

Wilson, John R. M. *Herbert Hoover and the Armed Forces: A Study of Presidential Attitudes and Policy*. Dissertation. Chicago, IL: Northwestern University, 1971.

ENDNOTES - CHAPTER 3

1. Paul K. MacDonald and Joseph M. Parent, "Graceful Decline? The Surprising Success of Great Power Retrenchment," *International Security*, Vol. 35, No. 4, 2011, p. 11.

2. On the need for retrenchment, see Barry R. Posen, "The Case for Restraint," *American Interest*, Vol. 3, No. 1, November/December 2008, pp. 7-17; Christopher Layne, "From Preponderance to Offshore Balancing: America's Future Grand Strategy," *International Security*, Vol. 22, No. 1, Summer 1997, pp. 86-124, among others.

3. On the need for renewal, see Robert Kagan, "Not Fade Away: The Myth of American Decline," *The New Republic*, Janu-

ary 11, 2012; G. John Ikenberry, Stephen G. Brooks, and William C. Wohlforth, "Don't Come Home, America: The Case against Retrenchment," *International Security*, Vol. 37, No. 3, among others.

4. Ellis Wayne Hawley, *The Great War and the Search for a Modern Order: A History of the American People and Their Institutions, 1917-1933*, 2nd Ed., The St Martin's Series in 20th-Century US History, New York: St. Martin's Press, 1992, pp. 30-38.

5. John Donald Hicks, *Republican Ascendancy, 1921-1933*, 1st Ed., The New American Nation Series, New York: Harper & Row, Publishers, 1960, p. 23.

6. Hawley, p. 38.

7. Robert W. D. Boyce, *The Great Interwar Crisis and the Collapse of Globalization*, Basingstoke, UK: Palgrave Macmillan, 2009, p. 11.

8. Melvyn P. Leffler, *The Elusive Quest: America's Pursuit of European Stability and French Security, 1919-1933*, Chapel Hill, NC: University of North Carolina Press, 1979, pp. x, 79.

9. Benjamin D. Rhodes, *United States Foreign Policy in the Interwar Period, 1918-1941: The Golden Age of American Diplomatic and Military Complacency*, Praeger Studies of Foreign Policies of the Great Powers, Westport, CT: Praeger, 2001, p. 45.

10. Rhodes, p. 45.

11. David M. Kennedy, *Freedom from Fear: The American People in Depression and War, 1929-1945*, The Oxford History of the United States, New York: Oxford University Press, 1999, p. 78.

12. Quoted in *ibid*.

13. Liaquat Ahamed, *Lords of Finance: The Bankers Who Broke the World*, New York: Penguin Press, 2009, pp. 13, 162-163.

14. *Ibid.*, pp. 162-163.

15. Leffler, p. 26.

16. *Ibid.*, pp. 62, 176.

17. Rhodes, p. 45.

18. Amity Shlaes, *The Forgotten Man: A New History of the Great Depression*, 1st Harper Perennial Ed., New York: Harper Perennial, 2008, p. 36.

19. Leffler, pp. 48-49.

20. Richard Hofstadter, *The American Political Tradition and the Men Who Made It*, New York: Vintage Books, 1954, p. 379.

21. Akira Iriye, Vol. 3, William Cohen, ed., *The Globalizing of America, 1913-1945*, The Cambridge History of American Foreign Relations, Cambridge, UK: Cambridge University Press, 1993, p. 113.

22. Emily S. Rosenberg, *Financial Missionaries to the World: The Politics and Culture of Dollar Diplomacy, 1900-1930*, American Encounters/Global Interactions, Durham, NC: Duke University Press, 2003, pp. 188-198; Rhodes, p. 45.

23. Shlaes, p. 38.

24. Leffler, pp. 23, 42.

25. Boyce, p. 11; Leffler, pp. 19, 79.

26. See George H. Nash, Vol. 1, "The Life of Herbert Hoover," *The Life of Herbert Hoover: The Engineer, 1874-1914*, New York: W. W. Norton & Co., 1983.

27. See also *The Life of Herbert Hoover: The Humanitarian, 1914-1917*, Vol. 2, *The Life of Herbert Hoover*, New York: W. W. Norton & Co, 1988; *The Life of Herbert Hoover: Master of Emergencies, 1917-1918*, Vol. 3, *The Life of Herbert Hoover*, New York: W. W. Norton & Co, 1996.

28. Hawley, p. 63.

29. See Kendrick Clements, *The Life of Herbert Hoover: Imperfect Visionary, 1918-1928*, Vol 4, *The Life of Herbert Hoover*, New York: Palgrave, MacMillan, 2010.

30. Herbert Hoover, *American Individualism*, Garden City: Doubleday, Page & Company, 1922, pp. 9-10.

31. *Ibid.*, p. 32.

32. *Ibid.*, pp. 44-45.

33. Clements, p. 109.

34. Terms used respectively in Hawley, pp. 54-55; John R. M. Wilson, *Herbert Hoover and the Armed Forces: A Study of Presidential Attitudes and Policy*, Dissertation, Chicago, IL: Northwestern University, 1971, pp. i-ii.

35. David Hamilton, *From New Day to New Deal: American Farm Policy from Hoover to Roosevelt, 1928-1933*, Chapel Hill, NC: University of North Carolina Press, 1991, p. 32.

36. Quoted in Hofstadter, p. 387.

37. David Burner, *Herbert Hoover: A Public Life*, 1st Atheneum Ed., New York: Atheneum, 1984, p. 238.

38. Quoted in Clements, p. 198.

39. Anne L. Foster, *Projections of Power: The United States and Europe in Colonial Southeast Asia, 1919-1941*, American Encounters/Global Interactions, Durham, NC: Duke University Press, 2010; Clements, p. 4.

40. Quoted in Joan H. Wilson, *Herbert Hoover: Forgotten Progressive*, Library of American Biography, Boston, MA: Little, Brown, 1975, p. 48; Nash, p. 1.

41. *The Life of Herbert Hoover: The Humanitarian, 1914-1917*, p. 293-294.

42. Shlaes, p. 18.

43. Hawley, p. 84.

44. Douglas Irwin, *Peddling Protectionism: Smoot Hawley and the Great Depression*, Princeton, NJ: Princeton University Press, 2011, pp. 16-17.

45. Leffler, p. 194.

46. Quoted in Burner, p. 286.

47. John R. M. Wilson, p. 175.

48. *Ibid.*, pp. 182-192.

49. *Ibid.*, p. 11.

50. Hamilton, p. 37.

51. Irwin, p. 7.

52. *Ibid.*, p. 105.

53. *Ibid.*

54. Burner, p. 248.

55. Hofstadter, pp. 392-393.

56. Kennedy, p. 57.

57. Burner, pp. 248-252.

58. *Ibid.*, p. 263.

59. Hawley, p. 173.

60. Burner, pp. 267-268.

61. *Ibid.*, pp. 265-270.

62. Shlaes, p. 103; Kennedy, p. 66.

63. Ahamed, *Lords of Finance*, p. 453; Boyce, pp. 300-304.

64. Quoted in *Lords of Finance*, p. 383.

65. Quoted in Kennedy, p. 76.

66. Shlaes, pp. 90-91.

67. Kennedy, p. 85.

68. *Ibid.*, pp. 83-84.

69. *Ibid.*, p. 85.

70. Shlaes, p. 117.

71. Burner, pp. 276-277.

72. Hawley, p. 197.

73. Leffler, pp. 312-313.

74. Iriye, p. 141.

75. Vol. 3, *The Globalizing of America, 1913-1945*, p. 129.

76. Liaquat Ahamed, "Currency Wars, Then and Now: How Policymakers Can Avoid the Perils of the 1930s," *Foreign Affairs*, Vol. 90, No. 2, 2011.

77. J. H. Wilson, pp. 210-216.

78. Burner, pp. 280-282.

79. John R. M. Wilson, pp. 195-196.

80. Thomas R. Davies, *The Possibilities of Transnational Activism: The Campaign for Disarmament between the Two Wars*, Boston, MA: Martinus Nijhoff Publishers, 2007, p. 127.

81. John R. M. Wilson, p. 69.

82. Margot Louria, *Triumph and Downfall: America's Pursuit of Peace and Prosperity, 1921-1933*, Westport, CT: Greenwood Press, 2001, p. 183.

83. John R. M. Wilson, pp. 9-10.

84. Kennedy, p. 55.

85. Irwin, pp. 164-180.

CHAPTER 4

STRATEGIC CALCULATIONS IN TIMES OF AUSTERITY: RICHARD NIXON

Megan Reiss

Richard Nixon entered the presidency with constrained resources because America was in financial, political, and cultural turmoil. Because of the understanding that the United States would be most effective when placing its resources in areas of greatest strategic importance, Nixon developed a détente strategy for containing the Soviets, which achieved significant successes. Austerity focused goal creation, which led to opportunities. The main tenets of détente include a decision to negotiate with the Soviets, a calculation to "link" goals, a decision to open China, and the development of the Nixon Doctrine. After assessing that the Vietnam War was a result of poor strategic decisionmaking and overextension of resources, Nixon and Henry Kissinger developed the Nixon Doctrine to consolidate resources in areas of greatest strategic importance. The failures of the Nixon presidency came from a muddled hierarchy of application of détente strategies, failures to recognize and develop goals for areas of strategic importance, an overemphasis on credibility, and an overconcentration of power in the chief executive.

RICHARD NIXON'S PRESIDENTIAL ENTRANCE: SALIENT PROBLEMS

The year of the unsettled giant was 1968; American domestic and international policies were in turmoil. Starting in 1965, public opinion polls started showing a disturbing trend: Americans were losing faith in their government, their military, and their political leaders.[1] The American public was so shocked by the abilities of the Viet Cong during the Tet Offensive that support for the Vietnam War, and the President, waned. President Lyndon Johnson chose not to run for reelection. Race riots in 130 cities followed the assassination of Martin Luther King, Jr.[2] Inflation rose 4 percent from the previous year (and 12 percent since 1964).[3] Johnson and the Union of Soviet Socialist Republics (USSR) agreed to begin talks on limitations of ballistic missile defense and nuclear weapons delivery systems, but the August 1968 invasion of Czechoslovakia halted the plans for negotiations. Nixon won the majority of the popular vote for President by only a little over 500,000 votes.[4] With this slim margin of political support, Nixon took office with a country divided not only by political party, but by economics, race, and war.

Nixon famously created a partnership with Henry Kissinger, first as the National Security Advisor and later as the Secretary of State, and together Nixon and Kissinger devised a series of strategies to bring the country out of its ongoing turmoil. Kissinger's goals in shaping strategic policy were premised on the view that in the previous administrations, "the debate has concentrated on our commitments and not our interests. It is really our interests that should get us involved, not our commitments."[5] The principle strategy of the

Nixon administration thus became the preservation of the balance of power and order, while taking actions which align with America's strategic interests and recognizing the Soviets as the primary threat to America.[6] Nixon and Kissinger actively worked to concentrate power in the executive branch so as to best deal with the turmoil, consistently returning to the strategy of balancing while pursuing American interests as they saw fit. While the difficult times provided for different methods and options than a prosperity president, Nixon used his time as President to work toward the ultimate goal of successfully containing the Soviet Union through the methods he saw fit. Nixon had the choice: must the United States retrench, or could it fight austerity? Ultimately, although Nixon's obsession with power and credibility weakened his ability to accomplish goals, the Nixon presidency faced the times of austerity as an opportunity to focus goals and steer the course of American history.

Defining the Terms.

Nixon entered his presidency with the assumption that before a President formats the details of a strategy, he needs first to assess the goals of the strategy. This observation is not as obvious as one may posit; notably, during the Johnson and John Kennedy administrations, the purpose of policy was sometimes not the end goal but the policy process. In the policy process, strategy becomes:

> the calculated relationship of ends and means . . . where calculations become more important than relationships being calculated, where means attract greater attentions than ends-then what one has is not so much bad strategy as no strategy at all.[7]

Nixon wished to turn that trend back to a focused calculation of end goals, because by creating goals and assessing and reassessing the reasons for actions, the United States would avoid wasting its resources in areas where it did not intend to get involved.

Nixon's goal assessments began with the premise that the military strategy for Vietnam did not align with Johnson's goal of "unconditional negotiations." In effect, the military acted as a bureaucratic entity which enacted a plan without incorporating clear goals or significant readjustments as needed, leading Kissinger to observe that "strategy divorced from foreign policy proved sterile."[8] The reality of conflict did not reflect the assertion of benchmarks for negotiations. The Nixon administration instead worked to create operational meanings for goals like superiority and stability.

Even with the purported necessity to define terms for strategy making, Kissinger is criticized by authors for setting out lofty goals without giving clear guidance on how to reach them.[9] The Vietnam conflict highlights the difficulty in shifting goals and actions from a previous administration. Nixon and Kissinger campaigned for the United States to leave Vietnam with dignity, while maintaining U.S. credibility abroad. In a worst-case scenario, loss of American credibility could lead to "global totalitarianism" and would equate to giving the Soviet leaders a "blank check" for expansionism. In fact, during this period, there was resurgence in Soviet thought to be in the Kremlin for increased Soviet activity abroad, countering the domestic retrenchment that took place beginning in 1965.[10] However, much of the fear of losing credibility was rooted in psychological, not real, threats.

What is more, perceptions of leaving with dignity was also rooted in domestic perceptions. "Dignity" could only be achieved through an agreement that would allow them to "save face" so that the American military deaths would not be in vain. The goal for exiting Vietnam was not to exit due to goal attainment of on-the-ground circumstances, but to exit when public perceptions aligned so the United States could maximize its perceived power and so Nixon could maximize his perceived power. The psychological aspect of understanding threats in this Cold War era made goal definition difficult during the Nixon era.

Kissinger, despite the image as a visionary, did not imagine a world beyond the Soviet-U.S. competition. However, despite failures in establishing goals with operational meanings or seeing beyond the status quo competition as it existed, the Nixon-Kissinger partnership did successfully achieve strategic foreign policy objectives by defining their objectives for détente, and those successes were rooted in a definition of goals.

Nixon and Détente.

Nixon and Kissinger's strategy for containing the USSR moved from the principle of "flexible response" (tactical flexibility, especially with regards to nuclear weapons) as described under the Kennedy and Johnson administrations to the principle of détente. Détente (as understood by the administration) was a strategy of containing the Soviets through the variety of tools at the president's disposal with the goal of convincing "Kremlin leaders that it was in their country's best interest to be 'contained'."[11]

John Lewis Gaddis describes the implementation of détente as a four-pronged approached: First, the

United States would engage the USSR in negotiations, and in the process, discard the outdated notions that the United States should wait until it regained the relative strength it had in comparison to the Soviets in the 1950s. The decision to negotiate could not and would not be seen as a weakness.[12]

The second aspect of détente was to shape Soviet behavior through the concept "linkage," allowing the administration to "link" negotiations in one area, such as economics, to an unrelated area.[13] This strategy was based on Nixon's assumption that "since U.S.-Soviet interests as the world's two competing nuclear superpowers were so widespread and overlapping, it was unrealistic to separate or compartmentalize areas of concern."[14] Kissinger argued that allowing the Soviets to get what they want in one arena should depend on the "good behavior" that they follow in another. In Nixon's first press conference about Strategic Arms Limitation Talks (SALT I), he envisioned "strategic arms talks in a way and at a time that will promote, if possible, progress on outstanding political problems at the same time."[15] Through this process, weapons systems negotiations could be linked to settling the Berlin problem. Linkage, effectively, "enlarged the scope" of elements which could be "traded in an international bargain."[16]

The third aspect of détente was to open ties with China in order to further pressure the USSR.[17] Nixon's decisionmaking regarding China aligned with Kissinger's philosophy that, in the triangular diplomacy between the Americans, the Soviets, and the Chinese, the United States should align with the weakest entity and prevent the USSR and China from forming an alliance that would alter the global balance of power.[18] Additionally, by recognizing China, the United States could conserve the diplomatic resources being spent on pressuring other countries from giving recognition to China.[19]

The final part of Nixon's strategy became known as the Nixon Doctrine: The United States would phase out of commitments in the world which did not align with U.S. strategic interests.[20] This doctrine was controversial for allies because there was, and remained, an expectation by American allies, especially America's European allies, that the United States would serve as a protector. America found itself in a position of being the protector for half the world's nations, and those states wanted and needed American security guarantees. Nixon and Kissinger recognized the reason for U.S. involvement in places such as Vietnam, with Kissinger stating that:

> conflicts among states merge with division within nations; the dividing line between domestic and foreign policy begins to disappear . . . [so that] states feel threatened not only by the foreign policy of other countries but also . . . by domestic transformations.[21]

However, they recognized that strategic calculations, not overblown threats, must steer U.S. policy. The Nixon Doctrine became a template for understanding how to balance obligations to half the world with pursuing interests of prime importance to America. The United States vowed to "keep all its treaty commitments" and "provide a shield if a nuclear power threatens the freedom of a nation allied with us or a nation whose survival we consider vital to our security."[22] However, if an ally was threatened or attacked with conventional forces, the United States would react with economic and military assistance but require the ally to take the majority of the responsibility in providing soldiers to protect the threatened or attacked nation. Nixon thus attempted to reassure allies that the United States would continue to honor its commitments and protect nervous European allies, especially through its military and nuclear weapons. However, Nixon publicly required American allies to take on part of the burden of their own defense.

The execution of these four points of Nixon's détente strategy shows certain flaws. For instance, the Nixon Doctrine plus years of a badly mangled war led to the January 1973 Paris Peace Accords agreement to let the U.S. exit from Vietnam. The signing resulted in the fulfillment of the Nixon Doctrine's goal of reigning in an overextended United States, but it left the international community unsure of the strength of an American alliance. Additionally, the Nixon Doctrine was sometimes viewed as an excuse to follow the most politically palatable course of action by exiting Vietnam without bringing peace.[23] The Nobel Prize awarded jointly to Kissinger and his North Vietnamese counterpart, Le Duc Tho, was rejected by Le Duc Tho because he insisted that there was no peace yet. When the United States exited, it left in its wake a South Vietnam plunged into recession with the lost revenue from the American military. With American aid cut off by Congress in 1975, the South Vietnamese were left still fighting a war with the North Vietnamese until they were overrun by the North.[24] In practice, Congress followed the Nixon Doctrine, so that by 1975 "Congress simply did not believe the future of Vietnam was very important to the United States."[25] Though the war ended with a general fulfillment of the Nixon Doctrine, an unsavory message can be gleaned from the end of the war: When a region is no longer vital, the United States may simply discard an ally and remove aid.[26]

The Nixon Doctrine, simple to describe, did not always lead to obvious conclusions about deciding America's strategic interests now and especially in the future. Domestic politics and personal political goals tended to interfere with pure strategic foreign policy goals. For instance, in 1970, due to emerging political circumstances at home and abroad such as "crime, busing, international terrorism, and mistreatment of Soviet Jews," the traditional Democratic allegiance of the Jewish population was cracking.[27] Nixon started to see support of Israel as a potentially important part of getting him reelected in 1972. When the Arab-Israeli War broke out in 1973, Kissinger wanted to keep Israel from returning territory gained in the 1967 conflict in order to prevent Soviet allies from gaining rewards from the war, and worked toward that end. He also worked to prevent strains on the American-Israeli relationship.[28] Nixon and Kissinger failed to see the future consequences of angering the Arab populations. A combination of political calculations for his reelection and calculations about preventing Soviet gains led to an Israel policy which strengthened the U.S. commitment to Israel rather than producing a more flexible strategy for the future.

Finally, the complexity of foreign affairs did not always permit a clear application of Nixon and Kissinger's détente strategies, leading to the failures and over-assumption of threats that repeatedly plagued Cold War Presidents. For instance, although he was neutral publicly, Nixon sent arms to Pakistan in 1971 to help the Pakistani army suppress the secessionist movement of East Pakistan (Bangladesh).[29] The actions of the Pakistani army caused a massive refugee flow into India and horrible human rights violations. The Bangladeshis were supported by Indians, and the Indians had an Indo-Soviet Treaty of Peace, Friendship, and Cooperation from August 1971.[30] The action was thus viewed through an anti-Soviet expansion lens, despite the weakness of the Indian-Soviet partnership.[31] The United States did calculate that, because of the China-Pakistan alliance, supporting the Pakistanis would help with opening China. However, the support also created a further tilt away from the Indians, which effectively helped widen a rift with India, while forging ties with China.[32]

With the massive human rights violations and public disapproval stemming from a publicity blitz originating with the likes of U.S. Senator Ted Kennedy and the Beatle's George Harrison, the U.S. support of Pakistan became an embarrassment to the United States.[33] In private, while Nixon disapproved of Pakistani leader Yahya Khan, he expressed anger with the Indians for the conflict, saying "The Indians put on this sanctimonious, peace, Gandhi-like, Christ-like attitude (like) they're the greatest, the world's biggest democracy and Pakistan is one of the most horrible dictatorships" and that "India's hands are not clean. They're caught in a bloody bit of aggression."[34] Yet, Nixon could not regain public support for his Pakistan policy, and Congress passed a bill to ban the sale of arms to the Pakistani army. Eventually, the Pakistanis were defeated.[35] The United States went on to recognize the state of Bangladesh on April 4, 1972.[36] The Bangladesh conflict highlights the potential discrepancies of détente strategy since one element could conflict with another, and the only basis of hierarchy rests in the recognition that any actions must work to contain the supreme threat of the Soviets. In the conflict, the United States focused on containing the Soviets and siding with the Chinese. However, the United

States overestimated the impact it could have in the conflict and did not adhere to the Nixon Doctrine, eventually coming out on the wrong side of history by siding with Pakistan and its human rights violations.

NIXON AND THE DECLINE OF AMERICAN POWER

The United States maintained the largest proportion of power in the world while Nixon was president, but perceptions of losing power grew. Between 1960 and 1970, Americans watched the Soviet economy expand to roughly half the size of the American economy, although growth rates declined over the decade. Some measures of "world power" showed a Soviet decline from 17 percent to 13 percent of world power during that decade. On the other hand, the United States saw its share of "world power" only decline from 22 percent to 21 percent over the same time period.[37] Alongside concerns of the loss of power were concerns, even obsessions, over perceptions of credibility: Could the United States act on its own or on behalf of its allies when necessary? Thus, while the United States was not facing a serious decline in power, it witnessed an increase in Soviet economic capabilities despite a decrease in relative Soviet power. Authors such as Jonathan Schell argue that, during this time period, credibility and perceptions of power ruled American foreign policy. He claimed that:

> from January of 1961, when John Kennedy took office, until August of 1974, when Richard Nixon was forced to leave office, the unvarying dominant goal of the foreign policy of the United States was the preservation of what policymakers throughout the period called the credibility of American power.[38]

Speculations about where the power trends would lead forced the United States to face the prospect of evolving great power status, with Kissinger arguing that when bipolarity ends, multipolarity will be reestablished. Thus, the Nixon's presidency focused heavily on preserving American power and credibility, even when it led to consequences such as prolonging the Vietnam War.

Despite the continued preponderance of U.S. power, the United States was particularly sensitive to real and perceived losses of relative power during the Nixon era. This was rooted in some actual corrosion of nuclear and economic power dominance. Notably, Nixon focused on nuclear power as central to his strategic calculations but gave only limited attention to the economy, using primarily political (as compared to broad strategic) calculations to make economic decisions. Nixon seemed to view American credibility in action primarily through a military, as compared to an economic, lens.

Maintaining superiority in nuclear missiles, both in number and technology, was a consistent concern for Cold War Presidents. Although it was Kennedy who ran for President with the determination to close the missile gap between the United States and the USSR (a gap which he discovered did not exist),[39] it wasn't until 1965 and 1966 that the Soviets started to approach the strength of U.S. strategic forces.[40] The missile gap became a reality when the USSR overtook the United States in production of intercontinental ballistic missiles (ICBMs). The gap in ICBMs, which was only one aspect of the nuclear race, did not equate to American decline. However, when coupled with domestic and external strife, the United States faced a shrinking power separation between the two superpowers.

Nixon faced the shrinking power gap through strength and diplomacy, not only because this was the best course of action for the United States, but because he believed that this was the only position the Soviets would respect. Even though the loss of an overwhelming position of strength could have been a detriment to the United States, it actually became an asset because the Soviets were more willing to negotiate when they would not be locked into a vastly inferior treaty-based position as a result of negotiations. Nixon's calculations for negotiations are well reflected in the process of the SALT I negotiations.

During the Nixon years, U.S. and USSR strategic weapons systems were asymmetrical, with the USSR overtaking the United States in numbers of land-based ICBMs by 1972, but this asymmetry reflected a change of technologies, not systemic American decline.[41] The Soviets increased their ICBMs from 1,000 to 1,500 from 1969-72, while the number of American ICBMs remained stagnant at 1,054.[42] However, when the United States stopped additional deployments of the strategic ICBMs in 1967, it turned instead to a system designed to inflict maximum damage from a single missile. The United States began employing multiple independently-targeted re-entry vehicles (MIRVs) which allowed a single missile to carry multiple warheads that could be sent to different targets.[43] The United States also held more long-range bombers than the Soviets, and had plans to increase the number of anti-ballistic missile (ABM) defense systems to counter the Soviet threat. Development of weapons systems highlighted a missile gap less as a reflection of American decline and more of the shifting macabre calculations of nuclear weapons systems.

On the very first day of the Nixon presidency, the Soviet Foreign Ministry extended a note probing the President's willingness to discuss arms limitations, and Nixon immediately expressed support for the proposition.[44] The Strategic Arms Limitation Talks (SALT I) started in Helsinki, Finland, in November 1969.[45] Notably, the discussions were private, allowing the negotiators to discuss candidly what they wanted. Private discussions hold the advantage of avoiding the trap of forcing negotiators to hold tight to government proclamations, and allow the results to be framed in a politically palpable manner when they are later presented to the public. Private discussions also concentrate power in the presidency and prevent the debate for nuances of well-versed advisers.

The difficulties of SALT I negotiations flowed from the same calculations which led to the asymmetry of weapons systems. The negotiations started with Soviets wanting to first define "strategic" weapons to best fit their aims. The United States needed to maintain its North Atlantic Treaty Organization (NATO) and other allied commitments, and thus had a variety of weapons capable of reaching the USSR located on ships or on European territory. When the USSR proposed to define "strategic" as weapons capable of reaching home territory, the limitations negotiated on strategic weapons would mean that those weapons on aircraft carriers and in Europe would be vulnerable to limitations through the talks.[46] However, the short- and mid-range Soviet weapons which could reach Europe but not make it across the ocean to the United States would not be subject to limitations. Clearly, this beginning stance was untenable for the United States, and was promptly rejected.[47] The talks would not place the United States in an inferior position.

For 2 years, the talks continued, with different amalgamations of proposals, including a call for limitations of ABMs by the Soviets and calls to limit offensive weapons by the Americans. Nixon and Kissinger insisted on linking offensive to defensive systems, despite the Soviet preference for discussions only on the defensive ABMs.[48] SALT I was in a virtual deadlock when Kissinger and his back channel diplomacy stepped in to keep SALT from collapsing.[49] Congressional opponents to the administration were supporting the ABM, defensive system-only negotiation, which Nixon thought would place American negotiators in an inferior position. His assessment that the Soviets would only negotiate from a position of strength, and thus the Americans must do the same, successfully led to the agreement in May 1971 that the United States and the USSR would concentrate talks on limiting ABMs and offensive systems. In the case of SALT I, the backchannel concentration of power led to success by avoiding the pitfalls of an overextended conversation. Finally, on May 26, 1972, Nixon and General Secretary Leonid Brezhnev signed the ABM Treaty, as well as the Interim Agreement and Protocol on Limitation of Strategic Offensive Weapons.[50] The ABM Treaty went into effect for unlimited duration, limiting each state to employ ABMs at only one site which could launch 100 interceptor missiles. The Interim Agreement had a 5-year time limit while negotiations continued, but in the meantime froze the number of ICBMs and submarine-launched ballistic missiles (SLBMs). During the 5 years, negotiations would continue, assuring that Kissinger could continue working for the best possible settlement on offensive weapons.

SALT I was a shining point for public relations and the Nixon presidency. He engaged in negotiations and concluded a treaty with the Soviets, he executed his strategy of linkage, and he successfully funneled negotiations to focus on the areas of greatest strategic importance to the United States. He also stood strong in the face of Soviet negotiators and American doves, and the agreement was the better for it. SALT I was only possible because of the willingness of the Nixon team to negotiate with America's greatest adversary and through a true understanding of the positions of both sides and a willingness to accept the strategic necessities of the Soviets. The United States negotiated from a position of power but accepted the power of the Soviets.

In contrast to the successes of Nixon's strategy for SALT, his failures as an economic President are rooted heavily in his lack of a strategy for the economy. Though in the general policy world the belief that America was losing power was premised not just on the faulty assumptions of the U.S. failure to compete with the USSR militarily but also on the faltering of the U.S. economy, the Nixon presidency did not focus on the U.S. economic states as the driving force for American power and credibility. Nixon focused his goals as President primarily on foreign affairs and imagining the multipolar world that would result from his détente strategies. However, Nixon's view of the economy kept his outlook anchored firmly in the near future. He wished to grow the economy and keep citizens working in order to maintain his office and allow him to continue involvement in foreign affairs.

Although Nixon firmly associated with the Republican Party, he did not hold the party line when it came to economic policy. For instance, in 1969, when Budget Director Robert Mayo pushed Nixon for "drastic cuts" to the budget, Nixon agreed only to small cuts to prevent causing a recession or alienating voters.[51] A notable exception to Nixon's aversion to drastic cuts affected the National Aeronautics and Space Administration (NASA). Neil Armstrong and Buzz Aldrin took *Apollo 11* to the moon on July 20, 1969.[52] Nixon is described as holding a keen understanding of the boost in prestige for America, and its space program, received through this historic event.[53] However, the following year, Nixon stated that "space expenditures must take their proper place within a rigorous system of national priorities," and oversaw a drop in NASA's budget from 4 percent to 1 percent of the federal budget by the time he left office, where it has stayed ever since.[54] Nixon's response to NASA and the moon landing fell squarely within his strategy of placing proper emphasis on American interests, and, in the process of cutting funding to the program, he effectively placed a value judgment that the power gained from NASA successes is not a key interest.

Nixon brought the conservative Democrat John Connally, Jr., into the cabinet as Secretary of the Treasury at the end of 1970. Although Connally was not an economist or a banker, Nixon calculated that the Democrat could help Nixon gain support among the Southern Democrats and potentially run as Nixon's vice president in the next election.[55] Connally eventually worked to get rid of gradualism, a policy advocated by Paul McCracken and George Shultz, which theoretically gets rid of inflation slowly while maintaining politically palatable levels of unemployment. Economic improvement was not swift in the early years of Nixon's presidency, and he worried about the 1972 election. Unemployment grew from 3.4 percent in January 1969 to 6.1 percent in December 1970. Nixon and Connally abandoned gradualism and turned to spending and price controls, a politically palatable move with fast economic gains.[56] Nixon did so without broadly consulting with advisers, including Schultz. By late summer of 1972, unemployment crept back down, hovering around 5.7 percent.[57] The decision to support Connally highlighted Nixon's preference for political goals over economics and foreshadowed his future failures to put in place people and policies to lead the economy for the long term.

Nixon's most notable act in his economic presidency was the single-handed reshaping of the international monetary system when, on August 15, 1971, Nixon controversially announced that the United States would entirely remove itself from the gold standard during an episode of the television program, Bonanza.[58] Since the Eisenhower administration, economists and Presidents alike worried that, because the United States ran a deficit with dollars held by countries outside the United States through the Bretton Woods system, any sudden run on the dollar could create a scenario whereby the United States would not be able to pay out gold for the dollars. The system made the U.S. inherently vulnerable.[59] In order to prevent a disaster scenario, an emergency cabinet study during December 1967 concluded that the best way to prevent a run on the dollar was that the United States would have to implement border taxes, export subsidies, travel taxes, and a variety of other measures to reduce the deficit. The result looked like a dangerous turn to isolationism for the United States and a turn away from America's laudatory free trade policies.[60]

In 1968, President Johnson introduced a balance of payments system to offset American deficits. Milton Friedman harshly criticized the program:

> The United States . . . prohibits its businessmen from investing abroad. . . . The United States, the wealthiest nation in the world, announces that its foreign policy will no longer be determined by its national interest and its international commitments but by the need to reduce spending abroad by $500 million.[61]

The economic problem of the gold standard fell squarely into the Nixon goals of focusing on the areas of greatest strategic importance to America. Key among the abilities to maintain U.S. policy interests abroad was the stationing of six army divisions in West Germany, a military placement central to containing the USSR.[62] The balance of payments process made bringing those troops home increasingly attractive financially, but the act would undermine NATO's strategy in facing down the Soviets. The boons of Nixon's New Economic Policy and going off the gold standard in 1971 included the increased flexibility of the Federal Reserve to print money in response to crisis situations. The United States would no longer feel pressured by the potential impact of a collective decision to turn in dollars for gold, and the subsequent national security consequences which would follow. What is more, with the Smithsonian Agreement of December 1971 whereby the Group of Ten finance ministers agreed to increase the price of their currency against the dollar to help with American deficits, the United States had temporary relief in easing its deficit.[63]

In the election year of 1972, Nixon turned away from his spending program designed to jump-start the economy and his policies of implementing price controls to Republican frugality. This transition was designed so that he could depict himself as "the very antithesis of the spendthrift Democrat against whom he would run."[64] Since the economic problems of unemployment and inflation looked under control, he steered the reelection debate to reduce the emphasis on the economy (and his record on the economy) in the election. He was reelected with 60 percent of the popular vote and the majority in every state except Massachusetts.[65] Nixon's economic decisions, motivated by future political calculations, paid off. He retained office, assuring future opportunities to continue his work in foreign affairs.

The success in the election did not lead to success in the economy and did not lead to a historical understanding of Nixon as a successful economic President. The price controls helped push an increased demand in raw materials, pushing up prices. Coupled with a "worldwide food commodity shortage," inflation skyrocketed.[66] American demand for energy increased by 5 percent in 1972, while supply diminished.[67] In response to American support for Israelis in the Yom Kippur War of 1973, the Saudis implemented an oil embargo, exacerbating the energy crisis.[68] Nixon's economic decisions based primarily in political calculations led not to a solid, coherent policy, but to a piecemeal policy subject to reversals. The calculations to take the United States off the gold standard was an anomaly in the ledger of the Nixon economic presidency. In the realm of the economy, Nixon did not lead, but was led. The Nixon presidency shows that, while the economy can lead to short-term political gains, a piecemeal strategy defined by producing those short-term gains is unlikely to lead to a strong American economy in the long term.

Finally, the power calculation made during Nixon's time revolved around America's future great power status. Statesmen including Kissinger were predicting the coming end to the existing great power structure in foreign relations. At the time, predictions centered on the eventual collapse of bipolarity and the potential repercussions of collapse. Kissinger conceived the possibility that, despite the remaining "overwhelming military strength" that the United States will maintain regardless of the change of great power status of other states, the United States will have to "evoke the creativity of a pluralistic world" in the sense that "political multipolarity makes it impossible to impose an American design" on international institutions or the domestic institutions of developing states.[69] The power calculations of multipolarity were, in fact, predictions of austerity of power, predictions which did not have immediately actionable results, but predictions which weighed heavy nonetheless.

Nixon In China.

A President's credibility may be determined both by past and current performance as well as by the history of the President's political party on a given issue. Neustadt argues "political reputation and public approval" are like a resource that is later spent when a President makes a decision.[70] Amassed political capital can allow a President to execute decisions that work against type; for instance, in the case of a President with political capital built up as a staunch anti-communist, the President may be given leeway by both the political establishment and the public in working with communists without massive political backlash or accusations of working with "the enemy."[71]

When Nixon came into office, he was known not just in political circles but in the general public as a staunch anti-communist, being described by Stephen Ambrose as "the world's best known anti-communist."[72] After being awakened to the threat of communism with the Soviet takeover of Hungary in 1947 and Czechoslovakia in 1948, Nixon began to view the USSR as the penultimate enemy to freedom.[73] Nixon's time in Congress included a stint on the House Un-American Activities Committee (HUAC), the committee charged by Congress to investigate real and suspected communists, where he drafted legislation requiring American communists to register publicly and give the source of all their printed materials, which could then be investigated.[74] Nixon's time on the HUAC allowed him to cultivate the image of an anti-communist, effectively removing criticism that he could be "soft" on communism.

What Nixon's "political capital" as an anti-communist allowed him to do was to open China without being labeled by American analysts as a communist sympathizer. China was ready to reenter the international community after the end of its isolation after the Great Cultural Revolution, and Nixon saw this as an opportunity.[75] In addition, the articulation of the Nixon Doctrine at Guam "publicized implicit administration affirmation of the principle that alliances and alignments were inherently conditional and subject to continued evaluation and adjustment."[76] The capital of a President and the articulation of a policy allowed for a shifting U.S. policy, and in 1970, Nixon and Kissinger first established back-channel communication with China to test the waters of creating a relationship with Beijing, with Kissinger taking a secret trip to China in 1971.[77]

While Kissinger often takes equal credit for the development and execution of Nixon's foreign policy successes, Nixon's goals for American relations with China predate the Nixon-Kissinger partnership. The ability to move quickly to change the U.S. policy toward a communist state stemmed from an already implanted seed in Nixon about the potential significance of Asia: Nixon's interest in China was partially based on a personal interest in Asia shaped by travels to the region. Asia was a part of Nixon's vision for what the world could look like when it moved beyond the stagnant bipolarity of the Cold War. Nixon first visited Asia in 1953, and repeated trips sparked a belief that this area of the world would become an increasingly pivotal area of American interest.[78] He took multiple trips to the region, often spending only 1 to 4 days in a country. However, despite these short periods of exposure, he personally experienced the economic and cultural transformations taking place. Nixon not only read about, but saw the astounding growth rates of Japan, South Korea, Taiwan, Thailand, Singapore, and Malaysia, and saw them as great opportunities for the United States. Perhaps it was this exposure that helped him articulate in a 1967 *Foreign Affairs* article the forward thinking idea that, despite the criticism levied at Asians for being too "different" to become a central focus of American concern, this criticism was "racial and cultural chauvinism that [did] little credit to American ideals, and it [showed] little appreciation either of the westward thrust of American interests or of the dynamics of world development."[79] The United States would need to see strategic interest in the continent which holds half of all the people in the world. He went on to argue that the long-term U.S. policy goal toward China must be to bring China "into the family of nations" and in the short term to discourage "imperial ambitions" and "foreign adventuring" and turn instead to "the solution of its own domestic problems."[80] The United States could not afford to allow

China to be, "self-exiled from society, stay exiled forever."[81] Finally, he argued that the "race for Asia" was between the United States, the USSR, and China. This vision laid the foundation for Nixon's power move to open China.

Opening China also fit clearly into the Nixon strategy of reassessing the major centers of American interest. He assessed that the USSR would consider it a failure if China and the United States align, and the USSR remain the prime U.S. adversary.[82] However, the idea of the United States and Asia holds a central U.S. interest in its own right. After assuming the presidency, Nixon secretly directed the National Security Council to study the implications of alternative policies toward China, and directed Kissinger to broach the topic of rapprochement.[83] In a pivotal discussion in Guam in July 1969, Nixon articulated his reasoning for moving toward Asia and laid the foundation for building political capital for the eventual move of reestablishing relations with China. Contrary to the Eurocentric tendencies of many Americans, Nixon argued that Asia could potentially pose the greatest threat to peace 20 years down the line.[84] He based this assertion on a quick read of history: World War II started (for the United States) in the Pacific, and the Korean and Vietnam Wars were among the points of the most intense conflicts for America in the 20th century. While he argued that America must retain a strong presence, he pointed to two changes in the region that should affect American policy. The first was that nationalism and regional pride surged since his first visit in 1953, and the second was the growing belief that Asians do not want America to dictate its policies. Thus, Nixon argued that "we should assist, but we should not dictate."[85] Finally, he argued again that America should develop a better understanding of its strategic interests and avoid getting dragged into long, protracted, and generally peripheral conflicts like that in Vietnam.

Opening China in February 1972, normalizing relations with the most populous country in the world, is one of the most lauded accomplishments of the Nixon presidency. This particular emphasis on China was not solely a continuation of the 1899 Open Door Policy toward Asia designed to open Asia to American trade, but as a key security element in Asia. Nixon, like many Presidents before him, saw China as a potentially huge boon for both American and Chinese trade. Nixon and Kissinger were able to make the prospect of normalizing relations with China an asset to both the United States and China, despite the severe differences since the communist revolution. Nixon acted on the transformations of Mao Zedong, recognizing and reassuring the Chinese that America's relations with Japan could hamper any renewal of Japanese aggression in the region. Nixon's strategic calculations about American priorities also led to closed-door assurances that the United States will stop asserting that the status of Taiwan is unknown, and that the United States will not support a Taiwanese independence movement. Nixon publicly shifted the United States from the Kennedy standard of being equipped to fight two and a half wars (the USSR and Eastern Europe and a China war) with conventional forces to one and a half wars, a proclamation which reassured Nixon's Chinese counterparts of his seriousness in strengthening ties between the two states.[86] Nixon's ultimate calculation that the Sino-Soviet split was an opportunity to create a permanent division in the world's largest communist countries is, perhaps, the ultimate success of Nixon's détente.[87]

The opening of China also showed the potential success of repeated, short-term trips across a substantial period of time in helping a President see the evolution of a region, an evolution which would not be as salient through simple reports. Seeing and understanding the evolution of states and governments will help a President recognize points where policy could turn or transition to something more amenable to the United States, or try to steer the tide away from a transition that is against American interests. Nixon also took care to reassure China about Japan and Taiwan, recognizing both the legitimate concerns of the Chinese and the ultimate U.S. strategic interests. The back-channel and closed door nature of the negotiations created an environment to produce diplomatic gains and reassurances about legitimate concerns without "crowing" about incremental gains or the other side's "losses." Such a strategy made the China negotiations politically feasible both for the governments and for citizens. When facing an adversary in negotiations, this strategy may be advisable in creating politically palatable results.

NIXON'S DOWNFALL

As seen over and over, Nixon attended to the major international and domestic political issues of the time with a strategic calculation: If Nixon considered the events important, he gave them proper recognition while placing them in the context of other strategic interests. If he had no regard for an event and its place in American strategy, he gave it little or no attention.

Nixon was a highly political man who saw politics as a roadblock to his success. He played up events which could increase his credibility and electability.

He used politics to his benefit when possible; for instance, he would refer to "the silent majority" when justifying policies which received public outcries, and is even purported to have White House staff write ghost editorials in support of him.[88] Nixon's presidency was not defined by fostering the will of the people, but by furthering his own agenda.

Nixon often downplayed or belittled events which could potentially hamper his ability to maintain office and pursue his chosen foreign policy goals. His years in office were marked by the cultural movements sweeping the big cities and college campuses. Although in his 1969 Inaugural Address Nixon claimed that he "know[s] America's youth" and he "believe[s] in them," the President was often dismissive of the student protesters.[89] Vice President Spiro Agnew freely demonized academics and peace protesters as people "encouraged to be an effete corps of impudent snobs who characterize themselves as intellectuals."[90] Since these groups opposed his policies, Nixon dismissed their impact. However, these movements and popular perceptions in general did have some sway on individual policies. General public opinion plus the Nixon Doctrine were together pivotal in removing the United States from Vietnam. For instance, the strategic bombing campaign of North Vietnam in 1972 was generally viewed by the American public as causing numerous civilian casualties. However, while the North Vietnamese did suffer about 13,000 civilian deaths, this level of casualties is unlikely to have pressured the North Vietnamese into the 1973 ceasefire which allowed the United States to leave Vietnam. Instead, in 1972, the U.S. ground troops stopped the progression of the North Vietnamese into South Vietnam. The North Vietnamese thereafter had an incentive to want the Americans to leave and create a power vacuum so the North Vietnamese could successfully take the South.[91] Without popular perception about the harm being inflicted on the civilian population and popular dismissal of the strategy of the North Vietnamese, the public may have read the decision about when and how to leave Vietnam differently.

Nixon was certainly not the first President to align political action with election calculations, as he did with his appointment of John Connally and his economic decisions at large. Campbell Craig and Frederick Logevall argue that the timing of many of Nixon's foreign policy decisions were likewise motivated by reelection calculations.[92] In his memoirs, he describes the announcement of Johnson to stop bombing North Vietnam as an "11th-hour masterstroke that almost won him [Hubert Humphrey] the election."[93] The decision did not come as a complete surprise because Kissinger, who was working for the Johnson administration, fed Nixon information about the bombing halt. The halt fell through due to the lack of support from South Vietnam, and Nixon won the presidency. The incident is less compelling for the facts and more for Nixon's disgust at the shady maneuver. Politics was a vessel for pursuing his policies, but there was a palpable loathing for politics at the heart of Nixon's actions. As a man who could never even dream of having the political charm of a Kennedy, Nixon came to disdain those who opposed him.

The time of austerity and unpopularity, coupled with Nixon's disdain for dissent in the political process, led to another defining characteristic of his presidency: the concentration of power, sometimes secretly held power, in the executive. From Kissinger's backchannel diplomacy in opening China to Nixon's economic policies, Nixon avoided or ignored the established political process. U.S. foreign policy, more than ever before, took place outside the knowledge of even the Secretary of State prior to Kissinger's placement in that position in 1973.

In painting a portrait of Nixon's time in office, Arthur M. Schlesinger, Jr., describes a President who disregards constitutional provisions regarding the division of power among the three branches of government, with Nixon "systematically" concentrating power in the executive. Nixon commandeered three powers constitutionally prescribed to Congress: "the war-making power, the power of the purse, and the power of oversight and investigation."[94] Although Harry Truman in Korea and Johnson in Vietnam provided the precedence of not requiring congressional approval for the dispatch of troops, Nixon additionally countered "the power of the purse by the doctrine of unlimited impoundment of appropriated funds" and avoided investigation through "the doctrine of unreviewable executive privilege."[95] In order to reach his goal of a balanced, full employment budget, in 1973, Nixon refused to "spend more than $12 billion in appropriated funds, an affront to its power so galling that Congress would soon debate whether impoundments warranted his impeachment."[96]

Nixon's disregard of the public and the Congress was overarching:

> the bureaucracy was shut out from key policy decisions, such as detente with the Soviet Union . . . the announcement of a new economic policy in August 1971, the trip to China, and the Vietnam peace negotiations.[97]

He viewed his goals as the President as U.S. goals, and did what he saw as best to achieve them, regardless of tradition, political logic, or legality. Congress and the American public were often either tools or obstacles to achieving objectives.

Although Nixon was never impeached, he resigned in disgrace on August 9, 1974. In the 2 years since members of the Committee to Reelect the President broke into the Democratic National Committee, Nixon obstructed justice by using political espionage and abuse of presidential power to cover up the crimes.[98] Kissinger attempted to save Nixon's job by telling the House Foreign Affairs Committee, which was conducting investigations, that Nixon was pivotal to the Middle East peace process and "this constant attack on domestic authority is going to have the most serious consequences for our foreign policy,"[99] but to no avail. The damage that the disrespect for the political process and the emphasis on secret, concentrated power had on the Nixon presidency forever eclipses the reputation of Nixon as "the foreign policy President." The United States put in place safeguards such as financial disclosure laws and Freedom of Information Act amendments after the Nixon presidency to assure that no President could again take advantage of the executive in the way Nixon did.

NIXON'S LESSONS FOR TODAY'S PRESIDENCY

Nixon's strategies and experiences showed that a President during times of austerity is capable of significant achievements, but Nixon's time in office also highlighted potential pitfalls other Presidents may face. The lessons that can be gleaned from history may not produce directly transferable solutions to present day policy dilemmas, but they can serve to inform the decisionmaking process around those dilemmas. For instance, the shift in goals of a war from one presidency to another may be littered with the same problems as the shift in Vietnam from Johnson to Nixon. Barack Obama's second term will see a comparable decision to be made in regards to the increasingly unpopular Afghanistan war. With the 2014 exit date for NATO combat troops, any change in the exit plan should come from clearly established goals and defined benchmarks, not a simple assessment that the "mission" is or is not accomplished.[100] Otherwise, although Obama will accomplish the U.S. exit from Afghanistan, he will have to accept the consequences of leaving a troubled state.

When Nixon brought the troops home from Vietnam while the civil war raged, the South Vietnamese questioned the loyalty of a U.S. partnership. The United States may face similar criticism when it leaves Afghanistan in 2014, depending on the political scenario and amount of conflict when it departs. American credibility with unstable allies may come into question. However, the United States must not overestimate the importance of American credibility. Nixon chose to stay in the Vietnam War, to continue putting American lives in danger through a deadly war, and to prop up the South Vietnamese government in order to salvage American credibility. As Schell puts it, Nixon wanted to "establish in the minds of peoples and their leaders throughout the world an image of the United States as a nation that possessed great power and had the will and determination to use it in foreign affairs."[101] Kennedy, Johnson, and Nixon all chose to make "Vietnam a 'test case' of American resolve" without considering that the Vietnam War was determined in large part not because of the strength of the communist movement emanating from the USSR, but because of the on-the-ground circumstances of Vietnam.[102] The United States chose to overemphasize the importance of Vietnam, and though the Nixon Doctrine specifically highlighted the necessity to avoid involvement in conflicts which weren't of strategic importance, Nixon fell into the peril of the sunk cost problem and prolonged the war to maintain the supposed credibility of American commitments instead of exiting sooner.

American leaders feared that if they lacked credibility, their allies may lose faith in American loyalty and ability to act and would fall to communism. Although Laos and Cambodia fell to the communist movement, there was not a general ricochet of falling dominoes, and America's strongest, mutually beneficial alliances with European countries did not suffer from the withdrawal.[103] Taking a lesson from Vietnam, although the United States should be concerned about maintaining perceptions of credibility to fulfill commitments, maintaining credibility should not come at the expense of real American interests. The United States should strive to leave Afghanistan in as good of shape as possible, but not choose to stay longer than necessary because of credibility calculations.

The United States is predicting massive military difficulties in Afghanistan after the U.S. exit. However, the exit from Vietnam leads one to anticipate another looming problem. As noted previously, when American troops left, they took with them a huge source of revenue for the Vietnamese government, leading to a Vietnamese recession with their own austerity measures. The United States has been in Afghanistan for more than 10 years now, and its exit will inevitably lead to a remarkable loss in the Afghani economy. If the United States loses interest in Afghanistan post-departure and chooses to reduce or eliminate aid, it should expect Afghanistan to institute its own austerity measures and struggle not just militarily but economically, with decreased functioning of many of the social institutions which were built up over the last decade.[104]

As the United States continues to support the internationally unpopular Israeli government today, the same problems crop up again and again: The strong, political American Jewish vote remains significant, and some Arab states remain hostile because of America's support for Israel. With the likelihood of Iran completing a nuclear weapon and the chance of an unpopular Israeli strike on Iran during the next presidential term, the United States will, implicitly or explicitly, face the calculations for action inherent in the Nixon Doctrine and must answer the question: What significance does Israel and a nuclear Iran hold among the array of American strategic interests?

The United States has not changed course since Nixon's time in assessing China as extremely important to American strategic interests. China's enormous economic gains, especially in the last 2 decades, were possible because of the normalized relations between the United States and China, emphasizing the potential gains of creating ties with an otherwise closed country. The United States is unlikely to have a repeat of Nixon's China moment, at least not one that could begin to match the economic gains brought on by reopening the Chinese markets. However, certain lessons can be garnered for the next presidential term based on the circumstances of the diplomatic process. First, Nixon's political capital as an anti-communist allowed him to establish ties with a Communist nation. Assuming the political capital of a President decreases with decisions made, the decision options available for the next term of the President will vary greatly based on the reputation, past performance, and political party of the President. A political area where the importance of political capital may become increasingly important in the next presidential term is related to the use of drones. The use of drones to target militants is a practice that theoretically fits with the hawkish character of the Republican Party, but as a Democrat, a lawyer, and a critic of the Iraq war, President Obama's political capital allowed him to greatly increase the use of drones across borders to target terrorists, despite the tenuous position of drones in international law. After the targeted killing of an American citizen, Obama's political capital diminished, and he now faces criticism for the lack of due process in targeting Americans and the secretive nature of the program.[105] These calculations of political capital will necessarily factor into the political decisions in the next presidency. Second, the opening of China points to the importance of negotiating with the Chinese from the point of equality. Nixon recognized that the Chinese needed respect in order to move forward, so when the United States enters negotiations with China in the future, it would be wise to follow the principles of treating the Chinese as equals and negotiating from a position of power, while developing a clear understanding of Chinese goals.

The United States could also learn from the linkage between offensive and defensive weapons of the SALT I negotiations. First, the United States must work toward gaining a clear understanding of the threats and needs of any country with which it enters into negotiations. Additionally, the United States could link one problem to another (like offensive and defensive weapons, or even two unrelated related subjects) and come to agreement on one subject with a temporary agreement with assured future negotiations on another subject. By using the first subject as "bait," the United States may eventually be more likely to achieve gains on the more controversial issue by coming to treaty-based temporary agreements with treaty-based assurances to future negotiations.

Kissinger's teachings on multipolarity are as relevant now as in the past: While America will maintain "overwhelming military strength" in the coming decades, the United States will have to to use creativity in dealing with the "pluralistic world" and avoid imposing American programs on developing states. Though the security of America in its great power status is not in question, questions today are repeatedly being asked about the potential influence of a rising China for creating a bipolar environment, or even the rise of lesser powers in creating a multipolar environment. However, while the insecurity of America in remaining the sole superpower repeatedly crops up during conversations about America's future, it is worth remembering that Kissinger's predictions about the world returning to multipolarity when bipolarity ended were wrong, and predictions made today should not be taken as an inevitability. For instance, while some authors predict bipolarity, others predict that the rise of nationalism or globalism will corrode the power of the state to the extent that great power status will not hold the same relevance in future years as it does today. While any of these predictions could come true, these types of predictions were made repeatedly over the last 40 or more years and have failed to produce the predicted results. Therefore, the United States should not assume bipolarity or multipolarity will reemerge, but it can, nonetheless, support nonradical cultural and political diversity in emerging domestic institutions of developing states and in international institutions.

Finally, the complicated ending of the Nixon presidency serves as a warning to all future Presidents. The embarrassment and failure of Nixon resulting from his concentration of executive power has not lead to an overwhelming timidity in concentrating power today. The emphasis on executive privilege related to rendition in the George Bush administration and the drone strikes under the Obama administration indicate that the United States can expect a continued wrangling for power between the executive, legislative, and judiciary branches. Presidents should assume, however, that whenever they take power which is not traditionally part of the executive, they will someday need to justify their decision.

ENDNOTES - CHAPTER 4

1. Seymour Martin Lipet and William Schneider, "The Decline of Confidence in American Institutions," *Political Science Quarterly*, Vol. 98, No. 3, Fall 1983, p. 380.

2. James T. Patterson, *Grand Expectations*, New York: Oxford University Press, 1996, p. 686.

3. Norman N. Bowsher, "1968-Year of Inflation," *Review*, St. Louis, MO: The Federal Reserve Bank of St. Louis, December 1968, available from *research.stlouisfed.org/publications/review/68/12/Inflation_Dec1968.pdf*.

4. Patterson, p. 704. Nixon received 31,785,480 votes, while Hubert Humphrey won 31,275,166 votes.

5. Henry A. Kissinger, "Central Issues of American Foreign Policy," *Foreign Relations of the United States, 1969-1976, Vol. I*, in *Foundations of Foreign Policy, 1969-1972*, Document 80, Washington, DC: Department of State, December 9, 1970.

6. John Lewis Gaddis, *Strategies of Containment*, New York: Oxford University Press, 2005, pp. 276.

7. *Ibid.*, p. 271.

8. Henry A. Kissinger, "Central Issues of American Foreign Policy," *Foreign Relations of the United States, 1969-1976, Vol. I*, in *Foundations of Foreign Policy, 1969-1972*, Document 4, Washington, DC: Department of State, 1968.

9. Robert D. Schulzinger, "The End of the Vietnam War, 1973-1976," Fredrik Logevall and Andrew Preston, eds., *Nixon in the World*, New York: Oxford University Press, 2008, p. 218.

10. Odd Arne Westad, *The Global Cold War: Third World Interventions an the Making of Our Times*, Cambridge, MA: Cambridge University Press, 2009, p. 202.

11. Gaddis, p. 287.

12. *Ibid.*, p. 288.

13. *Ibid.*, p. 290.

14. Richard Nixon, *The Memoirs of Richard Nixon*, New York: Grosset and Dunlap, 1978, pp. 346. Hereafter, *Memoirs*.

15. *Ibid.*

16. Edward A. Kolodziej, "Foreign Policy and the Politics of Interdependence: The Nixon Presidency," *Polity*, Vol. 9, No. 2, Winter 1976, p. 135.

17. Gaddis, p. 293.

18. *Ibid.*, p. 294.

19. Kolodziej, p. 140.

20. Gaddis, p. 295.

21. Kissinger, "Central Issues of American Foreign Policy," Document 4.

22. Gaddis, p. 296. Nixon delivered this outline of the Nixon Doctrine at a press briefing in Guam in July 1969.

23. Kolodziej, p. 131.

24. Schulzinger, pp. 205-206.

25. *Ibid.*, pp. 213.

26. *Ibid.*, pp. 213.

27. Salim Yaqub, "The Weight of Conquest: Henry Kissinger and the Arab-Israeli Conflict," *Nixon in the World*, New York: Oxford University Press, 2008, p. 230.

28. *Ibid.*, pp. 227.

29. "Candidates' Dads on Nixon Tapes," *CBS News*, February 11, 2009, available from *www.cbsnews.com/2100-250_162-244656.html*.

30. Mary Senteria, Chap. 3, *Indo-Soviet Relations 1971-1980: A Study of the Impact of the Treaty of Peace, Friendship and Co-operation on Bi-lateral Relations*, Kottayam, India: Mahatma Gandi University, 2010, available as an ebook from *shodhganga.inflibnet.ac.in/handle/10603/396?mode=full&submit_simple=Show+full+item+record*.

31. *Ibid.*, p. 81.

32. *Ibid.*

33. Joshua Keating, "How Ted Kennedy Helped Create Bangladesh," *Foreign Policy*, August 27, 2009, available from *blog.foreignpolicy.com/posts/2009/08/27/ted_kennedy_remembered_in_bangladesh*.

34. "Candidates' Dads on Nixon Tapes."

35. Keating.

36. "A Guide to the United States' History of Recognition, Diplomatic, and Consular Relations, by Country, since 1776: Bangladesh," Washington, DC: Department of State, Office of the Historian, available from *history.state.gov/countries/bangladesh*.

37. William C. Wohlforth, *The Elusive Balance: Power and Perception during the Cold War*, Ithaca, NY: Cornell University Press, 1993, p. 184.

38. Jonathan Schell, *The Time of Illusion: An Historical and Reflective Account of the Nixon Era*, New York: Random House, 1975, p. 341.

39. Richard Reeves, "Missile Gaps and Other Broken Promises," *New York Times*, February 10, 2009.

40. Vladislav M. Zubok, *A Failed Empire*, Chapel Hill, NC: The University of North Carolina Press, 2007, p. 205.

41. Bureau of Arms Control, Verification, and Compliance, "Strategic Arms Limitation Talks SALT I Narrative," Washington, DC: U.S. Department of State, available from *www.state.gov/t/isn/5191.htm*.

42. *Ibid.*

43. *Ibid.*

44. *Ibid.*

45. Henry Kissinger, *White House Years*, Boston, MA: Little, Brown and Company, 1979, p. 148.

46. *Ibid.*, pp. 101-149.

47. *Memoirs*, p. 523.

48. *Ibid.*

49. *Ibid.*

50. *Ibid.*, p. 524.

51. Allen J. Matusow, *Nixon's Economy: Booms, Busts, Dollars, & Votes*, Lawrence, KS: University Press of Kansas, 1998, p. 40.

52. John Noble Wilford, "Men Walk on Moon," *New York Times*, July 21, 1969, available from *www.nytimes.com/learning/general/onthisday/big/0720.html*.

53. John M. Logsdon, "Ten Presidents and NASA," *NASA 50th Magazine*, available from *www.nasa.gov/50th/50th_magazine/10presidents.html*.

54. Matusow. Quote taken from a March 7, 1970 statement.

55. *Ibid.*, p. 87.

56. *Ibid.*, pp. 10, 86.

57. Bureau of Labor Statistics, "Civilian Unemployment Rate," Washington, DC: U.S. Department of Labor, last updated October 5, 2012, available from *research.stlouisfed.org/fred2/data/UNRATE.txt*.

58. Adam Martin, "Remembering Nixon's Gold-Standard Gamble: Interrupting 'Bonanza,"' *The Atlantic-Wire*, August 15, 2011, available from *www.theatlanticwire.com/politics/2011/08/nixon-gold-standard-gamble-interrupting-bonanza/41278/*.

59. Francis J. Gavin, *Gold, Dollars, and Power: The Politics of International Monetary Relations, 1958-1971*, Chapel Hill, NC: University of North Carolina Press, 2004, pp. 3-4.

60. *Ibid.*, p. 3.

61. *Ibid.*, p. 4.

62. *Ibid.*, p. 8.

63. Council of Economic Advisers, "The Economy at Mid-1972," Washington, DC: Federal Reserve Archive, August 1972, p. 54.

64. Matusow, p. 204.

65. *Ibid.*, pp. 212-213.

66. *Ibid.*, pp. 220-222.

67. *Ibid.*, p. 246.

68. *Ibid.*, pp. 260-262.

69. *Ibid.*

70. Paul C. Light, "The President's Agenda: Notes on the Timing of Domestic Choice," *Presidential Studies Quarterly*, Vol. 11, No. 1, Winter 1981, p. 69.

71. Margaret MacMillan, "Nixon, Kissinger, and the Opening to China," *Nixon in the World*, New York: Oxford University Press, 2008, p. 107.

72. Iwan W. Morgan, *Nixon*, New York: Oxford University Press, 2002, p. 95.

73. *Memoirs*, p. 45.

74. *Ibid.*, p. 46.

75. Gaddis, p. 272.

76. Kolodziej, p. 133.

77. "The Beijing-Washington Back-Channel and Henry Kissinger's Secret Trip to China, September 1970-July 1971," William Burr, ed., *National Security Archive Electronic Briefing Book No. 66*, February 27, 2002, available from *www.gwu.edu/~nsarchiv/NSAEBB/NSAEBB66/*.

78. Richard Nixon, "Informal Remarks in Guam with Newsmen," The American Presidency Project, July 25, 1969, available from *www.presidency.ucsb.edu/ws/index.php?pid=2140*.

79. Richard Nixon, "Asia after Vietnam," *Foreign Affairs*, Vol. 46, October 1967, p. 112.

80. *Ibid.*

81. *Ibid.*, p. 123.

82. MacMillan, p. 109.

83. *Ibid.*, p. 113.

84. "Informal Remarks," p. 76.

85. *Ibid.*

86. Gaddis, p. 295.

87. Memorandum of Conversation in the Great Hall of the People, Peking, President Nixon *et. al.*, and Prime Minister Chou En-Lai *et. al.*, p. 5; Washington, DC: The White House, February 22, 1972, available from *www.gwu.edu/~nsarchiv/nsa/publications/DOC_readers/kissinger/nixzhou/12-05.htm*.

88. Kolodziej, p. 133.

89. Richard Nixon, "Inaugural Address," January 20, 1969, available from *www.presidency.ucsb.edu/ws/index.php?pid=1941*.

90. Patterson, p. 735.

91. John J. Mearsheimer, *The Tragedy of Great Power Politics*, New York: W. W. Norton & Co., 2001, p. 105.

92. Campbell Craig and Fredrik Logevall, *America's Cold War: The Politics of Insecurity*, Cambridge, MA: The Belknap Press, 2009, p. 272.

93. *Memoirs*, p. 322.

94. Arthur M. Schlesinger, Jr., *The Imperial Presidency*, Boston, MA: Houghton Miller, 2004, p. xv.

95. *Ibid.*

96. Matusow, p. 216.

97. Kolodziej, p. 139.

98. Morgan, p. 1.

99. Robert Dallek, *Nixon and Kissinger: Partners in Power*, New York: Harper Perennial, 2007, p. 535.

100. Mark Landler and Michael R. Gordon, "Obama Accelerates Transition of Security to Afghanistan," *New York Times*, January 11, 2013, available from *www.nytimes.com/2013/01/12/world/asia/us-can-speed-afghan-exit-obama-says.html?hpw&_r=0*.

101. Schell, p. 342.

102. Craig and Logevall, p. 276.

103. *Ibid.*, pp. 276-278.

104. Thomas E. Ricks, "Will Afghanistan Collapse after U.S. Troops Leave? Maybe, But Not Why You Think," *Foreign Policy*, February 16, 2012, available from *ricks.foreignpolicy.com/posts/2012/02/16/will_afghanistan_collapse_after_us_troops_leave_maybe_but_not_why_you_think*.

105. Noah Shachtman, "Obama Finally Talks Drone War, But It's almost Impossible to Believe Him," *Wired*, September 6, 2012, available from *www.wired.com/dangerroom/2012/09/obama-drone/*.

CHAPTER 5

JIMMY CARTER, RONALD REAGAN, AND THE END (OR CONSUMMATION?) OF DÉTENTE

Brian K. Muzas

I explore important continuities in the "détente" conducted by President Jimmy Carter and the "quiet diplomacy" practiced by President Ronald Reagan. The two Presidents agreed on the character of the Soviet threat, shared compatible visions of human nature, and pursued similar approaches in their foreign policy. Indeed, the Presidents were not only self-consistent over time (Carter before and after the Soviet invasion of Afghanistan, Reagan before and after the era of General Secretary Mikhail Gorbachev), but also remarkably consistent across administrations. However, the two leaders differed importantly as they conducted foreign affairs under a condition of austerity—a condition not so much of fiscal austerity but of "existential austerity," a term I coin to encompass not only losses of national pride, confidence, and sense of purpose, but also deficits of cultural and societal capital and vigor. The similarities and meaningful differences between Carter and Reagan lead me to conclude that détente did not collapse. Rather, détente was continued, changed, and ultimately consummated: The messaging and framework were transformed to address existential austerity, but the basic policy approaches persisted and ultimately succeeded. By exploring détente, quiet diplomacy, and sources and solutions for existential austerity, I reexamine the Carter-Regan era to seek similarities, differences, and lessons for today.

INTRODUCTION

In this chapter, I present a background of contemporaneous events which framed the U.S. foreign policy of détente as well as détente itself. I review what détente meant to Presidents Carter and Reagan by presenting their overarching views of détente (which remained constant for Carter before and after the invasion of Afghanistan and for Reagan before and after the era of General Secretary Gorbachev), by explaining what undergirded their views, and by comparing their substantive approaches to foreign policy. I observe essential similarity in the plans and implementations which Carter called "détente" and which Reagan called "quiet diplomacy." Taking into account the viewpoints of American allies and third-world heads of state, I re-harmonize the policies of Reagan and Carter to conclude that the Carter-Reagan approach to détente is a story of consummation rather than collapse. In my conclusion, I reflect on Carter and Reagan in terms of austerity and propose broadening the framework to include not only fiscal austerity, but existential austerity—that is, to consider not only constraints of U.S. monetary treasure and economic vigor, but also constraints of cultural treasure and societal vigor. I then remark upon similarities and differences in the world situations of the Carter-Reagan era and of today.

CONTEMPORANEOUS EVENTS AFFECTING U.S. FOREIGN POLICY AND ITS TOOLS

Détente did not happen in a vacuum. Events of the 1960s and 1970s that affected U.S. domestic and international politics must be borne in mind while investigating détente in the Carter and Reagan years. For example, the 1960s saw the civil rights movement crest and the Vietnam War deepen, and the 1970s saw the Watergate scandal and the oil crisis. These events—respectively human, military, institutional trust, and economic matters—taxed U.S. soft and hard reserves: Civil rights and Watergate caused upheavals in the American psyche, while Vietnam and the oil crisis, in addition to psychological shocks, were traditional security issues involving guns and dollars.

BACKGROUND OF DÉTENTE

In the early-1960s, there were compelling reasons for the United States and the Union of Soviet Socialist Republics (USSR) to ease their tense relationship. The U-2 incident occurred in 1960. The Bay of Pigs debacle occurred in April 1961, and the Berlin Wall went up 4 months later in August. The United States introduced missiles to Turkey in April 1962, 1 year after the Bay of Pigs; the Cuban Missile Crisis came to a head 6 months later in October. The tempo and seriousness of these crises pointed out the need for "relaxation"—the meaning of the French word "détente." Besides, both sides wished to decrease spending; the United States was increasingly concerned with fighting in Vietnam, and the Soviets were increasingly concerned about the Chinese on their southeastern border.

A countertrend of more cordial diplomatic relations arose thereafter. In 1963, the Partial Test Ban Treaty (PTBT) was signed on August 5, ratified by the U.S. Senate on September 24, and went into effect on October 10. President John Kennedy first used the word "détente" 9 days later, cautiously saying:

> For a pause in the cold war is not a lasting peace — and a detente does not equal disarmament. The United States must continue to seek a relaxation of tensions, but we have no cause to relax our vigilance.[1]

Yet relaxation and cooperation, or at least coordination, continued. The PTBT was followed by the Outer Space Treaty in 1967 and the Non-Proliferation Treaty (NPT) in 1968. Formal Strategic Arms Limitation Talks (SALT) began in 1969, culminating in the SALT I and Anti-Ballistic Missile (ABM) treaties in 1972. Soviet leader Leonid Brezhnev's visit to the United States in 1973 and the orbital meeting of American astronauts and Soviet cosmonauts through the Apollo-Soyuz Test Project in 1975 were visible, symbolic accomplishments, while the Helsinki Accords provided three items of substantive accomplishments in security, cooperation, and, notably, human rights.

Despite such developments, many aspects of détente were open to criticism when Carter came to the American presidency. Consider two arguments on the state of the U.S.-Soviet nuclear balance in the 1970s. Some argued the SALT I treaty was poorly conceived from a military point of view. By freezing the throw weight of missiles (and hence the weight of the warheads which could be carried by those missiles), the treaty locked in a potential four-fold Soviet advantage should Soviet warhead designers achieve sophistication equivalent to the lighter-weight American warheads in use at that time. Moreover, the treaty counted subsonic American B-52s as nuclear delivery systems but did not count supersonic Soviet *Backfire* bombers, which could strike roughly half of the continental United States (CONUS) unrefueled and the entire CONUS, given aerial refueling and the availability of Cuban airfields. Furthermore, there were indications the Soviets were violating the ABM treaty.[2]

Others argued the fundamental flaws of détente's signature negotiations and treaties were their failure to address the Soviet buildup dating to the Cuban Missile Crisis. These critics surmised the Soviets had decided never again to be in a position where they would have to back down during a crisis. Moreover, Soviet spending actually increased after SALT I—an indication that détente might not be the relaxation it appeared to be.[3] In addition, Soviet conventional superiority was telling not only in theory but in practice, for Soviet naval superiority in the Mediterranean Sea influenced U.S. bargaining over the Yom Kippur War in 1973.[4] Subsequently, a 1973 document called "Soviet Strategic Arms Programs and Detente: What Are They Up To?"[5] and a 1975 document called *Detente in Soviet Strategy*[6] appeared.

Given this background, President Carter recast détente. In the following pages, I contrast Carter's assessment of the Soviet view of détente with Carter's own overarching view of détente, I survey the principles Carter understood to undergird détente, and I compare Carter's substantive foreign policy before and after the Soviet invasion of Afghanistan.

Despite détente's association with the 1970s, the concept appeared consistently throughout President Reagan's two terms in the 1980s. Indeed, almost exactly 7 years separate Mexican President José Lopez Portillo's comments to Reagan in 1981 on "the detente of this world which is so complex and at times so absurd"[7] and journalist Helen Thomas' observation to Reagan in 1988 that the "world is applauding the initiative, the new détente that you and President Gorbachev have initiated."[8] Taking particular note of what Reagan called "quiet diplomacy," the following sections explore détente in the 1980s in parallel with Carter's approach in the 1970s.

Granted, there are differences between the approaches of Reagan and Carter, and the passages to follow illustrate distinctiveness as well as resemblance. In particular, I explore continuity in their political and philosophical realism insofar as Carter and Reagan ask the same questions of the superpower relationship and offer remarkably similar answers in broad strokes.

DÉTENTE, THE SOVIETS, AND THE FOREIGN POLICY APPROACHES OF CARTER AND REAGAN

According to Carter, the Soviets saw détente as "a continuing aggressive struggle for political advantage and increased influence" with "military power and military assistance as the best means of "expanding their influence abroad" as well as the use of "proxy forces to achieve their purposes."[9] Carter noted the excessive Soviet military increase, the violation of human rights (and thus the Helsinki agreement), and the closed nature Soviet society to further differentiate the United States and the USSR. In contrast, Carter continually made statements offering his view of détente, typically stating his desire that détente be "broad in scope" and "reciprocal."[10]

Some of Carter's understanding of détente can be gleaned from statements of what détente **is**, as when he said, "To me it means progress toward peace."[11] Indeed, when Carter used the term, he said he was "not speaking only of military security" but of:

> the concern among our individual citizens, Soviet and American, that comes from the knowledge . . . that the leaders of our two countries have the capacity to destroy human society through misunderstandings or mistakes.[12]

By relaxing this tension through reducing the nuclear threat, Carter claimed the world would be safer, and the superpowers would free themselves "to concentrate on constructive action to give the world a better life."[13] For Carter, détente related not only to military security, but to the peace of mind and better life people would experience as the specter of nuclear war declined.

Some of Carter's understanding of détente can be gleaned from quotations wherein he distinguished détente from **something else**, as when he said:

> Detente and arms control are necessary conditions, but not enough to build world peace upon solid foundations. To assert otherwise would be to give military matters an autonomy that it does not have, to give it primacy over the political, and to disengage politics from social matters. . . .[14]

Détente was not arms control; the two were distinguishable. Note also how détente was here presented as a condition of world peace.

In addition, Carter sought a definition of détente that was both expansive and flexible, "further defined by experience, as . . . nations evolve new means by which they can live with each other in peace."[15] Carter's sense of détente's breadth can be found in statements like, "We seek a world of peace. But such a world must accommodate diversity—social, political, and ideological. Only then can there be a genuine cooperation among nations and among cultures," and, "Our long-term objective must be to convince the Soviet Union of the advantages of cooperation and of the costs of disruptive behavior."[16]

Despite his insistence that détente be broadly conceived, sometimes Carter's usage painted a restricted, even anemic, portrait of détente as when he referred merely to "a pattern of détente," his only mention of détente in his 1979 State of the Union Address.[17] Another such example can be found in the Vienna Summit Communiqué released on the signing of the SALT II treaty. The communiqué implied détente was inadequately defined. Referring to détente as a process rather than a pattern, the communiqué mentioned the two sides "expressed their support for the process of international détente which in their view should become increasingly specific in nature."[18] Perhaps greater clarity can be found by exploring the rules or principles of détente as understood by Carter.

Carter's clearest statements on détente are found in his 1978 United States Naval Academy (USNA) commencement address—a speech he "largely wrote himself"[19] in which he sought to balance détente and resolve. In addition to calling for a broad definition of détente, he laid out the following principles for détente: reciprocity, restraint, meticulously honoring agreements; cooperation, arms limitation, freedom of movement and expression; protection of human rights, discarding the goal of attaining military supremacy, and forgoing the opportunities of military advantage.[20] Although some of these things are goals rather than principles, this articulation was the clearest statement of the foundations of détente as Carter envisioned them. Almost as clear was a later statement that "genuine détente . . . includes restraint in the use of military power and an end to the pursuit of unilateral advantage" and "must include the honoring of solemn international agreements concerning human rights and a mutual effort to promote a climate in which these rights can flourish."[21]

The noted quotations could suggest Carter's understanding of détente never really coalesced in his own mind. Moreover, even in Carter's time, observers heard "contradictory voices" in Washington, DC, regarding the Soviet Union. Nevertheless, Carter explained the apparent contradictions between détente and resolve as follows: "We have one basic policy that is complicated in itself."[22]

Just as Carter clarified détente's apparent tension of relaxation and resolve, much of Reagan's overall approach to détente can be expressed in terms of deterrence, dialogue, and signaling. To President Reagan, détente was not playing out well; hence, he was determined to change course. Reagan treated military power as a prerequisite for U.S.-Soviet negotiations, first to attract Soviet attention, second to deter Soviet aggression, and third to permit the United States to bargain from a position of strength. Reagan emphasized the importance of clear signaling through concrete action, noting in an interview that "the Soviet Union . . . during what was supposed to be a detente, has gone forward with the greatest military buildup in the history of man. And maybe we need to get their attention."[23]

On the one hand, then, Reagan read a clear signal from Soviet activity, faulted U.S. policy, and proposed a policy change to attract Soviet notice. At the midpoint of his presidency, Reagan reiterated the practical importance of commanding Soviet attention in the following critique:

> ... Mr. Brezhnev said that detente was serving their purpose and that by 1985, they would be able to get whatever they wanted by other means.
>
> So, I have no illusions about [the Soviets]. But I do believe that the Soviets can be dealt with if you deal with them on the basis of what is practical for them and that you can point out is to their advantage as well as ours to do certain things....
>
> Evil empire, the things of that kind, I thought ... it was time to get their attention, to let them know that I was viewing them realistically.[24]

On the other, however, Regan avoids a "just peace" approach,[25] for he believed strengthened U.S. military power was a prerequisite to fruitful U.S.-Soviet engagement.

> I believe that the United States ... went all out in various efforts at détente ... in which we unilaterally disarmed with the idea that maybe if we did this and showed our good faith, [The Soviets] would reciprocate by reducing their own [arms]. Well, they didn't. They've engaged in the most massive military buildup the world has ever seen. And therefore, the reason I believe that there is more security today is the redressing that we've done of our own military strength, the strength of the alliance, and the unity that we have.[26]

Strength precedes, originates, and fosters security in Reagan's view. Strength coupled with arms reductions were keys to productive U.S.-Soviet relations in Reagan's vision, but he also recognized that American public support for both was necessary to undergird and sustain them.

PHILOSOPHICAL UNDERPINNINGS OF CARTER'S AND REAGAN'S APPROACHES

The word "détente" evokes images of international politics. Carter, however, held the human person squarely in the center of his view of politics. To understand Carter's vision of détente, I explore Carter's philosophical anthropology—his theory of human nature—and how human rights, values, culture, morality, and religion interrelate according to his viewpoint.

After being characterized as an "enemy of détente" in the Soviet press, Carter was asked whether détente was possible without Soviet respect for human rights. Carter indicated that aggressive pursuit of human rights was even-handed aspect of détente, a standard which could and did apply equally to the Soviet Union and to the United States.[27] Carter further maintained, "There are no hidden meanings in our commitment to human rights;" moreover, American human rights emphasis was "specifically not designed to heat up the arms race or bring back the cold war." Rather, Carter argued:

> We must always combine realism with principle. Our actions must be faithful to the essential values to which our own society is dedicated, because our faith in those values is the source of our confidence that this relationship will evolve in a more constructive direction.[28]

Realism informed by principle and interests enlightened by values form a seamless whole in Carter's confident vision of foreign policy. Carter's realism is not only a political realism but also a philosophical realism, of which more follows in the following text.

Questioned on the Helsinki Accords and the fear that détente might cause the rights of the Baltic people to drop from the U.S. political scene, Carter stated, "As long as I'm in the White House, human rights will be a major consideration of every foreign policy decision that I make, and I might say, also, domestic."[29] He even reminded the North Atlantic Treaty Organization (NATO) that human rights and values "are the final purpose and meaning of our Alliance."[30] Thus, Carter interprets Helsinki as a development of détente which has incorporated human rights into the superpower relationship in an integral fashion.

For Carter, then, human rights and détente went hand in hand, although the two were independent issues to a degree. Nevertheless, Carter considered détente to serve human rights in an ultimate sense. Although Carter's emphasis on human rights may seem innovative since he was the first President to stress them so greatly in his international politics and policies, Carter considered the issue's importance already to have been highlighted. Carter's innovation thus is one of accent rather than development.

Moving from human rights to values, interests, culture, and the human person, Carter saw the relationship of values and interests as a question which exceeded the scope of superpower relations but which could not be bracketed from those relations. Dealing with interests and values simultaneously, Carter observed:

> [U.S.-Soviet] competition is real and deeply rooted in the history and the values of our respective societies. But... our two countries share many important overlapping interests. Our job... is to explore those shared interests and use them to enlarge the areas of cooperation between us on a basis of equality and mutual respect....
>
> ... But we will have no illusions about the nature of the world as it really is. The basis for complete mutual trust between us does not yet exist. Therefore, the agreements that we reach must be anchored on each side in enlightened self-interest....[31]

Carter thus exhibited philosophical realism (distinct from the term "realism" as used in international relations theory) insofar as he believes that it is possible for human beings to reach true judgments of fact and value. It is on such judgments that Carter based his approach to international politics and political realism. Dealing with the question of values from a U.S. perspective, Carter asserted the United States is a nation that "believes in peace," "values human life," and takes the lead to constrain nuclear weaponry among all nations, even ones that have not yet developed nuclear arms.[32] Dealing with interests, Carter stated:

> Our national security was often defined almost exclusively in terms of military competition with the Soviet Union.... But [military balance] cannot be our sole preoccupation to the exclusion of other world issues which also concern us both.[33]

Although Carter recognized variations in culture may affect the perceptions which influence judgments, he insisted on essential commonality: "Although there are deep differences in our values and ideas, we

Americans and Russians belong to the same civilization whose origins stretch back hundreds of years."[34] Herein lies a key to Carter's philosophical anthropology of a common human nature, perhaps best summed up by Carter's claim:

> Beyond all the disagreements . . . and beyond the cool calculations of mutual self-interest . . . is the invisible human reality that must bring us closer together. I mean the yearning for peace, real peace, that is in the very bones of us all."[35]

Such a view of human nature naturally moves our discussion to the crossroads of morality, human rights, and faith.

If human nature is shared as Carter suggests and if true judgments of fact and value can be reached as Carter holds, then it follows that Carter should contend that moral claims fall on both superpowers alike: "[w]e've moved to engage the Soviet Union in a joint effort to halt the strategic arms race. This race is not only dangerous, it's morally deplorable. We must put an end to it."[36] Indeed, Carter noted:

> When I took office, many Americans were growing disillusioned with detente—President [Gerald] Ford had even quit using the word. . . . I felt that it was urgent to restore the moral bearings of American foreign policy.[37]

Moreover, Carter linked human rights and religious faith, particularly in Africa, noting that Africans, whether Muslim or Christian, worship God:

> They recognize that the Soviet Union is a Communist and an atheistic nation, and it's a very present concern in the minds and hearts of Africans who, on a tempo-

> rary basis, will turn to the Soviets to buy weapons. . . .
> I'd rather depend on the basic commitment of American people to human rights, to religious commitment and freedom, and to a sense of equality. . . .[38]

Carter reiterated a week later, "The Soviets are atheistic, and most of the leaders in Africa are deeply religious people. They may be Christian, they may be Moslem, or otherwise. But I think they have a natural distrust of atheists."[39]

Carter was famously a born-again Christian, so naturally he made references to the authority of the Bible in some of his public statements: "With all the difficulties, all the conflicts, I believe that our planet must finally obey the Biblical injunction to 'follow after the things which make for peace'."[40] He also made biblical allusions and used biblical imagery in his speeches. Of particular note is the following: when at the Berlin Airlift Memorial, he mentioned three concrete principles of détente, Carter also made reference to the well-known "city on a hill" passage of the Bible,[41] foreshadowing Reagan's later effective use of the imagery.

Carter foreshadowed Reagan in more than just literary allusions, however. Indeed, if Reagan's military policy is seen as rebalancing of the superpower relationship in order to allow a secure relaxation of tensions, then Reagan's approach to the Strategic Arms Reduction Talks (START) is really a brand of détente. Reagan saw a serious disparity between the goals of relaxation and the results of détente as practiced in the 1970s—"a one-way street that the Soviet Union has used to pursue its own aims."[42] As a result, Reagan offered four points in a personal communication to Leonid Brezhnev. The United States would "cancel its deployment of Pershing II and ground-launch cruise missiles if the Soviets will dismantle their SS-20, SS-4, and SS-5 missiles," would readily "negotiate substantial reductions in nuclear arms which would result in levels that are equal and verifiable," would cooperate with the USSR "to achieve equality at lower levels of conventional forces in Europe," and would work to "reduce the risks of surprise attack and the chance of war arising out of uncertainty or miscalculation" — all of which were based on "fair-minded" principles of "substantial, militarily significant reduction in forces, equal ceilings for similar types of forces, and adequate provisions for verification."[43]

These four points were not framed by Reagan in the language of détente. However, President Luis Herrera Campíns of Venezuela was present when Reagan shared these points in a speech, and Herrera expressed his belief that "your speech . . . will be a great contribution to détente,"[44] thereby illustrating even in 1981, foreign leaders found continuity between Reagan's and Carter's admittedly different approaches to diplomacy and foreign policy.

One can move from proposals to principles by looking at a NATO statement offering carefully struck balances between the power reserved to states and the rights reserved to people, the freedom of travel of both ideas and of people, and the equilibrium and transparency of military relations.[45]

Reagan acknowledged the different manners in which the United States and Soviet Union treated détente. Once again, Reagan is in accord with Carter. A document issued by the North Atlantic Council read in part:

> The decade of so-called detente witnessed the most massive Soviet buildup of military power in history. They increased their defense spending by 40 percent while American defense actually declined in the same real terms. Soviet aggression and support for violence around the world . . . eroded the confidence needed for arms negotiations. While we exercised unilateral restraint, they forged ahead and today possess nuclear and conventional forces far in excess of an adequate deterrent capability.[46]

Speaking on disarmament, Reagan told the United Nations General Assembly, "We've seen, under the guise of diplomacy and detente and so forth in the past, efforts to kind of sweep the differences under the rug and pretend they don't exist." Rejecting the inevitability of war like Carter, Reagan noted both how START had surpassed SALT II and how progress had been made on Intermediate Nuclear Forces (INF) as well; he concluded, "I think that this just proves that maybe being willing, frankly, to recognize the differences between us and what our view is has proven that it's successful."[47]

When accused of "wrecking detente with the INF statement," Reagan again noted "detente, as it existed, was only a cover under which the Soviet Union built up the greatest military power in the world. I don't think we need that kind of a détente" while reiterating the United States was "ready at any time that they want to make it plain by deed, not word" that the Soviets were ready to progress.[48] In a similar vein, he addressed the role of the nonaligned movement and cautioned, "Pseudo nonalignment is no better than pseudo arms control."[49]

Reagan thus concluded that a firmer, better-armed United States is ultimately helpful to U.S.-Soviet bilateral relations and world peace, even to the extent of facilitating nuclear abolitionism.

> I think the Soviets . . . liked it the other way when under a kind of detente, they were having things their own way. Now they know that we're not going to make ourselves vulnerable. . . . But they also know . . . anytime they want to sit down, we are willing to start reducing these weapons. And my ultimate goal is—I think common sense dictates it—the world must rid itself of all nuclear weapons. There must never be a nuclear war. It can't—shouldn't be fought, and it can't be won.[50]

According to Reagan, he is not pursuing détente. Nevertheless, he seeks to abolish nuclear weapons. Like Carter, Reagan wished both to deter the Soviets and to constructively engage them. If this approach is not to be called détente, then perhaps Reagan's phrase, "quiet diplomacy," is a suitable label.

What the previous passages suggest should be made explicit. A good starting point is Reagan's Eureka College, Eureka, IL, speech. Reagan viewed the fruits of détente in the 1970s both in terms of the bilateral superpower relationship and in terms of the world as a whole, as follows: "If East-West relations in the detente era in Europe have yielded disappointment, detente outside of Europe has yielded a severe disillusionment for those who expected a moderation of Soviet behavior."[51] Questioned on his commitment to the idea of linkage, the "concept whereby you link arms control negotiations, East-West trade, summitry with the Soviet Union with political progress by the Soviet Union on things like Poland and Afghanistan,"

Reagan pointed out that, although the concept was not mentioned in his Eureka College speech, nevertheless:

> in the many times that I've spoken of that concept, I have never particularly linked it to something as specific as arms reductions talks. But it was done in the context of the summit meetings that have taken place with regard to trade and to features of détente. . ... The fact that you do not proclaim such subjects. . . does not mean that they can't be brought up when you're sitting at a table. I think sometimes that politically to publicly discuss things of that kind makes it politically impossible to get them, where maybe in what I've called quiet diplomacy you secure them.[52]

Quiet diplomacy may be the closest Reagan came to giving a name to his policies which included "features of detente."

Reagan also dealt with the limits of cooperation between the West and the East. Questioned about a communiqué stating one aim was "a more constructive East-West relationship aiming at genuine detente through dialog and negotiations and mutually advantageous exchanges," Reagan noted 19 arms reduction efforts since World War II, and efforts at persuasion, but:

> It seems to me that now, with the Soviets having the economic problems I mentioned, that this is an opportunity for us to suggest to them that there might be a better path than they've been taking. And if so, we'd like to explore that better path.[53]

Subsequently asking of the implications of the Polish announcement that Lech Walesa would be freed, that Brezhnev had died, and that new leaders would be coming to power in the USSR, the questioner asked whether any new initiatives to lessen tension were forthcoming. Reagan responded, "We have been trying to do that in the area of quiet diplomacy, tried in the summit conference, tried in the NATO conference, of various things.... But it's going to require some action, not just words."[54] Pressed on whether he was prepared to take a first step, Regan said, "Well, there are some people that have said I took the first step with lifting the grain embargo. Have we gotten anything for it?"[55]

Reagan insisted that superpower parity had to work both ways. He suggested "parallel paths" of deterrence and verifiable arms reductions to equal levels, noting that "never before have we proposed such a comprehensive program of nuclear arms control" and concluding:

> We ... want a constructive relationship with the Soviet Union, based on mutual restraint, responsibility, and reciprocity. Unfortunately, Soviet-backed aggression in recent years ... has violated these principles. But we remain ready to respond positively to constructive Soviet actions.[56]

As Carter had seen deterrence as necessary to détente, Reagan saw deterrence as required for relaxation.

Reagan's principles of "restraint, responsibility, and reciprocity" also strike a familiar, Carter-esque chord. Moreover, Reagan noted:

> From 1970 to 1979, our defense spending, in constant dollars, decreased by 22 percent....
>
> Potential adversaries saw this unilateral disarmament ... as a sign of weakness and a lack of will necessary to

protect our way of life. While we talked of detente, the lessening of tensions in the world, the Soviet Union embarked on a massive program of militarization. Since around 1965, they have increased their military spending, nearly doubling it over the past 15 years.[57]

Hence, Reagan saw the U.S. policy as one of rebalancing for relaxation. When pressed on whether he wanted "to contain [the Soviets] within their present borders and perhaps try to reestablish detente—or what goes for detente—or . . . roll back their empire," Reagan replied:

> I believe that many of the things they have done are evil in any concept of morality that we have. But I also recognize that as the two great superpowers in the world, we have to live with each other. . . . [B]etween us, we can either destroy the world or we can save it. And I suggested that, certainly, it was to their common interest, along with ours, to avoid a conflict and to attempt to save the world and remove the nuclear weapons. And I think that perhaps we established a little better understanding.
>
> I think that in dealing with the Soviet Union one has to be realistic. . . .
>
> The Soviet Union has been engaged in the biggest military buildup in the history of man at the same time that we tried the policy of unilateral disarmament, of weakness, if you will. And now we are putting up a defense of our own. And I've made it very plain to them, we seek no superiority. We simply are going to provide a deterrent so that it will be too costly for them if they are nursing any ideas of aggression against us. . . . There's been no change in my attitude at all. I just thought when I came into office it was time that there was some realistic talk to and about the Soviet Union. And we did get their attention.[58]

Thus, Reagan saw his policy as a recalibration of goals and a drawing of attention to this redirection. He characterized his policy in terms of morality, conflict avoidance, political and philosophical realism, and attention-getting.

Intertwined with Reagan's policy are principles of verification and reciprocity. Reagan stated arms reduction must not proceed "naively or pretending . . . that we can have a detente while [the Soviets] go on with their programs of expansion" but must rather "persuade them to, by deed, prove their contention that they want peace also."[59]

Reagan further clarified that the word détente had "been a little abused in the past in some ways. Yes, we would welcome such a thing as long as it was a two-way street. Our problem in the past has been that it has too much been a one-way street, and we were going the wrong way on that."[60] Indeed, one week before Gorbachev came to power, Regan emphasized reciprocity.[61] From such a standpoint, Reagan sounds much like Carter with less emphasis on leading by example and more emphasis on verifiability of actions. Note also that the U.S. military buildup, begun under Carter, is itself a U.S. action that the Soviets could verify, so one could additionally read this signal as a backhanded nod to reciprocity.

Like Carter, Regan's policies can best be understood by recognizing that, for both leaders, the roles of morality and human rights arise from their philosophical anthropology. In terms of morality, Reagan observed the Soviets:

> openly and publicly declared that the only morality they recognize is what will further their cause, mean-

ing they reserve unto themselves the right to commit any crime, to lie, to cheat, in order to attain that [goal], and that is moral, not immoral, and we operate on a different set of standards, I think when you do business with them, even at a detente, you keep that in mind.[62]

Building on what Reagan saw as the stark difference between Soviet and American understandings of morality, Reagan delineated how human rights ought to fit into superpower relations and American foreign policy in general by calling for consistently-applied standards. Reagan said, "I think human rights is very much a part of our American idealism . . . [but] we were selective with regard to human rights." Contrasting Cuba and the USSR—both human rights violators, yet some were proposing to better relations with Cuba anyway—Reagan argued for consistency: "I think that we ought to be more sincere about our position of human rights."[63]

Philosophical anthropology arose more explicitly in Reagan's approach to the Soviet Union when he responded to a question about "suggestions . . . made to the Soviets [concerning] ways they can improve their behavior [and so] get back to detente and reduce this war of words." Reagan said he had told Brezhnev "that sometimes it seems that the governments sometimes get in the way of the people" who essentially wish to raise families, choose a career, and exercise control over their own lives. He concluded, "I doubt that the people have ever started a war," so Reagan suggested that he and Brezhnev discuss what the people really wanted.[64]

In another venue, Reagan raised a philosophical point even more explicitly:

> [I]n the years of detente we tended to forget the greatest weapon the democracies have in their struggle is public candor: the truth.... It's not an act of belligerence to speak to the fundamental differences between totalitarianism and democracy; it's a moral imperative. It doesn't slow down the pace of negotiations; it moves them forward."[65]

Thus, like Carter, Reagan is a philosophical realist who wants to ground his foreign policy in true judgments of fact and value. To quote one of Reagan's favorite Russian proverbs, "Trust, but verify."

SUBSTANTIVE FOREIGN POLICY BEFORE AND AFTER AFGHANISTAN AND GORBACHEV

U.S. foreign policy and Carter's conception of détente were conjoint. Carter outlined the following principal policy goals in his USNA address: maintain equivalent nuclear strength; maintain judicious military spending; support global and regional organizations; seek peace, communication, understanding, cultural and scientific exchange, and trade; prevent nuclear weapons proliferation; and limit nuclear arms.[66] As means to these ends, Carter proposed a "combination of adequate American strength, of quiet self-restraint in the use of it, of a refusal to believe in the inevitability of war, and of a patient and persistent development of all the peaceful alternatives."[67] Note in passing the coherence of "quiet self-restraint" and "quiet diplomacy."

Carter had grand objectives for détente. These included SALT "reductions, limitations, and a freeze on new technology," a complete end to all nuclear tests, a ban on use and stockpiling of chemical and biological weapons, reduced conventional arms sales, arms limitations in the Indian Ocean, a ban on nuclear weapons in the southern half of the Western Hemisphere via the Treaty of Tlatelolco, Mexico, the Middle East peace promotion, NATO-Warsaw Pact force reductions in Europe, sharing of science and technology as well as cooperation in outer space, and world health improvement and hunger relief.[68]

In terms of nuclear strategy and declaratory policy, Carter made a stunning offer while toasting Leonid Brezhnev at the 1979 Vienna summit:

> I hope, Mr. President [Brezhnev], that détente, which has been growing in Europe because of your great work, can now encompass other regions of the world. . . . The SALT agreement . . . provides a good foundation. . . . Let us both agree never to use offensive weapons against any nation in an act of aggression.[69]

This quotation, taken from the official press release, is the closest thing to an offer of an American no-first-use policy of which I am aware. It therefore represents an amazing potential concession with implications for the credibility of U.S. extended deterrence. Bear these thoughts on credibility and extended deterrence when reading about Carter's response to the Afghanistan invasion in the following passages.

If nuclear bombs are indeed the ultimate weapon, then part of Carter's address at a 1980 Democratic National Committee fundraiser might be called an ultimate wish list. The first part of this list was free-standing and strikingly Reagan-like: Going further than his suggestion of nuclear no-first-use, Carter nearly called for nuclear abolition. He reached as far as effective nuclear abolition:

> We are eager to see that detente [is] not weakened but strengthened. And we are eager to control nuclear weapons, to reduce our dependence on them, and ultimately to eliminate nuclear weapons as a factor from the face of the Earth. This is our ultimate goal.[70]

Carter concluded with a restatement of Democratic Party platform commitments to peace, better relationships among peoples, control of nuclear weapons, and sound management of economic and energy issues.[71] Note that this 1980 statement antedates the Afghanistan invasion.

Most commentators proclaimed the death of détente with the Soviet's Christmas Eve invasion of Afghanistan in 1979. Not Carter. Just before entering his final full year in office, Carter declared:

> And my hope is to go out of this office having kept our country at peace; . . . with firm, sound friendship and detente between ourselves and the Soviet Union; . . . having enhanced human rights; . . . with alliances and friendships firmly established with as many people as possible on Earth; and . . . with nuclear arms under control.[72]

Carter addressed the previous statement to student leaders. Lest one think his remarks were tailored to impressionable youngsters, later the same day Carter told an audience of magazine editors:

> We're committed to the preservation of detente. Once the Soviet troops are withdrawn from Afghanistan and the threat of military action by them is removed, then we'll be very glad to pursue aggressively again further progress in the control of weapons and in the strengthening of our ties with all nations on Earth.[73]

Finally, Carter's toast of German Chancellor Helmut Schmidt reaffirmed commitments to "the control of weaponry" although they "have been shaken, but not changed, by the Soviet invasion of Afghanistan."[74] In returning the toast, Schmidt showed that Carter was not the only world leader who still held détente to be viable by noting the "necessity of a balance of military power in Europe and in the world as a prerequisite for detente" and judging that this prerequisite was, in fact, being met.[75]

Détente and deterrence remained intertwined for Carter in the aftermath of the Soviet invasion of Afghanistan. Within 1 month of the invasion, Carter's State of the Union message declared:

> An attempt by any outside force to gain control of the Persian Gulf region will be regarded as an assault on the vital interests of the United States of America, and such an assault will be repelled by any means necessary, including military force.[76]

Although Carter did not specifically mention a nuclear response, Carter wrote afterwards that he intended to signal the U.S. response would "not necessarily be confined to any small invaded area or to tactics or terrain of the Soviet's choosing."[77] In February, an administration official subsequently declared, "The Soviets know that this terrible weapon has been dropped on human beings twice in history and it was an American president who dropped it both times. Therefore, they have to take this into consideration in their calculus."[78] An ambiguous, but not ambivalent, mix of conventional and nuclear signaling took place in the form of 6 months of reconnaissance flights by B-52s.[79] These nuclear signals, although of limited significance to the American response overall, are noteworthy in light of détente. After all, many American elites had come to doubt the credibility of extended deterrence by the end of the 1960s, but the continuation of extended deterrence could be attributed to inertia, to the need for NATO solidarity, to the lack of danger in the era of détente, or to a combination of such factors. From this standpoint, then, the post-Afghanistan Carter doctrine is an innovation rather than a continuation, a unilateral action rather than a client-based action, and a decision undertaken in an unpredictable situation susceptible to miscalculation rather than in a business-as-usual context. Détente could have a hard nose.

After developing such a surprising policy, Carter reaffirmed the importance of deterrence in terms of détente, stating, "[I]f we continue to seek the benefit of detente while ignoring the necessity for deterrence, we would lose the advantages of both."[80] He emphasized the U.S. mission was:

> to promote order, not to enforce our will . . . to protect our citizens and our national honor, not to harm nor to dishonor others; to compel restraint, not to provoke confrontation; to support the weak, not to dominate them; to assure that the foundations of our new world are laid upon a stable superpower balance, not built on sand.[81]

Carter explained his post-Afghanistan actions as a choice to employ political and economic instruments "and to hold in reserve stronger action in the future, if necessary, to preserve peace in that troubled region."[82] His policies retained a less aggressive posture than some predecessors — less aggressive, but no less realistic since the United States had to "respond effectively and forcefully and, I believe, peacefully to Soviet aggression when it's so blatant and so immoral as is taking place at this very moment in Afghanistan."[83]

For Carter, then, détente survived Afghanistan with its essence intact. Carter's approach to détente can appear ambiguous at times: if it is simply a relaxation, then détente is not a policy but a policy goal, yet Carter occasionally treated détente as a means rather than an end. Nevertheless, Carter had a basically consistent focus for détente expressed by a consistent rhetoric. Reagan continued much of the Carter focus and rhetoric, especially when it came to topics and language dealing with religious, human rights, moral, and nuclear issues.

Toward the end of his presidency, Reagan summed up the "four legs" on which the "table" of the U.S.-Soviet relationship stood. Although he did not use the term "détente," Reagan set forth something rather like Carter's vision of a broad-based and reciprocal détente with four themes which would have been familiar to Carter: arms reduction, regional conflicts, human rights, and bilateral exchanges.[84] Moreover, Reagan criticized the détente of the early-1970s rather than the late-1970s over which Carter presided.

Combining his desire for relaxation and his steadfast adherence to principled foreign policy, Reagan, after noting expansionism in several places in the world, observed how Soviet leaders consistently "restated their goal of a one-world Socialist revolution, a one-world Communist state. And invariably, they have declared that the United States is the final enemy."[85]

Clearly Reagan was to tread cautiously. But tread forward he did, and between the Washington and Moscow summits, Reagan discussed the "fundamental approach to arms reduction" followed by the

United States. The remarks he made concerning arms reductions are worth quoting at length:

> At first, many critics viewed the goal of genuine arms reductions as unrealistic, even . . . misleading, even put forward in bad faith. . . . But by the autumn of 1985 . . . the media began reporting a Soviet willingness to consider a 25-percent, then a 40-percent, and finally a 50-percent reduction in strategic arms. . . .
>
> With regard to our zero-option proposal for intermediate-range nuclear forces . . . the critics again derided our position as unrealistic when we first advanced it in 1981. Today it's my hope that the Senate will . . . give its . . . consent to the INF treaty that Mr. Gorbachev and I signed last December in Washington so we can exchange instruments of ratification next month in Moscow.
>
> . . . You'll recall that the Soviets rejected [a 1977] American offer [of deep nuclear cuts] out of hand. Why? And what has changed in the meantime? . . .
>
> First, the United States in the 1970's slashed our defense budgets and neglected crucial defense investment. We were dealing . . . from a position of weakness. Well, today we're dealing from a position of strength. Second, the United States, those 11 years ago, had not yet shown what might be called a tough patience—a willingness to stake out a strong position, then stand by it as the Soviets probed and made their counteroffers, testing American determination. . . .
>
> . . . I said when I first ran for President that our nation needed to renew its strength. Some called me bellicose, even a warmonger. . . . Now we know, without doubt, that strength works, that strength promotes the cause of freedom and, yes, the cause of peace.[86]

A further, more concise retrospective view is provided by Reagan's farewell address. Reagan said, "The detente of the 1970's was based not on actions but promises," and he mentioned the gulag, Soviet expansionism, and proxy wars in Africa, Asia, and Latin America. He continued, "Well, this time, so far, it's different," and mentioned Gorbachev began internal reforms, started to withdraw from Afghanistan, and freed prisoners.[87]

Did Reagan provide retrospective structure, or was his narrative representative of how the United States approached foreign policy during his two terms? In fact, we can trace a number of the points raised throughout the Reagan-Gorbachev era, starting with Reagan's promise, "[W]e are not going to let them get enough advantage that they can ever make war."[88]

Although a military buildup began under Carter, Reagan intensified the buildup, using one of the tools that Carter was already employing. Moreover, Reagan's policies aspired to better the relations between the United States and the Soviet Union:

> [O]ur desire for improved relations is strong. We're ready and eager for step-by-step progress. We know that peace is not just the absence of war. We don't want a phony peace or a frail peace. We didn't go in pursuit of some kind of illusory detente. We can't be satisfied with cosmetic improvements that won't stand the test of time. We want real peace.[89]

Throughout his two terms, Reagan insisted on actual progress, not merely irenics. When it was pointed out to Reagan that "many Europeans consider Gorbachev the politician more aggressively looking for disarmament and detente than you," he was asked, "Is he [Gorbachev] simply a better communicator than you, or do you accept that view?" Reagan answered, "The last guest to arrive at a party usually gets the attention. . . . But the search for peace requires more than slogans and reassuring words; it requires genuine actions and concrete proposals that deal with real problems. . . ." He noted INF reduction and elimination were "[b]oth . . . in fact U.S. proposals" and that measures agreed to in Stockholm, Sweden, to improve military openness, to reduce the risk of surprise attack, and to discourage military intimidation were "based on NATO proposals. The Soviets wanted an empty, declaratory accord. We held out for something concrete that would enhance our security, and we got it."[90] For similar reasons, Reagan insists, "We do not want mere words; this time we're after true peace."[91] Shortly after his presidency ended, he got his wish: the Berlin Wall fell in 1989, and the Soviet Union dissolved in 1991.

DÉTENTE IN INTERNATIONAL PERSPECTIVE DURING THE CARTER-REAGAN YEARS

Lest the previous reading of the history of détente seem overly idiosyncratic, it is important to note how Carter's contemporaries understood both the man himself and his vision of détente. Certainly Prime Minister Giulio Andreotti of Italy felt he understood where Carter was coming from: he explained Carter's philosophy in terms of Carter's personal history:

> I do not think I am far off the mark, because the statesman is first of all a man, if I connect your reaffirmations for human rights not so much to a high political strategy but rather to your youthful experiences as a son of the Deep South — sensitive, with foreseeing clearness to the appeal of civil unity and of the equality of man.[92]

Andreotti additionally noted that Carter "made it clear, without equivocation, that there is no contrast between the repeated raising of the issue of human rights and international policy of detente, to which we are also faithfully and earnestly committed."[93] Moreover, as put by French Prime Minister Raymond Barre:

> France believes . . . that in the East-West relations a policy of detente, understanding, and cooperation is necessary now more than ever. France knows from her own long experience that vigilant trust is far preferable to distrust, to a refusal to enter into a dialog, and to incomprehension. The American people, motivated by a blend of tolerance and conviction, which gives it its moral strength, and of which you, Mr. President, are the exemplification, cannot fail to be so persuaded. . . . A world at peace must not only be a world without war; it must also be a world without violence and without tyranny, where the furthering of the human being is the prime objective of society. Peace is not established only upon the silence of man.[94]

Carter's contemporaries and peers understood détente's foundations, the requisite vigilant dialog, and the ultimate goal of peace without tyranny to be grounded in a view of the human person, a vision of the human person which they all shared.

From a thematic point of view, Carter's contemporaries saw détente as a process which had its own rules, principles, and logic. President Neelam Sanjiva Reddy of India stated: "Detente, coexistence, and even cooperation between countries with different political and social systems have come to be recognized as having an inexorable logic for our interdependent planet."[95] General Olusegun Obasanjo of Nigeria commented, "Africa is equally interested in the current efforts at detente between East and West, as this is the only dependable means of ensuring peace and stability in the world and development all around, especially in new states."[96]

Carter observed that President Josip Broz Tito of Yugoslavia understood:

> the true significance of this misunderstood word . . . that detente must be comprehensive, that it must be reciprocal in nature, and it must be a demonstration constantly by the super powers of mutual restraint and a constant search for peace.[97]

Tito himself described détente in terms of a process and even delineated a relationship between the nonaligned movement and détente:

> We are deeply convinced that detente can fulfill the expectations of all the peoples of our planet if it becomes a universal process and if it encompasses all the burning problems of the day — first and foremost political, military, and economic — as at present, we live in a world of such interdependence that its fate is ultimately common.
>
> The movement of nonaligned is a logical expression of the objective need of the present, still considerably divided world. It is an exceptionally important part, an active factor of the process of detente. . . .
>
> Therefore, every attempt at weakening the nonaligned movement and that linking its parts to one or the other bloc is inevitably directed against detente itself, against the strengthening and expansion of peaceful coexistence. . . .
>
> Any attempt to impose unilateral interests casts a shadow over the already attained level of confidence

> and throws us back into the past, while the very nature of the process of detente makes it incumbent on us, due to the accountability of all countries and peoples to themselves, to move constantly forward.[98]

The emphasis on interdependence coheres well with Carter's conception of a broad détente which was not to be narrowly bound to arms control or even to superpower relations.

The dressings of rhetoric may at first obscure the relationship between Carter's détente and Reagan's quiet diplomacy. Nevertheless, the continuity is deeper than first appearances would suggest; moreover, the continuity runs deeper than nuclear policy, for both Carter and Reagan forced the USSR to compete more broadly, especially on human rights. Consider the following elements of détente and quiet diplomacy through European eyes during Reagan's terms.

For similar reasons, Reagan insists on something deeper than the mere appearances of peace. This symbolism/substance dichotomy was observed by commentators. For example, Italian journalists wondered whether "a strong push by the Europeans for a summit conference, and possibly in the direction of a new detente, may create a situation in which the tactics of the summit may be more important than the substance of the discussions." Reagan wrote back:

> If nothing else, my most recent discussions with our allies and partners at the Bonn Economic Summit further convinced me that European leaders attach far more importance to the substance of East-West relations than to what you call tactics. Their stakes in a genuinely improved East-West climate are as strong — perhaps even stronger than our own, and they do not want such a critical relationship built on illusion, ambi-

guity, or misunderstanding. Despite what the Soviets themselves may be hoping or saying for propaganda purposes, the Western track record is impressive when it comes to sizing up our adversary and taking joint action in response. Allied firmness on commitment to the two-track NATO decision on intermediate-range missiles is eloquent proof of that.[99]

Thus, U.S. allies appeared to Reagan to be basically on the same page as he. Nevertheless, another journalist said "the Europeans have a great nostalgia of détente" and asked what was Reagan's "message to them at the eve of Geneva, and what's your vision of a new detente? Limits also?" Reagan replied:

If it is a real detente, if it is based on the elimination or reduction of the suspicions that now exist—but in the past, under the guise of detente, we saw the Soviet Union engage in the greatest military buildup in world history and at the same time that we were supposed to be talking as if we had friendly relations and had achieved some kind of a detente. And what was really, finally, going on was an arms race, because when they achieved an imbalance so great that we felt our own security was threatened, we had to get into the arms race. . . . And I know that Mr. Brezhnev at one point, to his own people, publicly made the statement that through detente they had gained enough that they would soon, shortly, be able to have their way and work their will throughout the world. Well, that isn't really detente.[100]

In addition, Reagan continued his emphasis on human rights during the Gorbachev period. Before a 1988 trip to Helsinki, a journalist noted that in 1975, "President Gerald Ford was criticized by going there and signing on to something that was cause of detente, which only served the Soviet interest, as it was said. How do you evaluate the document now?" The President replied:

> Well, I value it very much because it specified the agreement of a number of governments to recognize those basic rules of freedom for people. And since our country . . . is the first one that ever declared that government is the servant of the people, not the other way around, we heartily endorsed it.
>
> Right now our concern, as I'm sure the concern of a great many other people is that there has not been a complete keeping of those pledges in that agreement by some of the participants—by the Soviet Union, particularly—in recognizing the fundamental rights of people to leave a country, return to a country, worship as they will, and so forth.[101]

Thus, the parallels between Reagan and Carter are preserved. Carter and Reagan are both self-consistent across their respective presidencies, and Reagan follows Carter quite naturally in the sense that both employed the same tools. Moreover, non-superpower parties find détente the appropriate framework of reference throughout the presidencies of both Carter and Reagan. It thus seems plausible to conclude that the détente of the 1970s never truly collapsed. On the contrary, the label of détente was dropped, but the principles which the United States upheld and the goals which the United States sought under the umbrella term of détente were pursued under Reagan as they had been under Carter.

CONCLUSION: DÉTENTE WAS CONSUMMATED, NOT SIMPLY ENDED

At the beginning of this review, I mentioned the civil rights movement, the Vietnam War, the Watergate scandal, and the oil crisis. I used them as examples of human, military, trust, and economic matters of which the American public and politicians were conscious during the Carter-Reagan era. Carter's and Reagan's approaches to détente fit neatly under these categories. Human matters encompass human rights, morality and ethics, and faith and religion for both Presidents. Carter and Reagan both saw deterrence as providing protection on one hand and order in the world on the other. Granted, Carter's military posturing was less assertive than Reagan's. Nevertheless, both recognized the importance of arms reductions and sought to bring them about. In terms of matters of trust, both restraint and reciprocity were high priorities for both Presidents; verifiability, although valued by Carter, was more greatly emphasized by Reagan. In terms of détente, the difference between Carter's and Reagan's approaches to economics was one of degree: Carter saw economics as a tool while Reagan saw economics as a weapon.

The Soviet invasion of Afghanistan did not kill détente. Carter reaffirmed détente's principles; restated its essence; recast it a goal, a framework, a process; and brought to the fore a potent mix of anthropology, morality, and interest after the invasion just as he had before. Moreover, as he had once hinted at a no-first-use nuclear policy, Carter intimated a nuclear-zero policy. If anything, Carter doubled down on détente, broadly conceived.

Reagan, in contrast, looked at détente as a means used by the Soviets. The bulk of Reagan's critique of détente was directed toward the early-1970s and thus precedes Carter; instead, Reagan criticized Carter for lack of leadership. This distinction permitted Reagan to preserve continuity with Carter and maintain self-consistency: Reagan took Carter's mix of perspectives and tools but used quiet diplomacy for negotiating from strength rather than for attempting to lead by example because, from his view of the history of defense spending, the Soviets had not followed U.S. examples in the past. Reagan then took principles, values, interests, morality, anthropology, and other aspects of Carter's détente to pursue a foreign policy that sought not only to achieve better-than-SALT-II results but to drive the Soviet Union to the brink of collapse.

Reagan thus built on Carter's détente—and could perhaps even be said to have completed it—even though Reagan did not use that term to describe his policies, goals, or approaches. Certainly, Carter gave Reagan something on which to build. For this reason, the continuity and complementarity of their approaches is striking.

This viewpoint contrasts with other literature. Much ink has been spilled on internal friction within the two administrations—in Carter's, the conflict between Secretary of State Cyrus Vance and National Security Advisor Zbigniew Brzezinski is often repeated; in Reagan's, the Schultz-Weinberger conflict could perhaps be diversified to a manifold contrast of Central Intelligence Agency Director William Casey (proxy force in Central America), the Pentagon (decisive force in Lebanon), Secretary of State George Schultz (military power in support of diplomacy), and Secretary of Defense Caspar Weinberger (threats, norms, and politics). While such observations should not be minimized, I underscore continuities between Carter and Reagan to suggest that détente is a story of consummation, not collapse. Noting what is common across administrations allows differences to assume their true significance. Consider the following literature.

Fred Halliday thoroughly reviews the Cold War through 1985. Although he lists a number of explanations for the Cold War (which he divides into four periods: First Cold War 1946-53, Oscillatory Antagonism 1953-69, Detente 1969-79, and Second Cold War 1979 onward), Halliday assumes détente to be the default setting of the superpower relationship. As such, détente is not well explained.[102] For this reason, it makes sense to rely, as I do, on Carter's and Reagan's public statements to glean their understanding of détente and its dynamics.

Don Oberdorfer's extended journalistic account of the end of the Cold War, which he calls a contemporary history, spans 1983 to 1990. Fortified with key informant interviews from both the U.S. and Soviet side, some of his data were gleaned under not-for-attribution ground rules. As such, Oberdorfer's book should be considered a good first account and starting point. Although he does not offer a theory to explain how systemic factors, ideas, and personalities came together to form the rich history he relates, Oberdorfer leans toward highlighting the importance of the individual players who came together to negotiate and to reassess military power.[103] Bridging the coverage of Halliday and Oberdorfer allows one to better capture Regan's "détente-by-another-name" approach to Soviet policy.

Julian Zelizer sets out to catalog national security politics from the end of World War II to the War on Terrorism. Although he asks four overarching questions (to which his analysis never returns and by which his analysis is never structured), Zelizer's message-in-undercurrent is that any Cold War bipartisan consensus concerning foreign policy is a myth. If Zelizer's whole seems burdened by the sum of its parts, many of the parts are worthwhile. In particular, Zelizer does not see Reagan operating from a mandate, a strategic vision, or a moral vision. Rather, he sees Reagan, whose closeness with Gorbachev made conservatives indignant, as working from "a defensive posture borne out of the challenges of governance" and hampered by "the institutional and ideological obstacles that conservatives faced."[104] If Zelizer is right about the lack of bipartisan foreign policy consensus, and I believe he is, then the continuity I find between Carter and Reagan in strategic and moral outlook is all the more intriguing. Moreover, if Reagan's main constraints are governance, institutional, and ideological obstacles, then fiscal constraints fade in importance—or we need to devote more attention to this topic than has Zelizer.

Betty Glad takes a balanced look at the workings of Carter's administration (especially at contrasting how the gate-keeping Brzezinski, a dedicated Cold Warrior, kept Vance, tasked to realize the more idealistic objectives of Carter, from fully engaging with the President), but her either-or account of a shift between human rights and Cold War is too sweeping to ring true. Nor does Glad give full credit to Carter for having a genuine strategic vision.[105] While I recognize a certain lack of clarity in Carter's expressions regarding détente, I have tried to show his vision of foreign policy, especially the integration of detente and human rights, was thought through, consistent throughout time, and not at the mercy of internecine disagreements or gate-keeping.

Raymond Garthoff casts détente's apparent failure in terms of conflicting U.S.-Soviet conceptions of détente: The United States wanted to shepherd the Soviets into the era of parity, while the Soviets wanted to ease the United States into a less expansive international role. Each side thus wished to manage the other toward contrary directions. Overburdened by the expectations both of the public and of policymakers, adorned with general principles but bereft of specifics, the realistic political pursuits undertaken by the United States and the USSR disillusioned those who expected principle to be met in practice. Yet the inability to deliver upon the promise of détente means neither that it was tried and failed nor that it was never tried.[106] In this sense, Garthoff's approach comes closest to mine. Détente was certainly tried. I differ from Garthoff in that I stress how Carter brings something new to the table to modify détente—particularly in his appropriation of human rights, religion, and morality grounded in his philosophical anthropology—and how Reagan adopts and adapts much of Carter's tools to pursue détente-like quiet diplomacy by continuing to pursue realistic politics with openhanded offers of competition or cooperation. Ultimately, I claim détente was really tried, was really modified, and ultimately succeeded in bringing about a peaceful end to the Cold War thanks both to Carter and to Reagan. Did Reagan take "yes" for an answer from Gorbachev? Certainly he did on the INF proposal, but only after comparable offers of deep cuts had been rejected a decade earlier. Détente did not collapse: Détente was consummated.

One item noteworthy by its absence is the concept of austerity. In some sense, the approach staked out by Reagan and Carter is austerity-independent—and not just because there is no budget line for philosophical anthropology. Consider the following point: in the 1960s, a dispirited military had little external support. Nevertheless, by 1978, Carter's proposed 8 percent military budget increase was seen as, and criticized for being, a lack of support for the nation's military. Under pressure, the Congress added even more funds to Fiscal Year 1979 budget—the first such addition in 15 years![107] Reagan's buildup followed unabated despite the early-1980s recession. If, in a time of austerity the United States had to draw on softer power, then Carter's maneuvers at the very least prepared the way for Reagan to integrate the harder and softer potentials of U.S. power in a balanced combination that ultimately worked.

What conditions were necessary for détente/quiet diplomacy to succeed? From a material point of view, I find compelling Carter's and especially Reagan's understanding of the role of strength in a situation of fundamental mistrust—a situation in which both Presidents nevertheless sought opportunities to cooperate with the Soviets despite taking a hard line. Nevertheless, the Soviets judged the United States under Carter to be weak and lacking true room to maneuver, while the Soviets judged the United States under Reagan to be strong and capable of maneuvering freely.

This difference in perception allows us to expand our understanding of "austerity" beyond financial, economic, or budgetary austerity. I use the term "existential austerity"—that is, constraints arising not from a lack of U.S. monetary resources but from a deficit of cultural and moral capital (both in the sense of ethics and in the sense of morale). Existential austerity speaks to national pride, confidence, and purpose, and the difference between Carter and Reagan is the difference between "malaise" and "morning in America." Carter diagnosed, and tried to treat, a bad case of existential austerity. He identified a "crisis of confidence . . . that strikes at the very heart and soul and spirit of our national will."[108] Although Carter's televised speech is remembered, it is forgotten that the speech was initially well-received: only days after it was delivered, the *New York Times* ran an article titled, "Speech Lifts Carter Rating to 37%; Public Agrees on Confidence Crisis; Responsive Chord Struck."[109] Nevertheless, Carter failed to capitalize on this window of opportunity, and his request that his entire cabinet resign likely slammed the window shut. In contrast, Regan's televised campaign advertisement reinforced the message that the United States was "prouder and stronger and better,"[110] reflecting his efforts to restore to the populace a sense of vibrant optimism. Reagan dealt more effectively with existential austerity than did Carter, and this effectiveness fit hand-in-glove with traditional security concerns.

Note how the first perception mentioned previously is the Soviet perception. The adversary has a key role, for interaction is at the very core of the concepts of "strategy" and "strategic interaction." Note, too, how the previous discussion addressed the domestic aspects of existential austerity, for conditions of existential austerity could lead to a self-fulfilling prophecy of decline. Hence, Reagan's strategy included a message to the American public that things were not as bad as they seemed, a determination to bring all facets of national resources and power to bear, and a commitment to pursue both strength and conciliation in foreign policy toward the Soviet Union.

In a larger sense, the Carter-Reagan story illustrates how quickly shifts in international politics can occur. Moreover, the story demonstrates how asymmetric strategies can foster the two-step process of retrenchment and renewal under conditions of fiscal and existential austerity: Carter initially retrenched fiscally but advanced on a different dimension of power, opening a salient engagement on the human-rights front by wielding the Helsinki Accords. Reagan, following through where Carter's malaise speech began, took existential austerity seriously and balanced pressure for the USSR with inspiration for the United States. Foreign policy was not simply geopolitical for these Presidents: It was purposeful and mission-based as well. Carter's shift to a "moral foreign policy" exemplified by human rights was continued by Reagan. Carter and Reagan had differences (such as different approaches to economics and different emphases on verification), yet both Presidents sought to demonstrate that U.S. foreign policy, whether détente or quiet diplomacy, could play a constructive purpose in the world.

From another point of view, however, the state of play in the international system helped Carter and Reagan employ nonmilitary, noneconomic resources in a way that seems less accessible to contemporary American leaders. Then, the similarities among adversaries were greater than they are today. The Cold War on both sides of the Iron Curtain, as Carter noted, was centered on the European cultural universe. Both sides shared mutually intelligible understandings not only of science, history, and politics but of philosophy, ethics, and religion. Moreover, outside of Europe, the USSR was seen as atheistic, while the United States was seen as religion-friendly, a reality which probably did provide the United States the "natural" advantage Carter observed previously. Finally, it was generally recognized that the U.S. military, although not invincible, could be matched in a shooting fight only with help from big countries—the USSR, or at least China. Now, the differences among adversaries surpass the similarities. Europe, where commonality with the United States is greatest, is no longer the focus of international struggle. Moreover, the United States is seen as fundamentally different in the Middle and Far East. Indeed, rights, morality, and faith mean different things in Middle and Far East than in the United States. Furthermore, the past decade has seen much military use in exchange for comparatively modest achievement of aims. An important policy insight lies herein. Nonmilitary factors were heeded and used to advantage by Carter and Reagan. Existential austerity may have seemed to hold sway under Carter but not under Reagan. Perhaps the United States has become heedless of such factors of late.

To explore existential austerity is to imply that there are also such things as existential sufficiency and existential abundance; in other words, there could be societal and cultural capital sufficient or more than sufficient to allow the pursuit of particular goals, policies, and strategies. However, existential sufficiency or abundance does not guarantee per se the development and implementation of better policies or strategies: Just like fiscal and material assets, cultural and societal assets can be misapplied or squandered. Resources, fiscal or existential, do not in themselves assure good policy—although such plenty may allow unsustainable or counterproductive policies to be pursued with greater energy, or for a longer time, or both, than would otherwise be the case.

There are pressing human, military, trust, and economic issues in the United States today. Human issues include defining the institution of marriage and reforming immigration. Military matters range from repercussions of the wars in Iraq and Afghanistan to the pivot toward Asia. The Great Recession is the economic problem which overshadows everything else. Yet, institutional trust is perhaps the most intriguing concern. The falling trust in U.S. institutions has culminated in 2012 with record-low confidence in public schools, organized religion, banks, and television news; trust in Congress ranks lowest, with a scant 13 percent confidence rating. These ratings identify sources and symptoms of current U.S. existential austerity. Three-quarters of Americans, however, are confident in the military.[111]

Simply stated, what are the differences between the Carter-Reagan period and our own? Then, the similarities between disputants were greater than the differences; now, the opposite is true. When nonmilitary factors cannot be excluded from a rivalry, when do nonmilitary factors dominate? Herein are the crucial questions for policymakers. One should of course be cautious when offering evaluations, but no one less than Napoleon Bonaparte gave moral factors a 3:1 advantage over material factors, and Napoleon's contests were in a purely Western context.

ENDNOTES - CHAPTER 5

1. John F. Kennedy, "Address at the University of Maine," Orono, Maine, October 19, 1963, available from *www.presidency.ucsb.edu/ws/?pid=9483*.

2. Lawrence J. Korb, *The Fall and Rise of the Pentagon: American Defense Policies in the 1970s*, Westport, CT, and London, UK: Greenwood Press, 1979, pp. 143-144.

3. *Ibid.*, pp. 144-145.

4. *Ibid.*, p. 149.

5. "Soviet Strategic Arms Programs and Detente: What Are They Up To?" *Special National Intelligence Estimate* (SNIE) No. 11-4-73, September 10, 1973, available from *www.foia.cia.gov/sites/default/files/document_conversions/89801/DOC_0000268106.pdf*.

6. Wynfred Joshua, *Detente in Soviet Strategy*, Washington, DC: Defense Intelligence Agency, September 2, 1975.

7. Ronald Reagan, "Toasts of the President and President Jose Lopez Portillo of Mexico at the Luncheon Honoring the Mexican President," June 9, 1981, available from *www.presidency.ucsb.edu/ws/?pid=43926*.

8. Ronald Reagan, "The President's News Conference," December 8, 1988, available from *www.presidency.ucsb.edu/ws/?pid=35251*.

9. Jimmy Carter, "United States Naval Academy Address at the Commencement Exercises," June 7, 1978, available from *www.presidency.ucsb.edu/ws/?pid=30915*.

10. For just one example, see Jimmy Carter, "Berlin, Federal Republic of Germany Question-and-Answer Session at a Town Meeting," July 15, 1978, available from *www.presidency.ucsb.edu/ws/?pid=31087*. This formulation seems to be a common stock phrase often used by Carter at press conferences. It is often followed by concrete references; reducing or halting the buildup of military forces in the Indian Ocean is a common one.

11. Jimmy Carter, "University of Notre Dame—Address at Commencement Exercises at the University," South Bend, IN, May 22, 1977, available from *www.presidency.ucsb.edu/ws/?pid=7552*.

12. Jimmy Carter, "Charleston, South Carolina, Remarks at the 31st Annual Meeting of the Southern Legislative Conference," July 21, 1977, available from *www.presidency.ucsb.edu/ws/?pid=7852*.

13. *Ibid.*

14. Jimmy Carter, "Visit of President Perez of Venezuela Toasts of the President and President Perez at a Dinner Honoring the Venezuelan President," June 28, 1977, available from *www.presidency.ucsb.edu/ws/?pid=7738*.

15. Carter, "United States Naval Academy Address at the Commencement Exercises."

16. *Ibid.*

17. Jimmy Carter, "The State of the Union Annual Message to the Congress," Washington, DC, January 25, 1979, available from *www.presidency.ucsb.edu/ws/?pid=32735*.

18. Jimmy Carter, "Vienna Summit Meeting Joint U.S.-USSR Communiqué," Vienna, Austria, June 18, 1979, available from *www.presidency.ucsb.edu/ws/?pid=32497*.

19. John Lewis Gaddis, *Strategies of Containment: A Critical Appraisal of American National Security Policy During the Cold War*, revised and expanded Ed., New York: Oxford University Press, 2005, p. 347.

20. Carter, "United States Naval Academy Address at the Commencement Exercises."

21. Jimmy Carter, "Bonn, Federal Republic of Germany, Toast at the State Dinner," July 14, 1978, available from *www.presidency.ucsb.edu/ws/?pid=31083*.

22. Jimmy Carter, "Interview with the President Question-and-Answer Session with West German Reporters," July 11, 1978, available from *www.presidency.ucsb.edu/ws/?pid=31057*.

23. Ronald Reagan, "Interview with Western European Television Correspondents on the President's Trip to Europe," June 1, 1982, available from *www.presidency.ucsb.edu/ws/?pid=42592*.

24. Ronald Reagan, "Interview with Representatives of the Washington Times," November 27, 1984, available from *www.presidency.ucsb.edu/ws/?pid=39441*.

25. "Just peace" theory, so named to contrast with just war theory, contends that the good example of unilateral disarmament will so impress potential adversaries that they will follow suit and disarm, too.

26. Ronald Reagan, "Interview with Foreign Journalists," May 31, 1984, available from *www.presidency.ucsb.edu/ws/?pid=40006*.

27. Jimmy Carter, "The President's News Conference," June 13, 1977, available from *www.presidency.ucsb.edu/ws/?pid=7670*.

28. Carter, "Charleston, South Carolina Remarks at the 31st Annual Meeting of the Southern Legislative Conference."

29. Jimmy Carter, "Interview with the President Remarks and a Question-and-Answer Session with American Press Institute Editors," January 27, 1978, available from *www.presidency.ucsb.edu/ws/?pid=29850*.

30. Jimmy Carter, "North Atlantic Alliance Summit Remarks at the Opening Ceremonies," May 30, 1978, available from *www.presidency.ucsb.edu/ws/?pid=30868*.

31. Carter, "Charleston, South Carolina Remarks at the 31st Annual Meeting of the Southern Legislative Conference."

32. Jimmy Carter, "American Retail Federation Remarks at a White House Breakfast," Washington, DC, May 10, 1979, available from *www.presidency.ucsb.edu/ws/?pid=32318*.

33. Carter, "Charleston, South Carolina Remarks at the 31st Annual Meeting of the Southern Legislative Conference."

34. *Ibid.*

35. *Ibid.*

36. Carter, "University of Notre Dame—Address at Commencement Exercises at the University."

37. Carter, "Charleston, South Carolina Remarks at the 31st Annual Meeting of the Southern Legislative Conference."

38. Jimmy Carter, "Spokane, Washington, Remarks and a Question-and-Answer Session at a Town Meeting," May 5, 1978, available from *www.presidency.ucsb.edu/ws/?pid=30757*.

39. Jimmy Carter, "Interview with the President Remarks and a Question-and-Answer Session with Representatives of the Hispanic Media," May 12, 1978, available from *www.presidency.ucsb.edu/ws/?pid=30794*.

40. Carter, "Charleston, South Carolina Remarks at the 31st Annual Meeting of the Southern Legislative Conference." Carter is quoting Romans 14:9 as translated in the King James Version of the Bible.

41. Jimmy Carter, "Berlin, Federal Republic of Germany, Remarks at a Wreathlaying Ceremony at the Airlift Memorial," July 15, 1978, available from *www.presidency.ucsb.edu/ws/?pid=31086*.

42. Ronald Reagan, "The President's News Conference," January 29, 1981, available from *www.presidency.ucsb.edu/ws/?pid=44101*.

43. Ronald Reagan, "Remarks to Members of the National Press Club on Arms Reduction and Nuclear Weapons," November 18, 1981, available from *www.presidency.ucsb.edu/ws/?pid=43264*.

44. Ronald Reagan, "Remarks of President Reagan and President Luis Herrera Campins of Venezuela Following Their Meetings," November 18, 1981, available from *www.presidency.ucsb.edu/ws/?pid=43266*.

45. Ronald Reagan, "Documents Issued at the Conclusion of the North Atlantic Council Meetings Held in Bonn, Federal Republic of Germany," June 10, 1982, available from *www.presidency.ucsb.edu/ws/?pid=42621*.

46. Ronald Reagan, "Remarks in New York City Before the United Nations General Assembly Special Session Devoted to Disarmament," June 17, 1982, available from *www.presidency.ucsb.edu/ws/?pid=42644*.

47. Ronald Reagan, "Interview with Henry Brandon of the London Sunday Times and News Service on Domestic and Foreign Policy Issues," March 18, 1983, available from *www.presidency.ucsb.edu/ws/?pid=41072*.

48. Ronald Reagan, "Interview with American and Foreign Journalists at the Williamsburg Economic Summit Conference in Virginia," May 31, 1983, available from *www.presidency.ucsb.edu/ws/?pid=41406*.

49. Ronald Reagan, "Address Before the 38th Session of the United Nations General Assembly in New York, New York," September 26, 1983, available from *www.presidency.ucsb.edu/ws/?pid=40523*.

50. Ronald Reagan, "Interview with Brian Farrell of RTE-Television, Dublin, Ireland, on Foreign Issues," May 28, 1984, available from *www.presidency.ucsb.edu/ws/?pid=39976*.

51. Ronald Reagan, "Address at Commencement Exercises at Eureka College in Illinois," May 9, 1982, available from *www.presidency.ucsb.edu/ws/?pid=42501*.

52. Ronald Reagan: "Interview with Representatives of Western European Publications," May 21, 1982, available from *www.presidency.ucsb.edu/ws/?pid=42572*.

53. Ibid.

54. Ronald Reagan, "The President's News Conference," November 11, 1982, available from *www.presidency.ucsb.edu/ws/?pid=41985*.

55. Ibid.

56. Ronald Reagan, "Responses to Questions Submitted by Latin American Newspapers," November 30, 1982, available from *www.presidency.ucsb.edu/ws/?pid=42046*.

57. Ronald Reagan, "Remarks at the Recommissioning Ceremony for the U.S.S. *New Jersey* in Long Beach, California," December 28, 1982, available from *www.presidency.ucsb.edu/ws/?pid=42153*.

58. Ronald Reagan, "Debate Between the President and Former Vice President Walter F. Mondale in Kansas City, Missouri," October 21, 1984, available from *www.presidency.ucsb.edu/ws/?pid=39296*.

59. Ronald Reagan, "Interview with Western European Television Correspondents on the President's Trip to Europe," June 1, 1982, available from *www.presidency.ucsb.edu/ws/?pid=42592*.

60. Ronald Reagan, "The President's News Conference," January 9, 1985, available from *www.presidency.ucsb.edu/ws/?pid=38344*.

61. Ronald Reagan, "Interview with Morton Kondracke and Richard H. Smith of *Newsweek Magazine*," March 4, 1985, available from *www.presidency.ucsb.edu/ws/?pid=38303*.

62. Ronald Reagan, "The President's News Conference," January 29, 1981, available from *www.presidency.ucsb.edu/ws/?pid=44101*.

63. Ronald Reagan, "Excerpts From an Interview with Walter Cronkite of CBS News ," March 3, 1981, available from *www.presidency.ucsb.edu/ws/?pid=43497*.

64. Ronald Reagan, "Remarks on Signing the Economic Recovery Tax Act of 1981 and the Omnibus Budget Reconciliation Act of 1981, and a Question-and-Answer Session with Reporters," August 13, 1981, available from *www.presidency.ucsb.edu/ws/?pid=44161*.

65. Ronald Reagan, "Remarks and a Question-and-Answer Session at the University of Virginia in Charlottesville," December 16, 1988, available from *www.presidency.ucsb.edu/ws/?pid=35272*.

66. Carter, "United States Naval Academy Address at the Commencement Exercises."

67. *Ibid.*

68. Carter, "Charleston, South Carolina Remarks at the 31st Annual Meeting of the Southern Legislative Conference."

69. Jimmy Carter, "Vienna Summit Meeting Toast at a Working Dinner Hosted by the Soviet Delegation," June 17, 1979, available from *www.presidency.ucsb.edu/ws/?pid=32494*.

70. Jimmy Carter, "Portola Valley, California Remarks at a Democratic National Committee Fundraising Dinner," July 3, 1980, available from *www.presidency.ucsb.edu/ws/?pid=44727*.

71. *Ibid.*

72. Jimmy Carter, "Meeting with Student Leaders Remarks and a Question-and-Answer Session," February 15, 1980, available from *www.presidency.ucsb.edu/ws/?pid=32938*.

73. Jimmy Carter, "Interview with the President Remarks and a Question-and-Answer Session with Magazine Editors," February 15, 1980, available from *www.presidency.ucsb.edu/ws/?pid=32946*.

74. Jimmy Carter, "Visit of Chancellor Schmidt of the Federal Republic of Germany Toasts at the State Dinner," March 5, 1980, available from *www.presidency.ucsb.edu/ws/?pid=33110*.

75. *Ibid.*

76. Jimmy Carter, The State of the Union Address Delivered Before a Joint Session of the Congress, 23 January 1980, available from *www.presidency.ucsb.edu/ws/index.php?pid=33079&st=&st1=*.

77. Jimmy Carter, *Keeping Faith: Memoirs of a President*, New York: Bantam Books, 1982, p. 483.

78. Quoted in Robert Jay Lifton and Greg Mitchell, *Hiroshima in America: Fifty Years of Denial*, New York: G. P. Putnam, 1995, p. 220.

79. Barry Blechman and Douglas Hart, "Dangerous Shortcuts," *New Republic*, July 26, 1980, pp. 14-15.

80. Jimmy Carter, "American Society of Newspaper Editors Remarks and a Question-and-Answer Session at the Society's Annual Convention," April 10, 1980, available from *www.presidency.ucsb.edu/ws/?pid=33248*.

81. *Ibid.*

82. Jimmy Carter: "Interview with the President Question-and-Answer Session with Foreign Correspondents," April 12, 1980, available from *www.presidency.ucsb.edu/ws/?pid=33269*.

83. *Ibid.*

84. Ronald Reagan, "Remarks and a Question-and-Answer Session at a Luncheon with Radio and Television Journalists," June 8, 1988, available from *www.presidency.ucsb.edu/ws/?pid=35945*.

85. Ronald Reagan, "Interview with Representatives of College Radio Stations," September 9, 1985, available from *www.presidency.ucsb.edu/ws/?pid=39083*.

86. Ronald Reagan, "Remarks at the Annual Convention of the National Association of Broadcasters in Las Vegas, Nevada," April 10, 1988, available from *www.presidency.ucsb.edu/ws/?pid=35650*.

87. Ronald Reagan, "Farewell Address to the Nation," January 11, 1989, available from *www.presidency.ucsb.edu/ws/?pid=29650*.

88. Ronald Reagan, "Remarks and a Question-and-Answer Session with Students and Faculty at Gordon Technical High School in Chicago, Illinois," October 10, 1985, available from *www.presidency.ucsb.edu/ws/?pid=37893*.

89. Ronald Reagan, "Address Before a Joint Session of the Congress Following the Soviet-United States Summit Meeting in Geneva," November 21, 1985, available from *www.presidency.ucsb.edu/ws/?pid=38088*.

90. Ronald Reagan, "Written Responses to Questions Submitted by Deutsche Presse-Agentur of the Federal Republic of Germany," June 2, 1987, available from *www.presidency.ucsb.edu/ws/?pid=34366*.

91. Ronald Reagan, "Remarks and a Question-and-Answer Session with Area High School Seniors in Jacksonville, Florida," December 1, 1987, available from *www.presidency.ucsb.edu/ws/?pid=33751*.

92. Jimmy Carter, "Visit of Prime Minister Andreotti of Italy Toasts of the President and Prime Minister Andreotti at a Dinner Honoring the Prime Minister," July 26, 1977, available from *www.presidency.ucsb.edu/ws/?pid=7873*.

93. Ibid.

94. Jimmy Carter, "Visit of Prime Minister Barre of France Remarks of the President and the Prime Minister at a Working Dinner for the Prime Minister," September 15, 1977, available from *www.presidency.ucsb.edu/ws/?pid=6639*.

95. Jimmy Carter, "New Delhi, India Toasts of the President and President N. S. Reddy at a State Dinner," January 2, 1978, available from *www.presidency.ucsb.edu/ws/?pid=30733*.

96. Jimmy Carter, "Lagos, Nigeria Toasts at the State Dinner," April 2, 1978, available from *www.presidency.ucsb.edu/ws/?pid=30605*.

97. Jimmy Carter, "Visit of President Josip Broz Tito of Yugoslavia Remarks at the Welcoming Ceremony," March 7, 1978, available from *www.presidency.ucsb.edu/ws/?pid=30462*.

98. Jimmy Carter, "Visit Of President Tito of Yugoslavia Toasts at the State Dinner," March 7, 1978, available from *www.presidency.ucsb.edu/ws/?pid=30463*.

99. Ronald Reagan, "Written Responses to Questions Submitted by *Il Tempo* of Italy," May 23, 1985, available from *www.presidency.ucsb.edu/ws/?pid=38690*.

100. Ronald Reagan, "Interview with Foreign Broadcasters on the Upcoming Soviet-United States Summit Meeting in Geneva," November 12, 1985, available from *www.presidency.ucsb.edu/ws/?pid=38044*.

101. Ronald Reagan, "Interview with Foreign Television Journalists," May 19, 1988, available from *www.presidency.ucsb.edu/ws/?pid=35848*.

102. Fred Halliday, *The Making of the Cold War*, 2nd Ed., London, UK: Verso Editions and NLB, 1986.

103. Don Oberdorfer, *The Turn: From the Cold War to the New Era, The United States and the Soviet Union 1983-1990*, New York: Poseidon Press, 1991.

104. Julian E. Zelizer, *Arsenal of Democracy: The Politics of National Security – From World War II to the War on Terrorism*, New York: Basic Books, 2010, p. 354.

105. Betty Glad, *An Outsider in the White House: Jimmy Carter, His Advisors, and the Making of American Foreign Policy*, Ithaca, NY: Cornell University Press, 2009.

106. Raymond L. Garthoff, *Détente and Confrontation: American-Soviet Relations from Nixon to Reagan*, Rev. Ed., Washington, DC: The Brookings Institution Press, 1994.

107. Korb, p. xv.

108. Jimmy Carter, "Address to the Nation on Energy and National Goals: 'The Malaise Speech,'" July 15, 1979, available from *www.presidency.ucsb.edu/ws/?pid=32596*.

109. Adam Clymer, "Speech Lifts Carter Rating to 37%; Public Agrees on Confidence Crisis; Responsive Chord Struck," *New York Times*, July 18, 1979, p. A1.

110. A digital audiovisual copy entitled "Ronald Reagan TV Ad: 'Its morning in america again'" [sic], available from *www.youtube.com/watch?v=EU-IBF8nwSY*. The official name of the advertisement is "Prouder, Stronger, Better."

111. Catherine Rampell, "Losing Faith in American Institutions," *Economix: Explaining the Science of Everyday Life* (blog), *New York Times*, June 21, 2012, available from *economix.blogs.nytimes.com/2012/06/21/losing-faith-in-american-institutions/*. See also Jeffrey M. Jones, "Confidence in U.S. Public Schools at New Low: Confidence also at new lows for organized religion, banks, and TV news," *Gallup Politics* (blog), June 20, 2012, available from *www.gallup.com/poll/155258/Confidence-Public-Schools-New-Low.aspx*. The methodology, full questions, and trend data are available from *www.gallup.com/file/poll/155261/Confidence_Institutions_Overview_120620.pdf*.

CHAPTER 6

IS IT TIME FOR RETRENCHMENT? THE BIG DEBATE ON AMERICAN GRAND STRATEGY

Ionut C. Popescu

The U.S. grand strategy since the end of the Cold War has been premised on the overarching idea that Washington can and should act as the preeminent global power, and that it is in its best interest to bear the costs of maintaining this position of leadership and keep protecting and expending the current international order for as long as possible. Whether this vision for American grand strategy has been successful or not continues to be a matter of intense debate in the academic community, but, for better or worse, the majority of leading policymakers in both parties subscribed to this view of U.S. leadership. In recent years, however, a series of events (the prolonged expensive wars in Iraq and Afghanistan, the financial crisis/Great Recession, the looming debt crisis) led more and more scholars to call for a major shift from the current grand strategy of global leadership to a less ambitious and (arguably) less expensive one of retrenchment and restraint. While many of these voices called for such a shift throughout the post-Cold War era, their arguments are gaining more traction now in the context of an increasing concern with the possibility of America's decline from its place as the sole superpower due to its economic problems at home and the relative rise of other powers abroad. The most recent wave in the literature on "American decline" increases the appeal of a grand strategy of retrenchment as a suitable response to such a shift in the strategic environment, but the debate is far from settled. The current grand strategy continues to hold a great appeal for most Republican policymakers and opinion shapers, and for a significant number of Democratic ones. At times, the Barack Obama administration found itself in the first category, and at other times it went in the opposite direction.[1]

Throughout the 1990s "post-Cold War" era, scholars have generally identified four major theoretical schools of thought in American grand strategy: primacy/hegemony, institutional liberalism, selective engagement, and offshore balancing/isolationism.[2] In the last few years, however, the debate found advocates of the four schools largely selecting themselves into two broad categories, which could be called Renewal and Retrenchment. As Barry Posen, Christopher Layne, and Peter Feaver independently observed, the differences between advocates of primacy and institutional liberalism are more of nuance than of principle and their actual policies when in office are largely similar: Both the leadership of Republican and Democratic parties converged on a grand strategic approach of global leadership and international activism that replaced the Cold War era Containment.[3] The advocates of continuing this grand strategy, with minor adaptations, favor Renewal. On the other side of the debate, the critics of this strategy (found among advocates of the former categories of selective engagement, offshore balancing, and isolationism) represent a growing chorus calling for a Retrenchment grand strategy, which would represent a significant shift from the grand strategy of global leadership and international activism to one focused on reducing international commitments and the range of interests to be pursued abroad. These critics have recently been joined in their advocacy of restraint by influential members of the Washington foreign policy establishment such as Fareed Zakaria or Richard Haass, thus giving their arguments more prominence in Washington circles than used to be the case.

Therefore, the first and most important axis of disagreement at the highest level of analysis is between continuing an approach predicated on American global leadership and primacy, albeit with some small changes to account for certain recent developments—the "Renewal" option—or instead shift to a grand strategy of restraint and much more selective engagement with the outside world, the "Retrenchment" option. Broadly speaking, the advocates of Renewal fall into two further subcategories: the Republican-leaning primacy advocates who emphasize U.S. exceptionalism and are more comfortable with the use of military force, and the Democratic-leaning liberal institutionalists who favor more multilateral approaches to the use of force and as a general principle of foreign policy. The advocates of Retrenchment also vary to some degree on the extent to which they think this restraint should dominate U.S. foreign policy, from a more "selective engagement" view at one end to neo-isolationism at the other. The chapter will present both of these views and highlight the differences among their advocates.

The Renewal and Retrenchment advocates disagree on both their assessment of the external strategic environment, and also on their view of the domestic conditions impacting U.S. behavior on the world stage. This chapter will detail how the advocates of each grand strategy disagree on these two main axes of analysis—internal and external assessments of the constraints on U.S. grand strategy. In addition, the chapter also highlights two other contested areas about which the Renewal and the Retrenchment advocates have contrasting views: the size and shape of the defense budget and the idea of a uniquely American role in the global promotion of democracy and human rights.

RETRENCHMENT VS. RENEWAL

Overview.

The grand strategy of Retrenchment has become more and more present in public debates because it claims to allow the United States to secure its interests at a lower cost than the current grand strategy, and moreover it claims to represent a necessary adaptation to what many perceive to be an unavoidable geopolitical shift in international power from a period of unipolarity to a more multipolar world.[1] These two overarching principles, an emphasis on shifting resources from foreign to domestic priorities and a view of America as inexorably declining in power and influence, are common across the variety of scholars and analysts who favor Retrenchment, and they represent two of the most fundamental differences with the proponents of Renewal. In addition to these two main issues, the Retrenchment grand strategy also differs from the current grand strategy in two other critical ways derived from these two core assumptions. First, they advocate a reduced range of missions for U.S. military forces in both geographic focus and also in the kinds of conflicts they should prepare for fighting. Second, Retrenchment is grounded in skepticism about American exceptionalism and Washington's unique leadership role in defending freedom, democracy, and human rights. One subtle difference between advocates of Retrenchment in the academic world and those in the policy community and think tank world is that the latter tend to view it as a prelude to further renewal once America gets its internal house in order, while the former would favor a permanent retrenchment to a role of a great power among many. Therefore, the grand strategic "ends" of the Retrenchment advocates in the policy world are not so different than the ones favored by proponents of Renewal, but the former have a much longer time frame to achieve them and consider a short-term retrenchment to be necessary.

The advocates of a grand strategy of Renewal consider that the global leadership role played by the United States since the end of World War II served the American people remarkably well, and despite certain important domestic and international challenges facing Washington in both the short and long terms, a continuation of a grand strategy predicated on U.S. leadership of a liberal world order is still both possible and desirable.[5] In their internal assessment of U.S. strength, advocates of Renewal judge that the United States has the needed resources to finance such a grand strategy, as long as it is willing to address some structural problems independent of the realm of national security and foreign policy, i.e., the rise in the costs of entitlement programs, particularly in the health sector. Renewal proponents also differ in their view of American "decline" and the emerging shape of the international system: rather than perceiving a significant shift from unipolarity to multipolarity or nonpolarity, they generally continue to believe that the United States can and should maintain its current primacy for at least the next few decades as long as it chooses to implement the needed policies to achieve this, rather than becoming complacent and making decline a "self-fulfilling prophesy." The greatest policy debate nowadays among the advocates of Renewal and Retrenchment is in the realm of defense strategy and spending, where the former are attempting to limit, or better yet reverse, the spending cuts proposed by the Obama administration. Lastly, advocates of Renewal are also worried that Retrenchment would lead to an abandonment of the traditional belief in American exceptionalism as it pertains to a vigorous promotion of American values such as political and economic freedom and the defense of human rights in the face of gross abuses such as the ones in Syria.

Internal Assessment.

Retrenchment: The current grand strategy is now unaffordable; the United States needs to curtail spending on defense and foreign affairs, and shift economic resources to domestic priorities.

A grand strategy of Retrenchment is needed, according to its proponents, because U.S. current and projected future economic circumstances make it unaffordable to stay on the current path, particularly when it comes to defense spending. In a recent book-length treatment of this particular issue, Michael Mandelbaum argues that the economic recession precipitated by the collapse of Lehman Brothers in September 2008, together with the impact of rising government spending on so-called "entitlements" (i.e., Social Security, Medicare, and Medicaid) and interest payments on ever-higher levels of debt, represent a watershed change in American grand strategy: an era of scarcity has arrived that will impose serious limits on what the United States will be able to do abroad. As a result of all of these trends:

> American foreign policy will change in a fundamental way. . . . The international activities of ordinary countries are restrained by, among other things, the need to devote the bulk of their collective resources to domestic projects, such as roads, schools, pensions, and health care. For decades, the United States was exceptional in remaining free of such restraints, and the foreign policies that this freedom made possible did a great deal to shape the world of the 21st century. That era is now ending. In the future the United States will behave more like an ordinary country.[6]

The new limits call for a reduction in the scope of American grand strategy, at the very least until the United States will recover its economic strength and vitality at home. This trade-off between "guns and butter" is now more acute than in the past, the advocates of Retrenchment argue, and it is time to refocus government spending toward "nation-building here at home," as President Obama called it on more than one occasion. Moreover, he regards a fairer society and economy as key preconditions for economic renewal and the ability to compete internationally, and therefore he considers more traditional domestic policy choices in the realm of taxation, education, and infrastructure as having a clear impact on America's ability to have a global leadership role in foreign affairs in the long run. Echoing this theme is Richard Haass' advocacy for a foreign policy doctrine of **restoration**: "The goal would be to rebalance the resources devoted to domestic challenges, as opposed to international ones, in favor of the former."⁷ Similarly, Charles Kupchan argues that "the United States must rebalance means and ends by pursuing a judicious retrenchment; the nation needs to bring its strategic commitments back into line with its interests, resources, and public will." More specifically, leadership abroad must be first preceded by a series of domestic measures:

> Reviving economic growth, reducing unemployment and income inequality, improving education. . . . The first principle of a progressive agenda is that political and economic renewal at home is the indispensable foundation for strength abroad.⁸

In an article penned by two military strategists under the pseudonym of "Mr. Y," a reference to George Kennan's famous X Article, the authors make the same point that the United States needs a new grand strategy of "sustainment," by which they mean a strategy that refocuses American efforts from international to domestic priorities:

> We need to focus on sustaining ourselves in ways that build our strengths and underpin credible influence. That shift in turn means that the starting point for our strategy should be internal rather than external. The 2010 National Security Strategy did indeed focus on national renewal and global leadership, but this account makes an even stronger case for why we have to focus first and foremost on investing our resources domestically in those national resources that can be sustained, such as our youth and our natural resources (ranging from crops, livestock, and potable water to sources of energy and materials for industry).⁹

Lastly, Fareed Zakaria welcomes the deep cuts to defense spending, even if they would rise to $600-

$700 billion in addition to the ones already enacted, because he believes this will lead to a less militaristic foreign policy:

> Let the guillotine fall. It would be a much-needed adjustment to an out-of-control military-industrial complex. . . . Defense budget cuts would also force a healthy rebalancing of American foreign policy. Since the Cold War, Congress has tended to fatten the Pentagon while starving foreign policy agencies. . . . The result is a warped American foreign policy, ready to conceive of problems in military terms and present a ready military solution.[10]

Renewal: The United States faces serious budgetary problems due to domestic entitlements and a slow recovery, but it cannot and should not try to solve the fiscal crisis by turning inwards and abandon its role as global superpower: defense and foreign affairs spending at present levels is still affordable and well worth it.

The advocates of Renewal counter the Retrenchment view of the need to shift resources from foreign to domestic priorities by bringing up two main counterarguments. First, the roots of the fiscal crisis lie outside the realm of increases in defense spending, which are only a "drop in the bucket" compared to entitlements, and so the solution also lies in addressing the unsustainable trends in domestic programs. Second, the current investment in maintaining America's role as global superpower is still a very good deal compared to the potential costs of failing to continue to support the current U.S.-shaped world order. Many advocates of Renewal, particularly the ones on the Republican side of the political spectrum, are also traditionally skeptical that federal spending on infrastructure projects or education is key to America's future economic success, and therefore they are less inclined to accept the need to reduce foreign affairs spending in order to allow for more resources to go into those areas.

The overarching mantra of the Renewal advocates was well captured by Charles Krauthammer, who introduced to Washington's policy community a few years ago the slogan that "Decline is a Choice."[11] In a recent book arguing against the wisdom of Retrenchment, Karl Lieber elaborates in extensive detail on this particular point of the importance of political leadership and policy choices on whether the United States will move away from its current place of world leader or not. He criticizes Mandelbaum's thesis that the United States must reduce foreign spending in order to pay for domestic programs, by highlighting that this would be a choice leaders need to make between alternative options, not something inevitable.[12] As he sees it, "America's ability to avoid serious decline and the significant international retrenchment that would be a result of severely reduced resources becomes a matter of policy and will."[13] Tom Donnelly also echoes this criticism of assuming that U.S. leaders have no choice but to succumb to international Retrenchment, and he goes on to make the case that Washington's current and future fiscal problems have little to do with defense spending:

> Conventional wisdom in Washington has it that we are now in an 'Age of Austerity'—at least when it comes to defense budgets—as though it were a geological fact rather than a political choice. To be sure, the federal government's finances are a mess. But what is destroying the balance sheet is the growth of entitlements and other forms of 'mandatory'

spending, not military spending. The facts are that the Pentagon consumes about 20 percent of federal spending and less than 5 percent of gross domestic product (GDP); mandatory spending is about 60 percent of federal spending and getting close to 15 percent of GDP. Thanks to slow economic growth and aging Baby Boomers, those pie slices are getting ever bigger. The current defense budget debate is an example of looking through the wrong end of the telescope.[14]

In addition to arguing that maintaining the current level of spending is affordable because it represents a small share of overall government spending, Renewal advocates also argue that this commitment is worth it because it helps sustain a global leadership role that served America and the world well for the better part of 7 decades. As Robert Kagan put it:

> Whatever the nature of the current economic difficulties, the past 6 decades have seen a greater increase in global prosperity than any time in human history. Hundreds of millions have been lifted out of poverty. Once-backward nations have become economic dynamos. And the American economy, though suffering ups and downs throughout this period, has on the whole benefited immensely from this international order. One price of this success has been maintaining a sufficient military capacity to provide the essential security underpinnings of this order. But has the price not been worth it? In the first half of the 20th century, the United States found itself engaged in two world wars. In the second half, this global American strategy helped produce a peaceful end to the great-power struggle of the Cold War and then 20 more years of great-power peace. Looked at coldly, simply in terms of dollars and cents, the benefits of that strategy far outweigh the costs. The danger, as always, is that we don't even realize the benefits our strategic choices have provided.[15]

The United States is indeed facing a crisis because of reckless spending at home, but Washington leaders could make this problem worse by abandoning a grand strategy that proved successful over the decades:

> The United States may be in peril because of its spiraling deficits and mounting debt, but it will be in even greater peril if, out of some misguided sense that our national security budgets must "share the pain," we weaken ourselves even further.[16]

External Assessment.

Retrenchment: The geopolitical landscape is moving away from unipolarity, and Retrenchment is a grand strategy better suited for the coming multipolar world.

In addition to being considered too expensive given the demands of other competing domestic priorities, the current grand strategy is also considered by Retrenchment advocates to be ill-suited for the emerging multipolar structure of the international system. "The United States is declining as a nation and a world power,"[17] as Leslie Gelb began one of his *Foreign Affairs* articles, and therefore American officials are well advised to adapt their strategy to this new state of affairs where Washington is no longer the sole superpower in a unipolar world.[18] The theme of American decline dominated the pages of prominent foreign policy journals such as *Foreign Policy* and *Foreign Affairs* in the past few years, and a number of books made the case that America's so-called "unipolar moment" is over, and, as two authors have put it, "this time is for real."[19]

Christopher Layne, one of the foremost advocates of Retrenchment for the past decade, wrote earlier this year that the Pentagon's latest Defense Strategic Guidance (DSG) finally implies a recognition that "a profound power shift in international politics is taking place, which compels a rethinking of the U.S. world role." Layne, echoing arguments made by other proponents of Retrenchment such as prominent academic realists John Mearsheimer, Stephen Walt, Robert Pape, and Barry Posen, describes two drivers that should compel the United States to move from the current leadership/primacy approach to one of offshore balancing and restraint:

> First, the United States is in economic decline and will face a serious fiscal crisis by the end of this decade. . . . The second driver behind the new Pentagon strategy is the shift in global wealth and power from the Euro-Atlantic world to Asia. As new great powers such as China and, eventually, India emerge, important regional powers such as Russia, Japan, Turkey, Korea, South Africa and Brazil will assume more prominent roles in international politics. . . . The country needs to adjust to the world of 2025 when China will be the number-one economy and spending more on defense than any other nation. . . . The central strategic preoccupation of the United States during the next 2 decades will be its own decline and China's rise.[20]

Finally, Layne predicts that "the DSG is the first move in what figures to be a dramatic strategic retrenchment by the United States over the next 2 decades," and the triumph of the offshore balancing he and other realists have been arguing for in anticipation of the coming multipolar world.[21]

Other scholars and commentators who favor a slightly more active U.S. involvement than the academic adherents of offshore balancing, a group who would fall under the "selective engagement" category in the 1990s, nevertheless now echo the same theme of a profound shift in the configuration of the international system requiring a change in U.S. grand strategy. Bruce Jentleson talks about a "Copernican World" that no longer has the United States at its center as a "Ptolomeic" system had in the past.[22] In this new world configuration where diffusion of power (both hard and soft) is away from the United States toward the East and South, Washington will need to learn to accept important new limits. In response to the accusation of being a "declinist" that is made by proponents of primacy against people who advocate a lesser U.S. role, Jentleson calls them in return "denialists" for failing to account for what he perceives as a fundamental shift in world politics. Robert Art, one of the most eloquent advocates of "selective engagement" as a grand strategy, began a recent update of his grand strategy with the contention that "America's unipolar moment is over. It began with the breakup of the Soviet Union in December 1991 and ended with the collapse of Lehman Brothers on September 15, 2008."[23] He contends that the diffusion of power, combined with America's fiscal crisis, will force it to do less than it was able to do in the past, particularly when it comes to forceful exercises in nation-building. Lastly, Joseph Parent and Paul MacDonald recently argued a common theme for Retrenchment advocates in *Foreign Affairs* by stating that "As other states rise in prominence, the United States' undisciplined spending habits and open-ended foreign policy commitments are catching up with the country," and that "the United States has fallen into a familiar pattern for hegemonic powers: overconsumption, overextension, and over-optimism." As such, its leaders need to "fully embrace retrenchment as a policy and endorse deep spending cuts (especially to the military), redefine Washington's foreign policy priorities, and shift more of the United States' defense burdens onto its allies."[24]

Renewal: The United States will be able retain its position as sole superpower for at least the next few decades, and therefore it continues to be best served by a grand strategy of primacy and global leadership.

The recent wave of literature on American decline is accompanied by a new wave of anti-declinist arguments.[25] The scholars and commentators who argue America will continue to retain its position as the world's most important actor do not deny that its relative advantage across certain domains of power, such as economic power, has diminished in recent years. However, they contend that America retains other advantages, for example in superb military power, an entrepreneurship culture and higher education, new technology fields, natural resources, immigration, and demographics, which, when taken together, leads them to believe the United States will continue to be in a class of its own in the near- to medium-term. Even on economics, they are skeptical of forecasts assuming a continuation of linear growth on the part of rising challengers such as China, and point out to the very poor records of such forecasts in the past and to China's many potential problems that could derail its ascent. If America can get its own house in order by addressing its fiscal imbalances, there is no reason to expect the United States to be any less dominant in the coming decades as it has been in the recent ones.

In a study designed to explain America's "contested primacy" and to examine critically the notion of "American decline," Eric Edelman examined systematically the United States and all its other potential competitors (China, India, Russia, Brazil, and Europe) across a number of dimensions of power, including economic, military, demographic, soft power, and others. Summarizing his findings, he writes that:

> The period of unipolarity has been based on a singular fact: the United States is the first leading state in modern international history with decisive preponderance in all the underlying components of power: economic, military, technological, and geopolitical. With the possible exception of Brazil, all the other powers face serious internal and external security challenges. Japan, with its economic and demographic challenges, must deal with a de facto nuclear-armed, failing state (the DPRK [the Democratic People's Republic of Korea]) nearby and must also cast an uneasy glance at a rising China. India has domestic violence, insurgencies in bordering countries (Nepal and Bangladesh) and a persistent security dilemma with respect to China. The demographic challenges will be particularly acute for Europe, Japan, and Russia in the areas of military manpower and economic growth. The results will either diminish overall military strength or, in the case of Russia, impose a greater reliance on nuclear weapons.[26]

His conclusion is that:

> it seems likely that U.S. predominance could continue in a unipolar system, albeit one where U.S. hegemony is less clear than it was in the 1990s. In this iteration, however, American primacy will be more constrained by U.S. domestic and international economic limitations and more contested by regional powers.[27]

The same broad conclusion is reached by Stephen Brooks and William Wohlforth in their book on the topic of U.S. primacy and the continued unipolarity of the international system: "Since the dissolution of the Soviet Union, no other power—not Japan, China, India, or Russia, nor any European country, nor the EU (European Union)—has increased its capabilities sufficiently to transform itself into a pole."[28] The rise of China in particular has been hotly debated in recent years, as anti-declinists countering the narrative the China's inexorable rise will change the configuration of the international system away from unipolarity.[29]

Writing in *Foreign Affairs*, Josef Joffe argues that the current crop of declinist literature is no more persuasive than previous waves of this recurring argument about the end of America's supremacy, the fifth such wave in the past 60 years by his count. He presents data showing that the United States is still far and away the largest economy and the largest military power, and casting doubt on the trend analysis of the declinists. He has two objections to the analysis performed by Goldman Sachs and others who show China overtaking the United States in the next decade or two, a statistic often quoted by proponents of Retrenchment such as Fareed Zakaria or Christopher Layne. First, such predictions are based on a Purchasing Power Parity (PPP) measure of GDP, which greatly inflates China's GDP: for example, in 2009 China's GDP of 5 trillion at market exchange value become 9.1 trillion in PPP terms.[30] As Joffe states, however, such comparisons are very problematic when talking about a country's geopolitical clout:

global standing is not measured by the low prices of nontradable goods, such as haircuts, bootlegged software, and government services. Think instead about advanced technology, energy, raw materials, and the cost of higher education in the West. These items are critical for growth and must be procured on the world market. Influence bought abroad, say, through foreign aid, also comes at exchange-rate prices, as does imported high-tech weaponry.[31]

Second, he criticizes the trendline analysis of U.S. and China's rates of growth for assuming that Beijing would be able to keep its current high rates (by historical standards), and offers a counter-hypothetical scenario:

> Perhaps it is time to play a different round of the compound-interest game so beloved by the declinists. Assuming China's economy grows at seven percent— twice the historical rate of the United States'—China's GDP will double between 2007 and 2015, from $3.3 trillion to $6.6 trillion, and then double again by 2025, to $13.2 trillion. By that time, assuming 3.5 percent annual growth for the United States (the historical average), U.S. GDP will have grown to $28 trillion. Given the myriad challenges China faces, this scenario is more realistic than projections based on China's recent growth rates. China, it seems, still has a way to go before it can dethrone the United States.[32]

Proponents of Renewal generally agree on their assessment of America's continued preeminence and the need for continued U.S. leadership, but they differ somewhat on what marginal modifications are needed to the current grand strategy. Republican-leaning commentators worry about the recent loss of American influence in the Middle East at the same time that Iran is gaining in influence in that region. They are also less concerned with strengthening the United Nations (UN) and more focused on bilateral relations with like-minded countries. Democratic-leaning commentators worry more about creating institutions and mechanisms for the current liberal world order that would remain in place even at some later point in the future when the United States will not be the sole superpower anymore. John Ikenberry argues that "liberal order building" should be the main focus of U.S. grand strategy:

> [W]e should be planting the roots of a liberal international order as deeply as possible ... The United States should work with others to rebuild and renew the international foundations of the liberal international order, and, along the way, reestablish its own authority as a global leader.[33]

Anne-Marie Slaughter frames the institutional arrangement rather differently, in terms of networks rather than organizations of states, but the final goal of placing the United States at the center of a liberal world order is the same:

> strategists should analyze states as the principal hubs of intersecting regional and global networks instead of as poles in a unipolar, bipolar, or multipolar system. A state's ability to position itself as close to the center of critical networks as possible and to mobilize, orchestrate, and create networks will prove a vital source of power. The United States should thus strive to be the most central node—the supernode—in the networks that are most important to advancing its interests and that are most connected to other networks.[34]

How Much Military Force Is Enough?

Retrenchment: The United States should reduce its hegemonic ambitions as global security guarantor and instead focus on keeping the balance of power in key regions mainly by air and naval capabilities.

The most important policy change a Retrenchment grand strategy would bring from a practical perspective in the near term would be a reduction in the size and capabilities of the U.S. military, and consequently in the missions U.S. armed forces would be expected to carry out. Rather than investing in second-to-none capabilities across the spectrum of military conflict and across all domains of combat (conventional and unconventional, land, sea, air, space, and cyber space), the advocates of Retrenchment would divest from Landpower in particular, and from some of the air, space, and naval capabilities outside of the three key geopolitical regions mentioned previously. They argue that the lessons of the last decade are that land campaigns such as Afghanistan or Iraq are too expensive for the benefits they could bring and that it would be sufficient for the United States to rely on its air and sea power to project power in a few key regions. In addition to avoiding land conflicts, the advocates of Retrenchment also generally do not believe it is wise for the United States to strive for global military hegemony in every part of the world: balance of power, not U.S. dominance, should be the main goal driving force requirements. On this particular point, the advocates of Retrenchment generally divide into two sub-schools of thought, with "offshore balancers" being more willing to advocate deep military cuts across the board than "selective engagers."[35] The main difference is that the former would have the U.S. military retreat from many forward deployed positions, while the latter would not. However, both groups agree with the shift from Landpower to naval and air power, and with the need to reduce the overall level of spending on defense.

Among the proponents of Retrenchment, Richard Betts has recently summarized their case for a new defense posture very eloquently: a near-term military retrenchment requires:

> mainly hollowing out the U.S. military presence in Europe; moving to a reliance on economic, diplomatic and intelligence operations rather than military involvement in the Middle East and South Asia[36]; and revising the scheme for deterrence in Northeast Asia. This shift will not enable all of the ambitious accomplishments that policymakers have sought in recent times, but it is a level of activism in line with properly restrained ambition.[37]

Layne agrees that "America's comparative strategic advantages rest on naval and air power, not on sending land armies to fight ground wars in Eurasia," and therefore "The United States must avoid future large-scale nation-building exercises like those in Iraq and Afghanistan and refrain from fighting wars for the purpose of attaining regime change."[38]

Gordon Adams and Matthew Leatherman go into further detail and make specific recommendations on how to cut the defense budget:

> Eliminating counterinsurgency, stabilization, and nation building as first-order tasks would allow for cuts in the number of ground forces. In particular, the buildup in ground troops that President George W. Bush announced in his 2007 State of the Union

address—an addition of 92,000 Soldiers and Marines for operations in Afghanistan and Iraq—could be reversed. Moreover, a revised assessment of U.S. needs in terms of nuclear deterrence and conventional warfare would allow for an additional drawdown of permanently stationed U.S. forces. In Europe, where the chances of a military conflict continue to decrease—and where military planners are consequently reducing and restructuring their forces—the U.S. presence could shrink by 50,000, from approximately 70,000 down to 20,000 troops. Deployments in Asia could be halved, from 60,000 to 30,000, to refocus U.S. presence in the region on its comparative advantage: strategic nuclear deterrence and naval operations. These changes would also rebalance U.S. permanent deployments overseas toward Asia, where war, although still very unlikely, is more possible than in Europe.[39]

Renewal: The United States should continue to invest in maintaining its military hegemony and presence worldwide, and across the spectrum of conflict.

Given America's large military advantage against any potential competitors, U.S. superiority at least in the near future is not a matter of debate. The big debate, rather, focuses on whether the United States should maintain the expensive military requirements of the present grand strategy or whether it should focus on a narrower set of scenarios. Particular controversy revolves around cutting the size of the land forces by the 92,000 troops added by the Bush administration, shifting away from investing in irregular/counterinsurgency Landpower capabilities in favor of relying on drone strikes and special operations forces, and the geographical pivot from the Middle East to East Asia. Many proponents of Renewal have been critical of these moves toward Retrenchment made by the Obama administration in the past 2 years.

A joint report by three prominent hawkish think tanks recently provide a comprehensive list of the military requirements embedded in the current grand strategy:

> America's military must be able to fulfill a wide range of disparate missions: defending the homeland; assuring access to the seas, in the air, in space and now in 'cyberspace;' preserving the peace in Europe, working to build a peace across the greater Middle East and preparing for the rise of new great powers in the Asia-Pacific. The United States has always seen an interest in advancing a global 'common good' through disaster relief and other forms of humanitarian assistance. . . . The primary purpose of the U.S. military is to defend the homeland and, when required, fight and win wars to protect our security interests. American military strength also deters enemies, shapes and influences would-be aggressors, and serves as a comforting signal of security and support to friends and allies around the world. The benefits America enjoys as the world's sole superpower flow from preserving that strength.[40]

A reduction in the military missions the United States should prepare for in order to save on defense spending poses six unwanted risks for the United States, according to Peter Feaver:

1. The risk that America's European allies will not adequately carry the burdens that the United States is shifting to their shoulders;

2. The risk that adversaries will exploit a crisis because they believe that a less-capable United States is tied down in one theater;

3. The risk that the United States will require large stabilization forces even though the strategy assumes it will not. In the past, U.S. leaders have often guessed

wrong about the kinds of forces they need for the next conflict and found the military ill-prepared, lacking the very capabilities it had even a few years before the conflict;

4. The risk that Iraq, Afghanistan, or Pakistan will unravel in ways that even a United States determined to "end" the wars will not be able to ignore, thus requiring a recommitment of larger resources — and that those resources will not be available because of deep defense cuts;

5. The risk that an under-resourced pivot will provoke China into an arms race that U.S. defense cuts would make harder to win because of foregone defense investments; and,

6. The risk that the United States will lack the political will to fight in the cheaper-but-dumber mode that defense cuts will require.[41]

In recent years, a new debate is also taking place on ways to fight the war on terror, the most direct threat to the American homeland. Both Retrenchment and Renewal advocates believe their grand strategy is best suited to address the question of how to fight against terrorism. Robert Pape argued that U.S. military presence in the Middle East and the Muslim world is key to inciting terrorists, and therefore a retreat from that region should greatly alleviate the problem. The Renewal advocates, on the contrary, believe that only by working closely with local partners, maintaining a military presence to train them and, when needed, fight side-by-side allied governments (particularly in Afghanistan) is the right approach and that relying solely on offshore firepower will not work.[42]

American Exceptionalism and American Values.

Retrenchment: The United States should move away from the emphasis on the spread of political-economic liberal values based on a belief in American exceptionalism, and instead act in accordance with a narrower view of national interest.

Another disagreement between proponents of Retrenchment and those who favor a Renewal of the current grand strategic course is the issue of the traditional American role in the global promotion of democracy and human rights. Most advocates of Retrenchment find such pursuits at best nonessential "nice to have" goals when they can be achieved on the cheap, and, at worst, counterproductive to national security and leading to a waste of precious resources in ill-fated "nation-building" adventures. Such a belief in the importance of spreading American values is blamed for encouraging Washington policymakers of both parties to engage in unnecessary prolonged counter-insurgency campaigns in Iraq and Afghanistan, and in general to adopt an expensive view of U.S. interests which cannot discriminate between what must be considered proper national security interests vs. peripheral concerns.

Even though an idealist influence has been present in American grand strategy since the foundation of the Republic,[43] Retrenchment advocate Stephen Walt argues that this American exceptionalism is a myth that we should move away from:

> Most statements of 'American exceptionalism' presume that America's values, political system, and history are unique and worthy of universal admiration.

They also imply that the United States is both destined and entitled to play a distinct and positive role on the world stage. The only thing wrong with this self-congratulatory portrait of America's global role is that it is mostly a myth.... U.S. foreign policy would probably be more effective if Americans were less convinced of their own unique virtues and less eager to proclaim them.[44]

John Mearsheimer is even more blunt, and he criticizes as "imperial" the current grand strategy followed by Bill Clinton, Bush, and Obama alike: "Washington should also get out of the business of trying to spread democracy around the globe, and more generally acting as if we have the right and the responsibility to interfere in the domestic politics of other countries."[45]

Renewal: The United States should continue its unique role as a strong promoter of democracy and free markets, as well as its role as a defender against grave human rights abuses.

Proponents of Renewal believe that spreading American values is not only the right thing to do, but also it is a core U.S. national security interest—an open international system is both more peaceful and more prosperous. They also believe the United States is at its best when it leads the international community to prevent genocide and other brutal human rights abuses. Republican and Democratic grand strategists alike embrace this principle. As Anne-Marie Slaughter notices approvingly, the promotion of American values has been considered an enduring U.S. national interest by all previous post-Cold War administrations:

all national security strategies over the past 2 decades have assumed that the spread of universal values is not only normatively desirable as a matter of human freedom and dignity but also instrumentally important for U.S. security. They assume that a world in which every human being is free to speak and worship and free from fear and want would be a much safer and more prosperous world, and a better place for Americans.[46]

CONCLUSIONS

For the first time since the end of the Cold War, or some would say since the end of World War II, there is a serious debate about changing the scope of America's grand strategy. The idea of America's global preeminence, long taken for granted, is now under debate in government and scholarly circles. Even though bureaucratic inertia remains a powerful force and dramatic grand strategic shifts are very hard to implement, this may indeed be one of those inflexion points where such a big shift could occur. If political leaders will impose an era of austerity on the resources available for defense and foreign affairs, the United States might fall into a strategy of Retrenchment through the back door by virtue of a reduction in military resources that will gradually force future leaders to adopt less and less ambitious objectives. The advocates of Retrenchment would welcome this change because it is what they have argued for decades, while the advocates of Renewal would deplore it. One thing that should be clear is that it is highly unlikely that the United States could maintain its current global primacy with a significant reduction in the amount of money it is willing to spend on its military, no matter how brilliant its U.S. defense planners and how skillful its diplomats.[47] Choosing a "middle path" of maintaining expensive objectives but underfunding them, while tempting for policymakers, is probably a worse outcome than either choosing Retrenchment or Renewal, two grand strategies that are at least coherent in their own internal logic. Such an approach could lead to launching military interventions "on the cheap," usually a recipe for much larger costs than initially expected, or strategic failure, or both. [48]

This literature review focused on big picture, grand strategic differences between the Retrenchment and Renewal advocates. Based on these differences in their understanding of the internal and external constraints on the United States, and on the proper vision for the United States going forward, the adherents of each group unsurprisingly arrive at different tactical recommendations on a large number of specific policy dilemmas. These principles provide plenty of hints on how the advocates of each strategy would approach current and future problems. Having said that, different members of each camp sometimes have idiosyncratic approaches toward one policy or another, depending on the issue, which is one reason why this chapter did not dwell on specific "hot" policy debates such as what (else) to do about Iran's nuclear program, whether to intervene in Syria, and, if so, how, or the endgame in the Afghanistan-Pakistan region.

The two groups also differ on the desirability of maintaining U.S. troops in Europe. One of the most common arguments of "offshore balancer" proponents is that the United States should shift more responsibility for maintaining a peaceful liberal world order and regional stability to its rich allies like Europe, Japan, or South Korea. On this issue, as on a number of other policies, the end of maintaining regional peace and stability is, of course, shared by advocates of both schools, but they differ on the most economical way to do this. Retrenchment advocates would bet that the U.S. allies will pick up the slack if the United States draws down, and do so in a way that would not lead to outcomes the United States would not want to have happened, such as an increase in nuclear weapons proliferation and regional arms races. The advocates of Renewal disagree that this is a risk the United States should take. Such "bets" on second-order questions about how the world works cause advocates of the two schools to advocate different policies, even when the final ends they seek are rather similar.[49]

The only current policy debate with long-term implications broad enough to warrant inclusion in this grand strategy analysis was the question of defense spending. That is so because its answer will determine what the United States will be able to do in any number of future policy dilemmas, some quite predictable, and some entirely unpredictable at this point. The size and shape of the future military, however, is much more predictable because it takes years, and even decades, to change force structure both in terms of people and especially capital weapon systems and platforms. Even though this is a debate about means and not ends, in the policy world, major shifts at the grand strategic level such as those proposed by academic scholars are rarely possible—the way grand strategic change occurs more frequently is through a series of decisions on resources which can induce future leaders to adapt their objectives to the newly constrained means. This is why the current defense spending debate could turn out to be of much more significance for the future of American grand strategy than it is often recognized.

ENDNOTES - CHAPTER 6

1. For some early reviews of Obama's grand strategy, see Daniel W. Drezner, "Does Obama Have A Grand Strategy?" *Foreign Affairs*, Vol. 90, No. 4, 2011, pp. 57-68; Martin S. Indyk, Kenneth G. Lieberthal, and Michael E. O'Hanlon, "Scoring Obama's Foreign Policy," *Foreign Affairs*, Vol. 91, No. 3, 2012, pp. 29-43; G. John Ikenberry, "The Right Grand Strategy," *The American Interest*, January/February 2010. Among the most important grand strategic pronouncements of the administration, see the White House *National Security Strategy*, Washington, DC: The White House, May 2010; Hillary Clinton, "America's Pacific Century," *Foreign Policy*, November 2011; Department of Defense (DoD), *Sustaining U.S. Global Leadership: Priorities for 21st Century*, Washington, DC: DoD, January 2012.

2. Barry R. Posen and Andrew L. Ross, "Competing Visions for U.S. Grand Strategy," *International Security*, Vol. 21, No. 3, Winter 1996-97, pp. 5-53; Robert J. Art, *A Grand Strategy for America*, Ithaca, NY: Cornell University Press, 2003.

3. Barry Posen, "A Grand Strategy of Restraint," Peter Feaver, "American Grand Strategy at the Crossroads: Leading From the Front, Leading from Behind, or Not Leading at All? *Finding America's Path*, Washington, DC: Center for a New American Security (CNAS), 2012; Christopher Layne, "From Preponderance to Offshore Balancing," *International Security*, Vol. 22, No. 1, Summer 1997, pp. 112-124;

4. Among the more prominent proponents of a Retrenchment grand strategy, broadly defined, see Barry Posen, "The Case for Restraint," Michelle Flournoy and Shawn Brimley, ed., *Finding our Way: Debating American Grand Strategy*, Washington, DC: CNAS, 2008; Michael Mandelbaum, *The Frugal Superpower: America's Global Leadership in a Cash-Strapped Era*, New York: Public Affairs Press, 2010; John J. Mearsheimer, "Imperial by Design," *The National Interest*, January/February 2011, pp. 16-34; Stephen Walt, *Taming American Power: The Global Response to U.S. Primacy*, New York: W. W. Norton & Company, 2005; Christopher Layne, *The Peace of Illusions: American Grand Strategy from 1940 to the Present*, Ithaca, NY: Cornell University Press, 2006; Stephen Van Evera and Sidharth Shah, eds., *The Prudent Use of Power in Ameri-*

can *National Security Strategy,* Cambridge, MA: The Tobin Project, 2010; Richard K. Betts, "A Disciplined Defense: How to Regain Strategic Solvency," *Foreign Affairs,* November/December 2007; and "American Strategy: Grand vs. Grandiose" in *America's Path,* Washington, DC: CNAS, 2012; Leslie H. Gelb, "Necessity, Choice, And Common Sense," *Foreign Affairs,* Vol. 88, No. 3, 2009, pp. 56-72; Charles Kupchan, *No One's World: The West, the Rising Rest, and the Coming Global Turn,* New York: Oxford University Press, 2012; and "Grand Strategy: The Four Pillars of the Future Foreign Affairs," *Democracy: A Journal of Ideas,* Winter, 2012; Bruce Jentleson, "Accepting Limits, How to Adapt to a Copernican World," *Democracy: A Journal of Ideas,* Winter 2012; Bruce Jentleson and Steven Weber, *The End of Arrogance: America in the Global Competition of Ideas,* Cambridge, MA: Harvard University Press, 2010; Richard Haass, "Bringing Our Foreign Policy Home," *Time,* August 8, 2011; Robert Art, *A Grand Strategy for America,* and "Selective Engagement in the Era of Austerity," *America's Path,* Washington, DC: CNAS 2012; Joseph M. Parent and Paul K. MacDonald, "The Wisdom of Retrenchment," *Foreign Affairs,* Vol. 90, No. 6, 2011, pp. 32-47; Patrick Cronin, *Restraint: Recalibrating American Grand Strategy,* Washington, DC: CNAS, June 2010.

5. Among the more prominent recent proponents of a Renewal grand strategy, broadly defined, see Robert Kagan, "The Price of Power: The Benefits of U.S. Defense Spending Far Outweigh the Costs," *The Weekly Standard,* January 24, 2011, p. 28; Charles Krauthammer, "Decline is a Choice," *The Weekly Standard,* October 9, 2009; Robert J. Lieber, *Power and Willpower in the American Future: Why the United States Is Not Destined to Decline,* Cambridge, MA: Cambridge University Press, 2012; Feaver, "American Grand Strategy at the Crossroads"; Eric Edelman, *Understanding America's Contested Primacy,* Washington, DC: Center for Strategic and Budgetary Assessments, 2010; Fred Kagan, "Grand Strategy for the United States," *Finding our Way: Debating American Grand Strategy,* Washington, DC: CNAS, 2008; Anne-Marie Slaughter, "A Grand Strategy of Network Centrality," *America's Path;* Joseph S. Nye, "The Future Of American Power," *Foreign Affairs,* Vol. 89, No. 6, 2010; John Ikenberry, *Liberal Leviathan: The Origins, Crisis, and Transformation of the American World Order,* Princeton, NJ: Princeton University Press, 2011.

6. Mandelbaum, p. 10.

7. Haass.

8. Kupchan.

9. Mr. Y, "A National Strategic Narrative," Washington, DC: The Woodrow Wilson Center, 2011, p. 2.

10. Fareed Zakaria, "Why Defense Spending Should Be Cut," *Washington Post,* August 3, 2011.

11. Charles Krauthammer, "Decline is a Choice," *Weekly Standard*, October 9, 2009.

12. Lieber, p. 5.

13. *Ibid.*, p. 4.

14. Thomas Donnelly, "We Can Afford to Spend More, and We Need To," *The New York Times,* September 9, 2012. For similar arguments, see Max Boot, "Cutting Defense Spending Could Hasten America's Decline as a World Power," *Commentary*, August 8, 2011; Gary Schmitt and Thomas Donnelly, "The Big Squeeze," *The Weekly Standard*, June 7, 2010; *Defending Defense: Setting the Record Straight on U.S. Military Spending Requirements*, Foreign Policy Initiative (FPI), Washington, DC: American Enterprise Institute (AEI), The Heritage Foundation, October 2010. For charts making the case against defense spending by showing how it is much smaller than other government spending and how future trends predict entitlement spending to be the major problem to U.S. fiscal solvency, see Alison Acosta Fraser, "Federal Spending by the Numbers," Washington, DC: The Heritage Foundation, available from *www.heritage.org/research/reports/2012/10/federal-spending-by-the-numbers-2012*.

15. Robert Kagan, "The Price of Power: The Benefits of U.S. Defense Spending Far Outweigh the Costs," *The Weekly Standard*, January 24, 2011, p. 28.

16. *Ibid.*, p. 33.

17. Gelb, "Necessity, Choice, and Common Sense," pp. 56-72.

18. For more on the theme of American decline, see Parag Khanna, *The Second World: Empires and Influence in the New Global Order*, New York: Random House, 2008; Kishore Mahbubani, *The New Asian Hemisphere: The Irresistible Shift of Global Power to the East*, New York: Public Affairs, 2008; National Intelligence Council, *Global Trends 2025: A Transformed World*, Washington, DC: U.S. Government Printing Office, November 2008; Fareed Zakaria, *The Post-American World*, New York: W. W. Norton, 2008; Christopher Layne, "The Waning of U.S. Hegemony—Myth or Reality?" *International Security*, Vol. 34, No. 1, Summer 2009, pp. 147–172; Ian Bremmer, and Nouriel Roubini, "A G-Zero World," *Foreign Affairs*, Vol. 90, No. 2, 2011, pp. 2-7; Leslie H. Gelb, "GDP Now Matters More Than Force," *Foreign Affairs*, Vol. 89, No. 6, 2010, pp. 35-43; Nancy Birdsall and Francis Fukuyama, "The Post-Washington Consensus," *Foreign Affairs*, Vol. 90, No. 2, 2011; Simon Serfaty, "Moving into a Post-Western World," *The Washington Quarterly*, Vol. 34, No. 2, pp. 7-23; Paul Kennedy, "American Power is on the Wane," *The Wall Street Journal*, January 14, 2009; Francis Fukuyama, "The Fall of America, Inc.," *Newsweek*, October 13, 2008; Fareed Zakaria, "Are America's Best Days Behind Us?," *Time*, March 3, 2011; Andrew Bacevich, "American Triumphalism: A Post-Mortem," *Commonweal*, January 26, 2009; Paul Starobin, *After America: Narratives for the Next Global Age*, New York: Viking Penguin, 2009, p. 6; Robert A. Pape, "Empire Falls," *The National Interest*, January/February 2009, pp. 21–23; Edward Luce, *Time to Start Thinking: American in the Age of Descent*, New York: Atlantic Monthly Press, 2012.

19. Gideon Rachman, "American Decline: This Time is For Real," *Foreign Policy*, January/February 2011.

20. Christopher Layne, "The (Almost) Triumph of Offshore Balancing," *The National Interest*, Online Commentary, January 21, 2012.

21. *Ibid.*

22. Jentleson, *Accepting Limits*.

23. Art, "Selective Engagement in the Era of Austerity."

24. Parent and MacDonald, "The Wisdom of Retrenchment."

25. Some of the recent works making the case against American decline include Stephen G. Brooks and William C. Wohlforth, *World Out of Balance: International Relations and the Challenge of American Primacy*, Princeton, NJ: Princeton University Press, 2008; Josef Joffe, "The Default Power," *Foreign Affairs*, Vol. 88, No. 5, 2009, pp. 21-35; Anne-Marie Slaughter, "America's Edge: Power In The Networked Century," *Foreign Affairs*, Vol. 88, No. 1, 2009; Eric Edelman, *Understanding America's Contested Primacy*, Washington, DC: Center for Strategic and Budgetary Assessments, 2010; Joseph S. Nye, "The Future Of American Power." *Foreign Affairs*, Vol. 89, No. 6, 2010, pp. 2-12; Robert J. Lieber, *Power and Willpower in the American Future: Why the United States Is Not Destined to Decline*, Cambridge, MA: Cambridge University Press, 2012; Charles Krauthammer, "Decline is a Choice," *The Weekly Standard*, October 19, 2009; Robert Kagan, "Not Fade Away: Against the Myth of American Decline," *The New Republic*, January 17, 2012.

26. Edelman, *Understanding America's Contested Primacy*, p. xvii.

27. Ibid., p. xix.

28. Brooks and Wohlforth, *World Out of Balance*, p. 13.

29. See Minxin Pei, "Think Again: Asia's Rise," *Foreign Policy*, July/August 2009; Arvind Subramanian, "The Inevitable Superpower," *Foreign Affairs*, Vol. 90, No. 5, 2011, pp. 66-78; Derek Scissors, "The Wobbly Dragon," *Foreign Affairs*, Vol. 91, No. 1, 2012, pp. 173-177; Salvatore Babones, "The Middling Kingdom," *Foreign Affairs*, Vol. 90, No. 5, 2011, pp. 79-88; Wang Jisi, "China's Search For A Grand Strategy." *Foreign Affairs*, Vol. 90, No. 2, 2011, pp. 68-79.

30. Numbers available from *www.heritage.org/research/reports/2011/04/the-united-states-vs-china-which-economy-is-bigger-which-is-better#_ftn4*.

31. Joffe, *The Default Power*.

32. *Ibid.*

33. Ikenberry, *Liberal Leviathan*, pp. 348-349. For more on this, see also "Forging a World of Liberty Under Law: U.S. National Security in the 21st Century," The Final Report of the Princeton Project on National Security, Princeton, NJ: Woodrow Wilson School of International Affairs, 2006; John G. Ikenberry, "The Future Of The Liberal World Order," *Foreign Affairs*, Vol. 90, No. 3, 2011, pp. 56-68.

34. Slaughter, "A Grand Strategy of Network Centrality," p. 46. See also Anne-Marie Slaughter, "America's Edge: Power In The Networked Century," *Foreign Affairs*, Vol. 88, No. 1, 2009.

35. For the most detailed account of how to achieve military retrenchement across all services, see Christopher Preble, *The Power Problem: How American Military Dominance Makes Us Less Safe, Less Prosperous, and Less Free*, Ithaca, NY: Cornell University Press, 2009.

36. For a recent analysis of the possible impact of a U.S. military withdrawal from the Middle East, see the chapters by Daniel Byman and F. Gregory Gause in *The Prudent Use of Power*.

37. Betts, "American Strategy: Grand vs. Grandiose," p. 37.

38. Layne, "The (Almost) Triumph of Offshore Balancing."

39. Gordon Adams and Matthew Leatherman, "A Leaner And Meaner Defense," *Foreign Affairs*, Vol. 90, No. 1, 2011, pp. 139-152.

40. AEI, Heritage Foundation, and FPI, *Defending Defense*, 2010.

41. Feaver, *America's Path*, p. 65.

42. For a careful assessment of U.S. counterterrorism efforts and grand strategic concerns, see Audrey Kurth Cronin, "U.S. Grand Strategy and Counterterrorism," *Orbis*, Vol. 56, No. 2, Spring 2012.

43. Walter Russell Mead, *Special Providence: American Foreign Policy and How It Changed the World*, New York: Routledge, 2002.

44. Stephen Walt, "The Myth of American Exceptionalism," *Foreign Policy,* November 2011.

45. Mearsheimer, *Imperial by Design,* p. 31.

46. Slaughter, "A Grand Strategy of Network Centrality," p. 57.

47. For more on this point, see Andrew Krepinevich, Simon Chin, and Todd Harrison, *Strategy in Austerity,* Washington, DC: Center for Strategic and Budgetary Assessments, 2012.

48. Colin Dueck, *Reluctant Crusaders: Power, Culture, and Change in American Grand Strategy,* Princeton, NJ: Princeton University Press, 2006.

49. Peter Feaver and Hal Brands, unpublished manuscript. Another examples of these bets would be: Can the United States "pivot" from one region to another, or do losses in one region undermine gains in another? Is the United States more threatened by a strong or weak China? Is the liberal world order and the benefits it confers to the U.S. sustainable without predominant U.S. military power?

ABOUT THE CONTRIBUTORS

ELEANORE DOUGLAS is currently at the LBJ School of Public Affairs after serving several years as a defense consultant in Washington, DC. She has most recently contributed to a published assessment of the Depaartment of Defense organizational transformation initiatives during the George W. Bush administration. Her research interests include international security, intelligence policy, defense strategy and policy. Ms. Douglas holds a master's degree in intelligence and international security from the Department of War Studies, King's College, University of London.

PETER FEAVER is a Professor of Political Science and Public Policy at Duke University. He is Director of the Triangle Institute for Security Studies (TISS) and also Director of the Duke Program in American Grand Strategy (AGS). From June 2005 to July 2007, he was Special Advisor for Strategic Planning and Institutional Reform on the National Security Council Staff at the White House, where his responsibilities included the national security strategy, regional strategy reviews, and other political-military issues. Dr. Feaver is the author of *Armed Servants: Agency, Oversight, and Civil-Military Relations* (Harvard Press, 2003) and of *Guarding the Guardians: Civilian Control of Nuclear Weapons in the United States* (Cornell University Press, 1992), along with several other books. Dr. Feaver holds a Ph.D. from Harvard University.

FRANCIS J. GAVIN is first Frank Stanton Chair in Nuclear Security Policy studies and Professor of Political Science at the Massachusetts Institute of Technology (MIT). Before joining MIT, he was the Tom Slick Professor of International Affairs and the Director of the Robert S. Strauss Center for International Security and Law at the University of Texas. From 2005 until 2010, he directed The American Assembly's multi-year national initiative, *The Next Generation Project: U.S. Global Policy and the Future of International Institutions*. Dr. Gavin has been a National Security Fellow at Harvard's Olin Institute for Strategic Studies, an International Security Fellow at Harvard's Kennedy School of Government, a Research Fellow at the Miller Center for Public Affairs at the University of Virginia, a Smith Richardson Junior Faculty Fellow in international Security and Foreign Policy, a Donald D. Harrington Distinguished Faculty Fellow at the University of Texas, a Senior Research Fellow at the Nobel Institute, and an Aspen Ideas Festival Scholar. He is a life member of the Council on Foreign Relations. Dr. Gavin is the author of *Gold, Dollars, and Power: The Politics of International Monetary Relations, 1958-1971* (University of North Carolina Press, 2004) and *Nuclear Statecraft: History and Strategy in America's Atomic Age* (Cornell University Press, 2012). Dr. Gavin holds a B.A. in Political Science from the University of Chicago, a Master of Studies in modern European history from Oxford University, and an M.A. and a Ph.D. in diplomatic history from the University of Pennsylvania.

WILLIAM INBODEN is Executive Director of the William P. Clements, Jr., Center for History, Strategy, and Statecraft at the University of Texas-Austin. He also serves as Associate Professor at the LBJ School of Public Affairs and Distinguished Scholar at the Robert S. Strauss Center for International Security and Law. He also worked at the Department of State as a Member of the Policy Planning Staff and a Special Advisor in the Office of International Religious Freedom, and has worked as a staff member in both the United States Senate and the House of Representatives. His current research includes working on a history of the National Security Council. Dr. Imboden is the author of *Religion and American Foreign Policy, 1945-1960: The Soul of Containment* (Cambridge University Press, 2008), as well as numerous articles and book chapters. Dr. Inboden holds an A.B. from Stanford University, and an M.A. and Ph.D. in history from Yale University.

CHARLES MILLER's areas of regional interest include China, the United States, and Australia. His research interests include military effectiveness, public opinion and foreign policy, and rational decisionmaking in strategic affairs. Dr. Miller is the author of such publications as *Endgame for the West in Afghanistan* (2010), an exploration of the causes of the decline in support for the Afghan mission in Australia, the United States, France, Germany, Canada, and the United Kingdom, and *The Political Science of Retrenchment* (2013), an outline of what political science and defense economics can teach policymakers about when and how to carry out retrenchment in defense spending, both produced through the Strategic Studies Institute of the U.S. Army War College. Dr. Miller holds an undergraduate degree from the University of Cambridge, an M.A. from the University of Chicago, and a Ph.D. in political science from Duke University.

BRIAN MUZAS is Assistant Professor of Diplomacy and International Relations at Seton Hall University. His Ph.D. dissertation focused on the role of religious cultural heritage in shaping nuclear policy decisions.

Dr. Muzas holds a Ph.D. in public policy from the University of Texas.

IONUT C. POPESCU is an Assistant Professor in the Robertson School of Government at Regent University. His research focuses on U.S. foreign policy and national security strategy, security studies, and international relations. He was the Duke American Grand Strategy Program Fellow. He worked for the Center for Strategic and International Studies in Washington, DC. Dr. Popescu has written articles appearing in such journals as *Orbis*, *Armed Forces Journal*, *Joint Force Quarterly*, and *Contemporary Security Policy*. Dr. Popescu graduated Summa cum Laude from Occidental College with a B.A. in diplomacy and world affairs, and holds a Ph.D. in international relations from Duke University. His dissertation examined the interplay of design and emergence in the making of American Grand Strategy in several strategic eras in U.S. history.

MEGAN REISS holds a Graduate Fellowship at the William P. Clements Center for History, Strategy, and Statecraft. She worked as a researcher at the Hoover Institution and for the Stanford Preventive Force Group, focusing on security, foreign policy, and international law. Ms. Reiss holds a B.A. from Stanford University and an LLM from the University of Nottingham, her thesis focused on the ability of regional organizations to work within and outside the legal framework of a Security Council mandate. She is a Ph.D. student in public policy at the Lyndon B. Johnson School of Public Affairs at the University of Texas-Austin, where she studies the role of presidential decisionmaking in nuclear proliferation policy.

JEREMI SURI is the Mack Brown Distinguished Chair for Leadership in Global Affairs at the University of Texas at Austin. He is a professor in the University's Department of History and the Lyndon B. Johnson School of Public Affairs. His research and teaching have received numerous prizes. In 2007, *Smithsonian Magazine* named him one of America's "Top Young Innovators" in the Arts and Sciences. He is also a frequent public lecturer and guest on radio and television programs. Professor Suri is the author of five books on contemporary politics and foreign policy, and his most recent book is *Liberty's Surest Guardian: American Nation-Building from the Founders to Obama* (September 2011), which analyzes the past and future of nation-building. His writings appear widely in blogs and print media.

U.S. ARMY WAR COLLEGE

Major General William E. Rapp
Commandant

*****

STRATEGIC STUDIES INSTITUTE
and
THE U.S. ARMY WAR COLLEGE PRESS

Director
Professor Douglas C. Lovelace, Jr.

Director of Research
Dr. Steven K. Metz

Editor
Peter Feaver

Editor for Production
Dr. James G. Pierce

Publications Assistant
Ms. Rita A. Rummel

*****

Composition
Mrs. Jennifer E. Nevil

www.ingramcontent.com/pod-product-compliance
Lightning Source LLC
Chambersburg PA
CBHW080535170426
43195CB00016B/2564